Microsoft Forefront Identity Manager 2010 R2 Handbook

A complete handbook on FIM 2010 R2 covering both Identity and Certificate Management

Kent Nordström

BIRMINGHAM - MUMBAI

Microsoft Forefront Identity Manager 2010 R2 Handbook

Copyright © 2012 Packt Publishing

All rights reserved. No part of this book may be reproduced, stored in a retrieval system, or transmitted in any form or by any means, without the prior written permission of the publisher, except in the case of brief quotations embedded in critical articles or reviews.

Every effort has been made in the preparation of this book to ensure the accuracy of the information presented. However, the information contained in this book is sold without warranty, either express or implied. Neither the author, nor Packt Publishing, and its dealers and distributors will be held liable for any damages caused or alleged to be caused directly or indirectly by this book.

Packt Publishing has endeavored to provide trademark information about all of the companies and products mentioned in this book by the appropriate use of capitals. However, Packt Publishing cannot guarantee the accuracy of this information.

First published: August 2012

Production Reference: 1170812

Published by Packt Publishing Ltd.
Livery Place
35 Livery Street
Birmingham B3 2PB, UK.

ISBN 978-1-849685-36-8

www.packtpub.com

Cover Image by Priyal Bhiwandkar (priyal.bhiwandkar@yahoo.in)

Credits

Author
Kent Nordström

Reviewers
Peter Geelen
Henrik Nilsson

Acquisition Editor
Dhwani Devater

Lead Technical Editor
Pramila Balan

Technical Editors
Veronica Fernandes
Merin Jose
Naheed Shaikh

Copy Editors
Brandt D'Mello
Insiya Morbiwala

Project Coordinator
Sai Gamare

Proofreader
Aaron Nash

Indexer
Tejal Daruwale

Graphics
Manu Joseph
Valentina D'Silva

Production Coordinator
Arvindkumar Gupta

Cover Work
Arvindkumar Gupta

About the Author

Kent Nordström wrote his first lines of code in the late 70s, so he's been working with IT for quite some time now. When Microsoft released its Windows 2000 operating system, he started a close relationship with them, which has continued ever since.

For many years now, Kent has been working part-time as a Sub-contractor to Microsoft Consulting Services, and has been doing many of the implementations of FIM and its predecessors for multinational companies and large organizations in Sweden. Apart from FIM, Kent is also well known within the community for his knowledge about Forefront TMG, Forefront UAG, and PKI. Find out more by visiting his blog at `http://konab.com`.

> I would like to thank my family for their patience during the many evenings and weekends I have spent writing this book.
>
> I would also like to thank Peter Geelen and Henrik Nilsson for taking the time to review my writing. Your feedback has been invaluable!

About the Reviewers

Peter Geelen is CISSP, CISA, MCT (Microsoft Certified Trainer), MCSE:Security, and MCSA:Security, ITIL & PRINCE2 foundation certified.

Peter has been working with ICT since 1997, with a solid base on the Microsoft Windows server platform, running IT and network projects with MS server management and network support, advanced troubleshooting, presales, and enterprise architecture.

Since 2005, he has also been working as a consultant in Security, Identity, and Access Management, delivering Microsoft product support for server and enterprise platforms, such as Windows server, SQL Server, Directory Services, MS Identity Integration Server, MS Identity Lifecycle Manager, Forefront Identity Manager 2010, Omada Identity Manager, PKI, TMG, IAG/UAG, ADFS, and other IDM systems; and single sign-on and security solutions, including Sentillion expreSSO and Vergence product suite, Identity Forge solutions, and BHOLD.

Peter is co-founder of Winsec.be, the Belgian Microsoft Security User Group (http://www.winsec.be). He has been awarded the MVP award for Identity Lifecycle Manager (now MVP Forefront Identity Manager) four times, since 2008.

He is currently working as a Premier Field Engineer, FIM and Security, at Microsoft. Peter blogs at http://blog.identityunderground.be. You may also catch him on LinkedIn, at http://be.linkedin.com/in/pgeelen.

Peter has also reviewed *FIM Best Practices Volume 1: Introduction, Architecture And Installation Of Forefront Identity Manager 2010,* by David Lundell (http://www.lulu.com/shop/david-lundell/fim-best-practices-volume-1-introduction-architecture-and-installation-of-forefront-identity-manager-2010/ebook/product-18334749.html).

Henrik Nilsson has been working with Forefront Identity Manager and its predecessors since 2006. Before that he had been working in the IT industry since 1997, mainly as a developer of Microsoft products. In 2010, Henrik was awarded the Microsoft Most Valuable Award for spreading his knowledge about FIM in the community.

Henrik works at Cortego as a consultant within the IDA area using Microsoft products. Cortego is a Swedish consulting company working explicitly with Identity and Access Management.

> I wish to thank my girlfriend Amanda, who coped with me not only while I was reviewing this book, but also during the times that I spent on the Identity and Access Management topic, which not only is my job but also my main interest.

www.PacktPub.com

Support files, eBooks, discount offers and more

You might want to visit www.PacktPub.com for support files and downloads related to your book.

Did you know that Packt offers eBook versions of every book published, with PDF and ePub files available? You can upgrade to the eBook version at www.PacktPub.com and as a print book customer, you are entitled to a discount on the eBook copy. Get in touch with us at service@packtpub.com for more details.

At www.PacktPub.com, you can also read a collection of free technical articles, sign up for a range of free newsletters and receive exclusive discounts and offers on Packt books and eBooks.

http://PacktLib.PacktPub.com

Do you need instant solutions to your IT questions? PacktLib is Packt's online digital book library. Here, you can access, read and search across Packt's entire library of books.

Why Subscribe?

- Fully searchable across every book published by Packt
- Copy and paste, print and bookmark content
- On demand and accessible via web browser

Free Access for Packt account holders

If you have an account with Packt at www.PacktPub.com, you can use this to access PacktLib today and view nine entirely free books. Simply use your login credentials for immediate access.

Instant Updates on New Packt Books

Get notified! Find out when new books are published by following @PacktEnterprise on Twitter, or the *Packt Enterprise* Facebook page.

Table of Contents

Preface	**1**
Chapter 1: The Story in this Book	**7**
The Company	**7**
The challenges	**8**
Provisioning of users	8
Identity lifecycle procedures	8
Highly Privileged Accounts (HPA)	8
Password management	9
Traceability	9
The solutions	**9**
Implement FIM 2010 R2	9
Start using smart cards	10
Implement federation	10
The environment	**11**
Moving forward	**12**
Summary	**13**
Chapter 2: Overview of FIM 2010 R2	**15**
The history of FIM 2010 R2	**16**
FIM Synchronization Service (FIM Sync)	**17**
Management Agents	19
Non-declarative vs. declarative synchronization	20
Password synchronization	20
FIM Service Management Agent	21
FIM Service	**21**
Request pipeline	22
FIM Service Management Agent	23
Management Policy Rules (MPRs)	23

FIM Portal	**24**
Self Service Password Reset (SSPR)	24
FIM Reporting	**25**
FIM Certificate Management (FIM CM)	**25**
Certificate Management portal	26
Licensing	**27**
Summary	**28**
Chapter 3: Installation	**29**
Development versus production	29
Capacity planning	**30**
Separating roles	**31**
Databases	31
FIM features	31
Hardware	**32**
Installation order	**32**
Prerequisites	**34**
Databases	34
Collation and languages	35
SQL aliases	36
FIM-Dev	38
SQL	38
SCSM	39
Web servers	41
FIM Portal	41
FIM Password Reset	42
FIM Certificate Management	44
Service accounts	45
Kerberos configuration	48
SETSPN	50
Delegation	52
System Center Service Manager Console	52
Installation	**53**
FIM Synchronization Service	53
FIM Service and FIM Portal	58
FIM Password Reset portal	67
FIM Certificate Management	70
SCSM management	71
SCSM Data Warehouse	76
Post-installation configuration	**80**
Granting FIM Service access to FIM Sync	80
Securing the FIM Service mailbox	80
Disabling indexing in SharePoint	80

Table of Contents

Redirecting to IdentityManagement	81
Enforcing Kerberos	81
Editing binding in IIS for FIM Password sites	82
Registering SCSM Manager in Data Warehouse	82
FIM post-install scripts for Data Warehouse	87
Summary	**87**
Chapter 4: Basic Configuration	**89**
Creating Management Agents	**90**
Active Directory	90
Least privileged	91
Directory replication	93
Password reset	93
Creating AD MA	93
HR (SQL Server)	105
Creating SQL MA	107
Run profiles	116
Single or Multi step	116
Schema management	**116**
FIM Sync versus FIM Service schema	116
Object deletion in MV	117
Modifying FIM Service schema	118
FIM Service MA	**120**
Creating the FIM Service MA	120
Creating run profiles	127
First import	128
Filtering accounts	128
Initial load versus scheduled runs	**130**
Moving configuration from development to production	**131**
Maintenance mode for production	132
Disabling maintenance mode	133
Exporting FIM Synchronization Service settings	134
Exporting FIM Service settings	134
Exporting the FIM Service schema	135
Exporting the FIM Service policy	135
Generating the difference files	136
Generating the schema difference	136
Generating the policy difference	136
Importing to production	137
Importing custom code	137
Importing the Service schema difference	137
Importing the Synchronization Service settings	137
Importing the FIM Service policy	140

PowerShell scripts	141
Summary	**141**
Chapter 5: User Management	**143**
Modifying MPRs for user management	**143**
Configuring sets for user management	**148**
Inbound synchronization rules	**150**
Outbound synchronization rules	**158**
Outbound synchronization policy	159
Outbound system scoping filter	159
Detected rule entry	160
Provisioning	**161**
Non-declarative provisioning	162
Managing users in a phone system	**163**
Managing users in Active Directory	**170**
userAccountControl	170
Provision users to Active Directory	173
Synchronization rule	174
Set	177
Workflow	178
MPR	181
Inbound synchronization from AD	183
Temporal Sets	**185**
Self-service using the FIM portal	**186**
Managers can see direct reports	188
Users can manage their own attributes	190
Managing Exchange	**194**
Exchange 2007	194
Exchange 2010	195
Synchronization rule for Exchange	195
Mailbox users	196
Mail-enabled users	197
Summary	**198**
Chapter 6: Group Management	**199**
Group scope and types	**199**
Active Directory	199
FIM	201
Type	201
Scope	202
Member Selection	202
Installing client add-ins	**206**
Add-ins and extensions	206
Modifying MPRs for group management	**210**

Table of Contents

Creating and managing distribution groups	**212**
Importing groups from HR	**219**
FIM Service and Metaverse	**222**
Managing groups in AD	**224**
Security groups	225
Distribution groups	229
Synchronization rule	229
Set	233
Workflow	234
MPR	236
Summary	**237**
Chapter 7: Self-service Password Reset	**239**
Anonymous request	**239**
QA versus OTP	240
Enabling password management in AD	**240**
Allowing FIM Service to set passwords	**242**
Configuring FIM Service	**246**
Security context	247
Password Reset Users Set	247
Password Reset AuthN workflow	248
Configuring the QA gate	249
The OTP gate	251
Require re-registration	254
SSPR MPRs	255
The user experience	**255**
Summary	**262**
Chapter 8: Using FIM to Manage Office 365 and Other Cloud Identities	**263**
Overview of Office 365	**263**
DirSync	267
Federation	273
PowerShell or Custom MA	277
Using UAG and FIM to get OTP for Office 365	279
Summary	**280**
Chapter 9: Reporting	**281**
Verifying the SCSM setup	**281**
Synchronizing data from FIM to SCSM	283
Default reports	**285**
The SCSM ETL process	**286**
Looking at reports	**289**
Allowing users to read reports	291

[v]

Modifying the reports	**294**
Summary	**296**
Chapter 10: FIM Portal Customization	**297**
Components of the UI	**298**
Portal Configuration	**301**
Navigation Bar Resource	**302**
Search scopes	**311**
Usage Keyword	311
Search Definition	313
Results	314
Creating your own search scope	315
Filter Permissions	**318**
RCDC	**319**
Summary	**323**
Chapter 11: Customizing Data Transformations	**325**
Our options	**325**
PowerShell	326
Classic rules extensions	326
SSIS	327
Workflow activities	328
Extensible Connectivity Management Agent	328
Managing Lync	**329**
Provision Lync Users	329
Managing multivalued attributes	331
Selective deprovisioning	**339**
The case with the strange roles	**340**
Summary	**345**
Chapter 12: Issuing Smart Cards	**347**
Our scenario	**347**
Assurance level	348
Extending the schema	**349**
The configuration wizard	**351**
Create service accounts	351
Create certificate templates for FIM CM service accounts	352
FIM CM User Agent certificate template	353
FIM CM Enrollment Agent certificate template	356
FIM CM Key Recovery Agent certificate template	356
Enable the templates	356
Require SSL on the CM portal	357
Kerberos again!	357
Install SQL Client Tools Connectivity	358

Run the wizard	359
Backup certificates	364
Rerunning the wizard	365
The accounts	365
The database	365
Configuring the FIM CM Update Service	**366**
Database permissions	**366**
Configuring the CA	**367**
Installing FIM CM CA files	367
Configuring Policy Module	368
Installing the FIM CM client	**371**
FIM CM permissions	**372**
Service Connection Point	372
Users and groups	374
Certificate Template	375
Profile Template object	377
Profile Template settings	378
Allowing managers to issue certificates for consultants	**379**
Creating a Profile Template for consultant Smart Cards	379
Configuring permissions for consultant Smart Cards	382
John enrolls a Smart Card	382
RDP using Smart Cards	**386**
CM Management Agent	**386**
Summary	**387**
Chapter 13: Troubleshooting	**389**
Reminder	**389**
Troubleshooting	**390**
Kerberos	390
Connected Data Sources	392
FIM Sync	393
FIM Service	398
Request errors	398
Sync errors	401
Reporting	404
FIM CM	405
Agent certificates	406
CA	407
FIM clients	407
Backup and restore	**408**
FIM Sync	408
FIM Service and Portal	409
FIM CM	409

Source code	410
Summary	**411**
Afterword	**413**
Index	**415**

Preface

Microsoft's Forefront Identity Manager simplifies enterprise Identity Management for end users by automating admin tasks and integrating the infrastructure of an enterprise with strong authentication systems.

The Microsoft Forefront Identity Manager 2010 R2 Handbook is an in-depth guide to Identity Management. You will learn how to manage users and groups, and implement self-service parts. This book also covers basic Certificate Management and troubleshooting.

Throughout the book we will follow a fictional case study. You will see how to implement IM and also set up Smart Card logon for strong administrative accounts within Active Directory. You will learn to implement all the features of FIM 2010 R2. You will see how to install a complete FIM 2010 R2 infrastructure, including both test and production environments. You will be introduced to Self-Service management of both users and groups. FIM Reports to audit the identity management lifecycle are also discussed in detail.

With the Microsoft Forefront Identity Manager 2010 R2 Handbook you will be able to implement and manage FIM 2010 R2 almost effortlessly.

What this book covers

Chapter 1, The Story in this Book: In this chapter, the author gives a short description of a fictive company, which he uses throughout the book as an example.

He also discusses some of the Identity Management-related challenges faced by the fictive company, solutions to these challenges, and the company's IT system infrastructure.

Preface

Chapter 2, Overview of FIM 2010 R2: In this chapter, the author gives an overview of the history of FIM 2010 R2, FIM Synchronization Service, FIM Service, FIM Portal, FIM Reporting, FIM Certificate Management, and licensing.

Chapter 3, Installation: In this chapter, we discuss the prerequisites for installing different components of FIM 2010 R2, see how to actually install the components, and look at a few post-installation steps to get it working.

Chapter 4, Basic Configuration: In this chapter, we discuss some of the basic configurations we need to look at, no matter how our environment looks or how we plan to use FIM 2010 R2. We focus on the initial configuration of FIM Synchronization Service and FIM Service, specifically topics such as creating Management Agents, schema management, FIM Service Management Agents, initial load versus scheduled runs, and moving configurations from the development to the production environment.

If you have an environment already set up, this chapter can act as a guide for you to verify that you have not missed any important steps that will cause your FIM environment to not work properly.

Chapter 5, User Management: User management is the primary goal for most FIM deployments. Synchronizing user information between different Management Agents, and managing user provisioning/deprovisioning is often the first thing we focus on in our FIM deployment.

In this chapter, we discuss how user management is set up in FIM Service and FIM Synchronization Service. We also discuss how to manage users in Active Directory, Microsoft Exchange, a fictive phone system, and how to enable users to do some self-service.

Chapter 6, Group Management: Once you have User Management in place, it is usually time to start looking at Group Management. In this chapter, we will look at the different group scopes and types in AD and FIM, how to manage groups using the Outlook add-in, and synchronizing groups between HR, AD, and FIM.

Chapter 7, Self-service Password Reset: In this chapter, we look at the Self-service Password Reset (SSPR) feature, which allows users to reset their own passwords if they have forgotten them.

We discuss how to enable password management in AD, allow FIM Service to set a password, and configure FIM Service. We also discuss the user experience of the Self-service Password Reset feature.

Chapter 8, Using FIM to Manage Office 365 and Other Cloud Identities: In this chapter, we see how FIM 2010 R2 might fit into the puzzle of managing Office 365 identities and also how FIM might play a role in Identity Federation scenarios.

Chapter 9, Reporting: One of the new features in FIM 2010 R2 is built-in Reporting support. In this chapter, we discuss how to verify the System Center Service Manager 2010 (SCSM) setup, the default reports that are automatically installed, and the SCSM ETL process. We look at the methods to check/verify and modify reports.

Chapter 10, FIM Portal Customization: In this chapter, we take a quick look at the components of the FIM Portal UI. We discuss how to modify the basic FIM Portal UI, and how to customize search scopes and forms.

Chapter 11, Customizing Data Transformations: In this chapter, we will discuss the overall need and options for data transformation and selective deprovisioning. We also look at an example of managing Microsoft Lync, and a case with strange roles.

Chapter 12, Issuing Smart Cards: In this chapter, we will take a look at how we can use FIM CM to issue Smart Cards. You will see how FIM CM adds a lot of functionality and security to the process of managing the complete lifecycle of your Smart Cards.

Chapter 13, Troubleshooting: In this chapter, we discuss how to go about troubleshooting issues, depending on where we see the failure and the type of failure. We also see how to perform backup and restore the various parts of FIM.

What you need for this book

In the book we install and configure a complete FIM 2010 R2 environment. In this book, all the installations and servers use the following operating system:

- Microsoft Windows Server 2008 R2 SP1 Enterprise Edition
- .NET Framework 3.5.1

The required software is as follows:

- Microsoft Forefront Identity Manager 2010 R2
- Microsoft SQL Server 2008 R2 SP1
- Microsoft Visual Studio 2008 SP1
- Microsoft SharePoint Foundation 2010
- Microsoft System Center Service Manager 2010

Apart from the software required to get FIM 2010 R2 up and running, the following software is also used or referred to in the book:

- Microsoft DirSync x64; this software is used to synchronize data with Office 365.

- Microsoft Active Directory Federation Services 2.0.
- Granfeldt PowerShell Management Agent 2.0 is used to demonstrate extensible connectivity. More info on this can be found at `http://aka.ms/PowerShellMA`.

Who this book is for

If you are implementing and managing FIM 2010 R2 in your business, then this book is for you. You will need to have a basic understanding of Microsoft-based infrastructure using Active Directory. If you are new to Forefront Identity Management, the case-study approach of this book will help you understand the concepts and implement them.

Conventions

In this book, you will find a number of styles of text that distinguish between different kinds of information. Here are some examples of these styles, and an explanation of their meaning.

Code words in text are shown as follows: "The public domain used by The Company is `company.com`; this is also the primary email domain used."

A block of code is set as follows:

```
<!-- hex-encoded certificate hash. -->
<add key="Clm.SigningCertificate.Hash" value="1F9AA53D5D15C17969ACA0A5C1FD102C61978E25" />
```

New terms and **important words** are shown in bold. Words that you see on the screen, in menus or dialog boxes for example, appear in the text like this: " Open up the **Security** tab in the domain.".

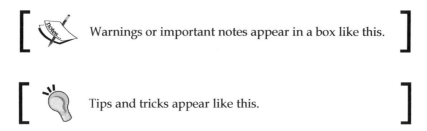

Warnings or important notes appear in a box like this.

Tips and tricks appear like this.

Reader feedback

Feedback from our readers is always welcome. Let us know what you think about this book—what you liked or may have disliked. Reader feedback is important for us to develop titles that you really get the most out of.

To send us general feedback, simply send an e-mail to feedback@packtpub.com, and mention the book title through the subject of your message.

If there is a topic that you have expertise in and you are interested in either writing or contributing to a book, see our author guide on www.packtpub.com/authors.

Customer support

Now that you are the proud owner of a Packt book, we have a number of things to help you to get the most from your purchase.

Downloading the example code

You can download the example code files for all Packt books you have purchased from your account at http://www.packtpub.com. If you purchased this book elsewhere, you can visit http://www.packtpub.com/support and register to have the files e-mailed directly to you.

Errata

Although we have taken every care to ensure the accuracy of our content, mistakes do happen. If you find a mistake in one of our books—maybe a mistake in the text or the code—we would be grateful if you would report this to us. By doing so, you can save other readers from frustration and help us improve subsequent versions of this book. If you find any errata, please report them by visiting http://www.packtpub.com/support, selecting your book, clicking on the **errata submission form** link, and entering the details of your errata. Once your errata are verified, your submission will be accepted and the errata will be uploaded to our website, or added to any list of existing errata, under the Errata section of that title.

Piracy

Piracy of copyright material on the Internet is an ongoing problem across all media. At Packt, we take the protection of our copyright and licenses very seriously. If you come across any illegal copies of our works, in any form, on the Internet, please provide us with the location address or website name immediately so that we can pursue a remedy.

Please contact us at `copyright@packtpub.com` with a link to the suspected pirated material.

We appreciate your help in protecting our authors, and our ability to bring you valuable content.

Questions

You can contact us at `questions@packtpub.com` if you are having a problem with any aspect of the book, and we will do our best to address it.

The Story in this Book

Microsoft Forefront Identity Manager 2010 R2 (FIM 2010 R2) is a tool that helps you with Identity Management. As you might know or are able to guess, Identity Management is, for the most part, process-oriented rather than technology-oriented. In order to be able to explain some concepts within this area, I have chosen to write this book using a fictive company as an example.

In this chapter, I will give you a description of this company and will talk about:

- The challenges
- The solutions
- The environment

The Company

The name of my fictive company is *The Company*. The Company is neither small nor big. I will not give you any numbers on the size of this company because I do not want you to take my example setup as being optimized for a company of a particular size.

As with many other companies, The Company tries to keep up with modern techniques within their IT infrastructure. They are a big fan of Microsoft and live by the following principle:

> *If Microsoft has a product that can do it, let's try that one first.*

The concept of *cloud computing* is still somewhat fuzzy to them, and they do not yet know how or when they will be using it. They do understand that in the near future this technology will be an important factor for them, so they have decided that, for every new system or function that needs to be implemented, they will take cloud computing into account.

The challenges

During a recent inventory of the systems and functions that the The Company's IT department supported, a number of challenges were detected. We will now have a look at some of the Identity Management (IdM)-related challenges that were detected.

Provisioning of users

Within The Company, they discovered that it can take up to one week before a new employee or contractor is properly assigned their role and provisioned to the different systems required by them to do their job.

The Company would like for this to not take more than a few hours.

Identity lifecycle procedures

A number of issues were detected in lifecycle management of identities.

Changes in roles took way too long. Access based on old roles continued even after people were moved to a new function or changed their job. Termination and disabling of identities was also out of control. They found that accounts of users who had left the company more than six months ago were still active.

After a security review, they found out that a consultant working with the HR system still had access using VPN and an active administrative account within the HR system. The access should have been disabled about six months ago, when the upgrade project was completed. They also found that the consultant who the company engaged to help out during the upgrade, didn't even work for the firm any more.

What The Company would like is not only a way of defining policies about identity management, but also a tool that enforces it and detects anomalies.

Highly Privileged Accounts (HPA)

Although The Company has been successful in reducing the number of strong administrative accounts over the last few years, a few still exist. There are also other highly privileged accounts and also a few highly privileged digital identities, such as code signing certificates. The concern is that the security of these accounts is not as strong as it should be.

The **Public Key Infrastructure (PKI)** within The Company is a one layer PKI, using an Enterprise Root CA without **Hardware Security Module (HSM)**. The CSO is concerned that it is not sufficient to start using smart cards, because he feels the assurance level of the PKI is not high enough.

Password management

The helpdesk at The Company spends a lot of time helping users who forgot their password. These are both internal users as well as partners, with access to the shared systems.

Traceability

They found that they had no process or tools in place to trace the status of identities and roles historically. They wanted to be able answer questions such as:

- *Who was a member of the Domain Admins group in April?*
- *When was John's account disabled and who approved that?*

The solutions

Once the challenges had been defined, The Company started looking for possible solutions.

When they were searching the globe for someone who might help them with their issues, they found a highly recommended consultant in Sweden, who had worked with identity management for more than a decade. We will now have a look at the solutions that he proposed for their major issues.

Implement FIM 2010 R2

By implementing Microsoft Forefront Identity Manager 2010 R2, The Company will be able to:

- Automate lifecycle management of identities all the way from creation to deletion
- Implement self-service password reset
- Strengthen the identity of highly privileged accounts, using smart cards
- Get traceability of the whole lifecycle of an identity

Start using smart cards

By using smart cards to store identities of the highly privileged accounts, the security for this type of account is increased. Even if the PKI does not have a high assurance level, it is more secure to use a smart card than to just use a password.

By implementing the **Certificate Management (CM)** part of FIM 2010 R2, The Company will get the control they would like when managing these strong identities.

Even if the PKI within The Company does not have high assurance levels, the use of smart cards will enhance the security of the highly privileged accounts. If the initial proof-of-concept of using smart cards works out, a redesign of the current PKI will be discussed.

Implement federation

All the services shared with the major partners were using Microsoft Sharepoint. The consultant therefore suggested that The Company should investigate if federation would work with these partners.

The Microsoft product used when implementing federation is **Active Directory Federation Services (AD FS)**. To get an overview of federation and AD FS, please visit http://aka.ms/ADFSOverview.

By implementing federation, it would be easier for The Company to move shared resources to the cloud. For example, moving the Sharepoint sites shared with partners, to Microsoft Office 365 cloud services. Read more about Office 365 at http://office365.microsoft.com.

> Within this book, I will not explain in detail how the implementation of federation using Active Directory Federation Services (AD FS) is made.

The use of FIM is vital in a federation scenario, as federation using claims-based authentication and authorization requires very good control on attributes and group/role membership changes of users.

The environment

The following diagram gives you an overview of the relevant parts of infrastructure within The Company:

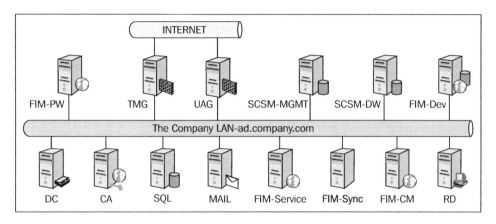

The servers you see do not in any way represent any scaling scenario, but rather show the different functions I will be using in my examples in this book.

In the following table, you will find a short summary of the systems involved, so that when they are referenced in the book later on, you will have an idea about their usage:

System	Usage	Products installed/to be installed
DC	Domain Controller for the Active Directory domain ad.company.com.	AD DS and DNS role installed.
CA	Enterprise Root Certification Authority. The Company uses only a one-layer PKI without any HSM.	AD CS, including Web Enrollment role, installed
SQL	Central Microsoft SQL Server used by many systems. Among these systems are the HR and Phone systems.	SQL Server 2008 R2, including Integration Services, installed.
MAIL	E-mail system.	Exchange 2010 installed.
RD	Remote Desktop system used by administrators.	Remote Desktop Services role installed.
TMG	The Company firewall.	Forefront Threat Management Gateway 2010 installed.

System	Usage	Products installed/to be installed
UAG	The remote access solution used by The Company.	Forefront Unified Access Gateway 2010 installed.
FIM-Dev	The test and development server for FIM.	SQL Server 2008 R2 and Visual Studio 2008. FIM Sync, Service and Portal will be installed.
FIM-Sync	The FIM Synchronization server.	FIM Synchronization Service will be installed.
FIM-Service	The FIM Web Service and Portal server.	FIM Service and FIM Portal will be installed.
FIM-CM	The FIM Certificate Management Server	FIM CM Service and Portal will be installed.
FIM-PW	The FIM Password Registration and Reset server.	FIM Password Registration and Reset will be installed.
SCSM-MGMT	SCSM Management Server. Used by FIM Reporting.	SQL Server 2008 R2 and System Center Service Manager will be installed.
SCSM-DW	SCSM Data Warehouse Server. Used by FIM Reporting.	SQL Server 2008 R2 and System Center Service Manager will be installed.

All systems have Microsoft Windows Server 2008 R2 as the operating system.

The products installed/to be installed show the status of the systems when we start our journey with The Company in this book. Details about the features and products already installed will be explained in *Chapter 2, Installation*.

The Active Directory domain within The Company is ad.company.com, using AD as the NetBIOS name. The public domain used by The Company is company.com; this is also the primary email domain used.

Moving forward

The CIO, CSO, and CTO of The Company found that the solutions explained to them by the consultant would indeed help The Company mitigate the challenges they were facing. They decided to implement FIM 2010 R2.

In this book, we will follow them as they implement FIM 2010 R2. We will see how the different features and functions of FIM 2010 R2 will, in the end, solve all the issues that the company has detected.

The use of digital identities, using smart cards, is very new to them, so they decide that this should initially be implemented as a proof of concept.

Summary

You now know a little about the company I will be using in this book to give you examples and to explain concepts. So let's go on and see how The Company implements Microsoft Forefront Identity Manager 2010 R2 in its environment.

In the next chapter, I will start off with an overview to give you some conceptual understanding of FIM 2010 R2.

Overview of FIM 2010 R2

Microsoft Forefront Identity Manager 2010 R2 (FIM 2010 R2) is not one product, but a family of products working together to mitigate the challenges regarding Identity Management.

The following picture shows a high-level overview of the FIM family and the components relevant to an FIM 2010 R2 implementation:

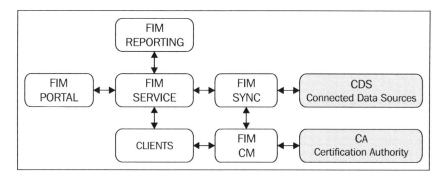

Within the FIM family, there are some parts that can live by themselves and others that depend on other parts. But, in order to fully utilize the power of FIM 2010 R2, you should have all parts in place.

At the center, we have **FIM Service** and **FIM Synchronization Service (FIM Sync)**. The key to a successful implementation of FIM 2010 R2 is to understand how these two components work—by themselves as well as together.

In this chapter, I will give you an overview of:

- The history of FIM 2010 R2
- FIM Synchronization Service (FIM Sync)
- FIM Service

- FIM Portal
- FIM Reporting
- FIM Certificate Management (FIM CM)
- Licensing

The history of FIM 2010 R2

Let me give you a short summary of the versions preceding FIM 2010 R2.

In 1999, Microsoft bought a company called Zoomit. They had a product called VIA—a directory synchronization product. Microsoft incorporated Zoomit VIA into **Microsoft Metadirectory Services (MMS)**. MMS was only available as a Microsoft Consulting Services solution.

In 2003, Microsoft released **Microsoft Identity Integration Server (MIIS)**, and this was the first publicly available version of the synchronization engine today known as FIM 2010 R2 Synchronization Service.

In 2005, Microsoft bought a company called Alacris. They had a product called IdNexus, which was used to manage certificates and smart cards. Microsoft renamed it **Certificate Lifecycle Manager (CLM).**

In 2007, Microsoft took MIIS (now with Service Pack 2) and CLM and slammed them together into a new product called **Identity Lifecycle Manager 2007 (ILM 2007)**. Despite the name, ILM 2007 was basically a directory synchronization tool with a certificate management side-kicker.

Finally, in 2010, Microsoft released Forefront Identity Manager 2010 (FIM 2010). FIM 2010 was a whole new thing, but as you will see, the old parts from MIIS and CLM are still there. The most fundamental change in FIM 2010 was the addition of the FIM Service component. In my opinion, the most important news was that FIM Service added workflow capability to the synchronization engine. Many identity management operations that used to require a lot of coding were suddenly available without a single line of code.

Many things in this book will be valid for FIM 2010, but this book will cover the R2 release of FIM 2010, released in 2012. In FIM 2010 R2, Microsoft added the FIM Reporting component and also made significant improvements to the other components.

Chapter 2

FIM Synchronization Service (FIM Sync)

FIM Synchronization Service is the *oldest* member of the FIM family. Anyone who has worked with MIIS back in 2003 will feel quite at home with it. Visually, the management tools look the same.

FIM Synchronization Service can actually work by itself, without any other component of FIM 2010 R2 being present. You will then basically get the same functionality as MIIS had, back in 2003.

FIM Synchronization Service is the heart of FIM, which pumps the data around, causing information about identities to flow from one system to another.

Let's look at the pieces that make up the FIM Synchronization Service:

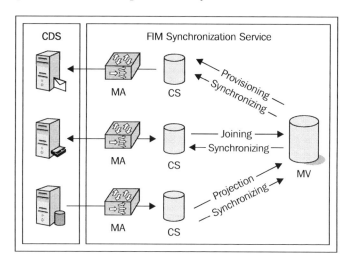

As you can see, there are lots of acronyms and concepts that need a little explaining.

On the right-hand side of **FIM Synchronization Service**, we have **Metaverse (MV)**. Metaverse is used to collect all the information about all the identities managed by FIM.

On the other side, we have **Connected Data Source (CDS)**. Connected Data Source is the database, directory, and file, among others, that the synchronization service imports information regarding the managed identities from, and/or exports this information to.

[17]

To talk to different kinds of Connected Data Sources, FIM Synchronization Service uses adapters that are called **Management Agents (MA)**. In FIM 2010 R2, we will start to use the term **Connectors**, instead. But, as the user interface in FIM Synchronization Manager still uses the term Management Agent, I will use that term throughout this book.

The Management Agent stores a representation of the objects in the CDS, in its **Connector Space (CS)**. When stored in the Connector Space, we refer to the objects as **holograms**. If we were to look into this a little deeper, we would find that the holograms (objects) are actually stored in multiple instances so that the Management Agent can keep a track of the changes to the objects in the Connector Space.

In order to synchronize information from/to different Connected Data Sources, we connect the objects in the Connector Space with the corresponding object in the Metaverse. By collecting information from all Connected Data Sources, the synchronization engine aggregates the information about the object from all the Connected Data Sources into the Metaverse object. This way, the Metaverse will only contain one representation of the object (for example, a user).

To describe the data flow within the synchronization service, let's look at the previous diagram and follow a typical scenario.

The scenario is this—we want information in our **Human Resource (HR)** system to govern how users appear in **Active Directory (AD)** and in our e-mail system.

1. **Import users from HR**: The bottom CDS could be our HR system. We configure a Management Agent to import users from HR to the corresponding CS.
2. **Projection to Metaverse**: As there is no corresponding user in the MV that we can connect to, we tell the MA to create a new object in the MV. The process of creating new objects in the MV is called **Projection**. To transfer information from the HR CS to the MV, we configure Inbound Synchronization Rules.
3. **Import and join users from AD**: The middle CDS could be Active Directory (AD). We configure a Management Agent to import users from AD. Because there are objects in the MV, we can now tell the Management Agent to try to match the user objects from AD to the objects in the MV. Connecting existing objects in a Connector Space, to an existing object in the Metaverse, is called **Joining**. In order for the synchronization service to know which objects to connect, some kind of unique information must be present, to get a one-to-one mapping between the object in the CS and the object in the Metaverse.

4. **Synchronize information from HR to AD**: Once the Metaverse object has a connector to both the HR CS and the AD CS, we can move information from the HR CS to the AD CS. We can, for example, use the employee status information in the HR system to modify the *userAccountControl* attribute of the AD account. In order to modify the AD CS object, we configure an Outbound Synchronization rule that will tell the synchronization service how to update the CS object based on the information in the MV object. Synchronizing, however, does not modify the user object in AD; it only modifies the hologram representation of the user in the AD Connector Space.

5. **Export information to AD**: In order to actually change any information in a Connected Data Source, we need to tell the MA to export the changes. During export, the MA updates the objects in the CDS with the changes it has made to the hologram in the Connector Space.

6. **Provision users to the e-mail system**: The top CDS could be our e-mail system. As users are not present in this system, we would like the synchronization service to create new objects in the CS for the e-mail system. The process of creating new objects in a Connector Space is called **Provisioning**.

Projection, Joining, and Provisioning all create a connector between the Metaverse object and the Connector Space object, making it possible to synchronize identity information between different Connected Data Sources.

A key concept to understand here, is that you do **not** configure synchronization between Connected Data Sources or between Connector Spaces. You synchronize between each Connector Space and Metaverse. Looking at the previous example, you can see that when information flows from HR to AD, you configure the following:

- HR MA to Import data to the HR CS
- Inbound synchronization from the HR CS to the MV
- Outbound synchronization from the MV to the AD CS
- AD MA to Export the data to AD

Management Agents

Management Agents, or Connectors as some people call them, are the entities that enable FIM to talk to different kinds of data sources. Basically, you can say that FIM can talk to any type of data source, but it only has built-in Management Agents for some. If the data source is really old, you might even have to use the extensibility platform and write your own Management Agent or buy a Management Agent from a third-party supplier. At http://aka.ms/FIMPartnerMA, you can find a list of Management Agents supplied by Microsoft Partners.

For a complete list of Management Agents built in and available from Microsoft, please look at http://aka.ms/FIMMA.

With R2, a new Management Agent for **Extensible Connectivity 2.0 (ECMA 2.0)** is released, introducing new ways of making custom Management Agents. I suppose that we will see updated versions of most third party Management Agents as soon as they are migrated to the new ECMA 2.0 platform. Microsoft will also ship new Management Agents using the new ECMA 2.0 platform.

Writing your own MA is one way of solving problems communicating with odd data sources. But, as I will discuss further in *Chapter 11, Customizing Data Transformation*, there might be other solutions to the problem that will require less coding.

Non-declarative vs. declarative synchronization

If you are using FIM Synchronization Service the old way, like we did in MIIS or ILM 2007, it is called non-declarative synchronization. I usually call that *classic* synchronization and will also use that term in this book. If we use the FIM Service logic to control it all, it is called declarative synchronization.

As classic synchronization usually involves writing code, and declarative does not; you will also find references calling declarative synchronization codeless.

In fact, it was quite possible, in some scenarios, to have codeless synchronization—even in the old MIIS or ILM 2007—using classic synchronization. The fact also remains that there are very few FIM 2010 R2 implementations that are indeed code free. In some cases you might even mix the two. This could be due either to migration from MIIS/ILM 2007 to FIM 2010 R2 or to the decision that it is cheaper/quicker/easier to solve a particular problem using classic synchronization.

The solutions I will describe in this book will be based on declarative synchronization, rather than the old-fashioned, classic ones. In *Chapter 11, Customizing Data Transformations*, I will show some examples in which classic synchronization is the best way to solve some problems.

Password synchronization

Let me first state that I am not a fan of using password synchronization. I believe that this should be the last resort to achieve some kind of **Single Sign On (SSO)**. Instead of implementing password synchronization, I try to make my customers look at other ways, such as Kerberos or Federation, to get SSO.

There are, however, many cases where password synchronization is the best option to maintain passwords in different systems. Not all environments can utilize Kerberos or Federation and therefore need the FIM password synchronization feature to maintain passwords in different Connected Data Sources.

The use of this feature is to have Active Directory by either installing and configuring **Password Change Notification Service (PCNS)** on Domain Controllers or using FIM Service as a source for the password change. FIM Synchronization Service then updates the password on the connected object in Connected Data Sources, which are configured as password synchronization targets. In order for FIM to set the password in a target system, the Management Agent used to connect to that specific CDS needs to support this. Most Management Agents available today support password management or can be configured to do so.

FIM Service Management Agent

A very special Management Agent is the one connecting FIM Synchronization Service to FIM Service. Many of the *rules* we apply to other types of Management Agents do not apply to this one. If you have experience working with classic synchronization in MIIS or ILM 2007, you will find that this Management Agent does not work as the others.

This Management Agent will be fully explained in *Chapter 4*, *Basic Configuration*. For now, let's just leave it at the fact that this is a special Management Agent.

FIM Service

If FIM Synchronization Service is the heart pumping information, FIM Service is the brain (sorry FIM CM, but your brain is not as impressive; I'll give you credit later).

FIM Service plays many roles in FIM, and during the design phase the capabilities of FIM Service is often on focus. FIM Service allows you to enforce the Identity Management policy within your organization and also make sure you are compliant at all times.

FIM Service has its own database, where it stores the information about the identities it manages.

Request pipeline

In order to make any changes to objects in the FIM Service database, you need to work your way through the FIM Service request pipeline. So, let's look at the following diagram and walk through the request pipeline:

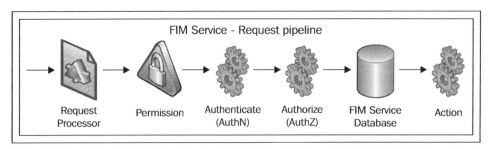

Every request is made to the web service interface, and follows the ensuing flow:

1. The **Request Processor** workflow receives the request and evaluates the token (who?) and the request type (what?).
2. Permission is checked to see if the request is allowed. Management Policy Rules are evaluated.
3. If **Authenticate** workflow is required, serialize and run interactive workflow.
4. If **Authorize** workflow is required, parallelize and run asynchronous workflow.
5. Modify the object in **FIM Service Database** according to the request.
6. If **Action** workflow is required, run follow-up workflows.

As you can see, a request to FIM Service may trigger three types of workflows. With the installation of FIM 2001 R2, you will get a few workflows that will cover many basic requirements, but this is one of the situations where custom coding or third-party workflows might be required in order to fulfill the identity management policy within the organization.

Authentication workflow (AuthN) is used when the request requires additional authentication. An example of this is when a user tries to reset his password—the AuthN workflow will ask the anonymous user to authenticate using the QA gateway.

Authorization workflow (AuthZ) is used when the request requires authorization from someone else. An example of this is when a user is added to a group, but the policy states that the owner of the group needs to approve the request.

Action workflow is used for many types of follow-up actions—it could be sending a notification email or modifying attributes, among many other things.

FIM Service Management Agent

FIM Service Management Agent, as we discussed earlier, is responsible for synchronizing data between FIM Service and FIM Synchronization Service. I said then that this MA is a bit special, and even from the FIM Service perspective it works a little differently.

A couple of examples of the special relationship between the FIM Service MA and FIM Service are as follows:

- Any request made by the FIM Service MA will bypass any AuthN and AuthZ workflows
- As a performance enhancer, the FIM Service MA is allowed to make changes directly to the FIM Service DB in FIM 2010 R2, without using the request pipeline described earlier

Management Policy Rules (MPRs)

The way we control what can be done, or what should happen, is by defining **Management Policy Rules (MPRs)** within FIM Service.

MPR is our tool to enforce the Identity Management policies within our organization.

There are two types of MPRs—Request and Set Transition.

A **Request** MPR is used to define how the request pipeline should behave on a particular request. If a request comes in and there is no Request MPR matching the request, it will fail.

A **Set Transition** MPR is used to detect changes in objects and react upon that change. For example, if my `EmployeeStatus` is changed to `Fired`, my Active Directory (AD) account should be disabled.

A **Set** is used within FIM Service to group objects. We define rules that govern the criteria for an object to be part of a Set. For example, we can create a Set, which contains all users with `Fired` as `EmployeeStatus`. As objects satisfy this criteria and transition in to the Set, we can define a Set Transition MPR to make things such as disabling the AD account happen. We can also define an MPR that applies to the transition out from a Set.

The Sets are also used to configure permissions within FIM Service. Using Sets allows us to configure very granular permissions in scenarios where FIM Service is used for user self service.

FIM Portal

FIM Portal is usually the starting point for administrators who will configure FIM Service. The configuration of FIM Service is usually done using FIM Portal, but it may also be configured using Power Shell or even your own custom interface.

FIM Portal can also be used for self-service scenarios, allowing users to manage some aspect of the Identity Management process.

FIM Portal is actually an ASP.NET application using Microsoft Sharepoint as a foundation, and can be modified in many ways.

Self Service Password Reset (SSPR)

The **Self Service Password Reset (SSPR)** feature of FIM is a special case, where most components used to implement it are built-in.

The default method is using what is called a QA Gate. FIM 2010 R2 also has built-in methods for using a **One Time Password (OTP)** that can be sent using either SMS, or e-mail services.

In short, the QA Gate works in the following way:

1. The administrator defines a number of questions.
2. Users register for SSPR and provide answers to the questions.
3. Users are presented with the same questions, when a password reset is needed.
4. Giving the correct answers identifies the user and allows them to reset their password.

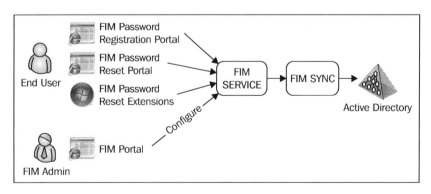

Once the FIM administrator has used **FIM Portal** to configure the password reset feature, the end user can register his answers to QA Gate.

If the organization has deployed **FIM Password Reset Extension** to the end user's Windows client, the process of registration and reset can be made directly from the Windows client. If not, the user can register and reset his password using the password registration and reset portals.

FIM Reporting

The Reporting component is brand new in FIM 2010 R2. In earlier versions of FIM, as well as the older MIIS and ILM, reporting was typically achieved by either buying third-party add-ons or developing their own solutions based on SQL Reporting Services.

The purpose of Reporting is to give you a chance to view historical data. There are a few reports built in to FIM 2010 R2, but many organizations will develop their own reports that comply with their Identity Management policies.

The implementation of FIM 2010 R2 will however be a little more complex, if you want the Reporting component. This is because the engine used to generate the reports is the Data Warehouse component of **Microsoft System Center Service Manager (SCSM)**.

There are a number of reasons for using the existing reporting capabilities in SCSM; the main one, I would guess, is that it is easy to extend.

Since the architecture of the Reporting component is quite complex, I will explain it in a dedicated chapter—*Chapter 9, Reporting*.

FIM Certificate Management (FIM CM)

Certificate Management is the *outcast* member of the FIM family. FIM CM can be, and often is, used by itself, without any other parts of FIM being present. It is also the component with the poorest integration with the other components.

If you look at it, you will find that it hasn't changed much since its predecessor, **Certificate Lifecycle Management (CLM)**, was released.

FIM CM is mainly focused on managing smart cards, but it can also be used to manage and trace any type of certificate requests.

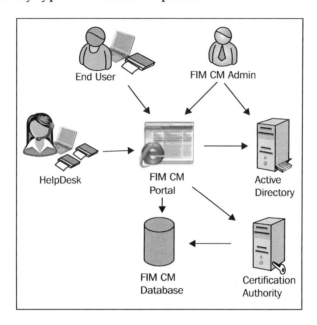

The basic concept of FIM CM is that a smart card is requested using the FIM CM portal. Information regarding all requests is stored in the FIM CM database.

The Certification authority, which handles the issuing of the certificates, is configured to report the status back to the FIM CM database.

FIM CM portal also contains a workflow engine, so that the FIM CM admin can configure features such as e-mail notifications as a part of the policies.

Certificate Management portal

FIM Certificate Management uses a portal to interact with users and administrators. The FIM CM portal is an ASP.Net 2.0 website where, for example:

- Administrators can configure the policies that govern the processes around certificate management
- End users can manage their smart cards for purposes such as renewing and changing PIN codes

- Help desks can use the portal to, for example, request temporary smart cards or reset PINs:

Common Tasks

Use this section to perform actions on users, such as enroll, revoke, recover, or view requests that need approval or completion. You will have to search on the user in order to perform an action on that user.

- Enroll a user for a new set of certificates or a smart card
- View requests that need approvals
- View requests that need completion

Manage Users And Certificates

Use this section to perform actions on a user or on a certificate. You will have to search on the user (or certificate) in order to perform an action on that user or certificate.

- Find a user to view or manage their information
- Find a certificate
- Find a certificate revocation list

Manage User Smart Cards

Use this section to manage a user's smart cards. You can view details of a smart card and perform actions on the smart card, such as unblock.

- Unblock a user's smart card
- Find a smart card
- View details of the smart card currently in the reader

Requests

Use this section to manage requests. You can cancel a request you initiated that is in the pending state, distribute one-time passwords for a request that is approved, and view request information

- Find a request
- Browse completed requests
- Distribute one-time passwords for a request

Administration

Use this section to manage profile templates.

- Manage profile templates

Licensing

I put this part in here, *not* to tell you how FIM 2010 R2 is licensed, but rather to tell you that it is complex. Since Microsoft has a habit of changing the way they license their products, I will not put any license details into writing.

Depending on what parts you are using and, in some cases, how you are using them, you need to buy different licenses. FIM 2010 R2 (at the time of my writing) uses both Server licenses as well as Client Access Licenses (CALs).

In almost every FIM project I have been involved with, the licensing cost has been negligible compared to the gain retrieved by implementing it. But even so, please make sure to contact your Microsoft licensing partner, or your Microsoft contact, to clear any questions you might have around licensing.

If you do not have Microsoft System Center Service Manager (SCSM), it is stated (at the time of my writing) that you can install and use SCSM for FIM Reporting usage without having to buying SCSM licenses.

Read more about FIM Licensing at `http://aka.ms/FIMLicense`.

Summary

As you can see, Microsoft Forefront Identity Manager 2010 R2 is not just one product, but a family of products. In this chapter, I have given you a short overview of the different components, and we saw how together they can mitigate the challenges that The Company has identified about their identity management.

But, as you can see, there are many components involved. In the next chapter, we will look at how to install all these components.

3
Installation

As we have already discussed, Microsoft Forefront Identity Manager 2010 R2 (FIM 2010 R2) is not *one* product, but a family of products.

This also means that there are many different ways of installing the product, depending on what parts you want and how you would like to separate them on different systems.

We can choose to separate the different components based on load or just because we like it clean.

As an example, we will look at the setup used by The Company. They are doing a split installation for the production environment, but for test and development around FIM Sync and FIM Service, they use a single-box approach.

In this chapter we will look at the following:

- Prerequisites for installing different components of FIM 2010 R2
- How to actually install the components
- A few post-installation steps to get it working

Development versus production

If you are using FIM Synchronization Service and FIM Service, you are likely in need of a test/development environment. As I will show you later, migrating from test to production is not that hard with FIM.

The problem is to make your test/development environment look as close as possible to the production environment. The problem with FIM in this case is Connected Data Sources. How to get a representation of each CDS in the test environment is a difficult problem.

Installation

Ideally, you would have a mirrored environment where all systems are represented. But that's not available to everyone. If you do, you're lucky!

The Company is running the test/development FIM Server parallel to the production environment using the same Active Directory. This gives them some special problems that we will discuss in this chapter.

Capacity planning

At the Microsoft download center, you can download the Forefront Identity Manager Capacity Planning Guide (http://aka.ms/FIMCapacityPlanning). I will not dig deep into capacity planning in this book, but rather make sure your setup is made in a way that allows you to easily make your FIM environment expand to cope with future needs.

If you look at the following table, you'll see that capacity planning is not easy since there is no straight answer to the problem. If I have 10,000 users, how should I plan my FIM environment? There are too many other parameters to look at.

Design factor	Considerations
Topology	The distribution of the FIM services among computers on the network.
Hardware	The physical hardware and any virtualized hardware specifications that you are running for each FIM component. This includes CPU, memory, network adapter, and hard drive configurations.
FIM policy configuration objects	The number and type of FIM policy configuration objects, which includes sets, **Management Policy Rules** (**MPRs**), and workflows. For example, how many workflows are triggered for operations, how many set definitions exist, and what is the relative complexity of each?
Scale	The number of users, groups, calculated groups, and custom object types, such as computers, to be managed by FIM. Also consider the complexity of dynamic groups, and be sure to factor in group nesting.
Load	Frequency of anticipated use. For example, the number of times that you expect new groups or users to be created, passwords to be reset, or the portal to be visited in a given time period. Note that the load may vary during the course of an hour, day, week, or year. Depending on the component, you may have to design for peak load or average load.

The fact that the FIM 2010 R2 release includes a number of performance improvements also makes it harder to find relevant facts, since so far most performance testing has been around earlier releases.

I would like to point out one fact, though. In the earlier versions of FIM, MIIS, and ILM, there where huge performance gains by co-locating the synchronization service database with the synchronization service itself. In modern 1-Gigabit networks, and with the changes in the design of FIM, this is no longer the case. And since centralized database servers tend to have better CPU and disk performance, you could even gain performance today by having the database and the service separated.

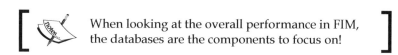

When looking at the overall performance in FIM, the databases are the components to focus on!

Separating roles

If we look at all the FIM features we are about to install, we need to understand that in theory, we might be able to put them all in one box. But, that is not practical, and in some cases is not even supported by Microsoft.

The example setup I use in this book, for The Company, can be used as a starting point.

Databases

As you will see, you will need quite a few databases. Depending on load and other factors, you can choose to install the databases locally on each box hosting a FIM feature or choose to have them all in a central Microsoft SQL server. Or, you can even mix the two approaches.

If you find that your initial approach was not optimal, don't be alarmed. Moving the databases is fully supported. In this book I will use so-called SQL aliases when referencing the databases; one reason for this is that it will make moving the databases simpler.

The System Center Service Manager Data Warehouse, required by the FIM Reporting feature, is usually using a separate SQL server.

FIM features

As with the databases, the FIM features can also be co-located or separated. The only issue here is that FIM Certificate Management should not be co-located with other parts of FIM. The main reason for this is that the FIM CM setup and configuration tool will *think* it owns its local web server (IIS). If you have other FIM features using IIS on the same box, you will get a conflict.

Also, the System Center Service Manager used for Reporting requires separate servers. Read more about that at http://aka.ms/SCSM2010Deployment.

If I were to give you all the possible scenarios for the ways you could separate the FIM features, in order to get fault tolerance, performance, and so on, I would have to add some 50 pages just to cover that topic. I suggest you take a good look at the Microsoft TechNet site (http://aka.ms/FIMPlanning), to find out how your company should separate or co-locate different parts.

In this book, The Company is using a design that can easily be expanded if the need arises. If you find that your company requires much better performance or maybe that you would only use part of the product or co-locate more services, this book will still be valid when it comes to the requirements and the setup procedures.

Hardware

Whether to virtualize or not is the question for many companies today. All components of FIM 2010 R2 can be virtualized. If you have chosen to virtualize your SQL servers, I guess every other service will be virtualized as well. A starting point for the discussion on virtualization is available at http://aka.ms/VirtualizationBestPractices.

If I have noticed one thing during my years as a consultant, it is that customers tend to give virtual machines only one virtual CPU. However, almost every FIM feature can benefit from multiple CPUs, and I would recommend giving at least two to three CPUs to your FIM servers, depending on how you co-locate different FIM features.

The FIM development server at The Company, for example, has two CPUs and 4 GB of RAM. If your test development server is to load and manage *all* your identities, you will likely need to add more RAM to that system.

Installation order

The FIM CM components can be installed regardless of the other FIM pieces.

If you have an existing SCSM environment, the SCSM Servers might already be in place but might still need some updates to support FIM 2001 R2 Reporting.

 At the time of writing, there is no official support for using SCSM 2012.

The following SCSM Servers need to be installed before we install the FIM Reporting feature:

- SCSM Management (if the FIM Reporting feature is to be used)
- SCSM Data Warehouse (if the FIM Reporting feature is to be used)

The FIM components also have some dependencies that make it logical to install them in a certain order. They should be installed in the following order:

1. FIM Synchronization Service
2. FIM Service
3. FIM Portals
4. FIM Reporting

If you have a setup similar to The Company, the order of installation could be to start off with the test/development environment. I am using the syntax *server name: feature to install*, in the following installation lists. The server names refer to the server names used in the description of the environment in *Chapter 1, The Story in this Book*.

1. FIM-Dev: FIM Synchronization Service
2. FIM-Dev: FIM Portal and FIM Service

You can now start testing and development of the FIM Synchronization and FIM Service solutions.

We then move on to install the production environment in the following order:

1. SCSM-MGMT: SCSM Management
2. SCSM-DW: SCSM Data Warehouse
3. FIM-Sync: FIM Synchronization Service
4. FIM-Service: FIM Service, FIM Portal, and FIM Reporting
5. FIM-PW: FIM Password Registration and Reset Portals

The FIM CM can be installed at any point, but it also has two components that I usually install in the following order, since there are dependencies within FIM CM as well:

1. FIM-CM: FIM Certificate Management
2. CA: FIM CM CA Files

Installation

Prerequisites

Before we can start installing any components, there are a number of prerequisites that we need to make sure we have in place.

The main reason for errors in FIM is mistakes made during this phase of the installation. Sometimes, it is hard to backtrack the errors, especially if you get Kerberos authentication errors.

Databases

The Company will have several servers running Microsoft SQL Server. The server names in the following list refer to the server names used in the description of the environment in *Chapter 1, The Story in this Book*:

- FIM-Dev: This SQL server will be used by the FIM Sync and FIM Service running on the FIM-Dev server. But, this instance will also be used to develop and test **SQL Server Integration Services** (**SSIS**) packages and test versions of SQL-based CDSs.
- SQL: This is the central SQL server holding all production databases. This will be used by the FIM-Sync, FIM-Service, and FIM-CM servers. This is also where SQL-based CDSs such as the HR system will be found.
- SCSM-MGMT: This SQL server will be used by SCSM for management. The Company does not have existing SCSM infrastructure and is implementing this for FIM reporting purposes only.
- SCSM-DW: This SQL server will be used by SCSM for data warehousing and reporting. The Company does not have existing SCSM infrastructure and is implementing this for FIM reporting purposes only.

All instances of SQL Server will be running the SQL Server 2008 R2 release. The R2 release of SQL Server 2008 is not a requirement. But since this is a new setup, why not use the latest version?

 At the time of writing there is no official support for using SQL Server 2012.

The technical requirements for the SQL servers are that they must have at least SQL Server 2008 SP2 (64-bit version) installed.

There are many resources on how to install SQL Server, but I have added my own guide here, since I would like to point out some things related to FIM 2010 R2.

Collation and languages

In this book, I will not go into the different SQL Server Collation settings to support different languages in FIM 2010 R2, or in System Center Service Manager 2010. Read more about FIM 2010 R2 language packs at `http://aka.ms/FIMLanguagePacks`.

For more information on SQL Server Collations, please take a look at `http://aka.ms/SQLCollations`. SCSM 2010 has its own collation problems, described at `http://aka.ms/SCSMCollations`.

One reason is that if I should cover one language and collation setting, I should cover them all, so I decided to cover none.

If you need support for other languages, read the information in the previous URLs. On the TechNet site (`http://technet.microsoft.com/en-us/library/hh332707`), the following information can be found to also act as guidance:

> *Work with your SQL Server database administrator (DBA) to determine the correct collation setting to use for your FIM Service database. The collation setting determines the sorting order and how indexing works.*

> *The default collation set during installation is SQL_LATIN1_General_CP1_CI_AS.*

> *If the server running Windows is using a character set that is different from the Latin alphabet, then you might consider a different collation.*

> *Ensure that the selected collation is case insensitive (indicated by _CI_).*

> *If you change the collation setting, ensure that the collation setting is the same on the FIM Service database and on the system databases master and tempdb.*

> *If you install the FIM Service and later decide to change the collation setting, you must manually change the collation setting on every table in the FIM Service database.*

I have so far only worked with customers using the Latin alphabet and therefore use the collation `SQL_LATIN1_General_CP1_CI_AS`, to begin with.

Since not all components of FIM 2010 R2 have the same list of supported languages, you need to figure out at what user interfaces other languages might be required within your organization, and if they are supported by the features of FIM you intend to use.

Installation

SQL aliases

It is highly recommended that you use SQL aliases for the database connections used by different FIM pieces. The reason for this is that it simplifies moves of databases to other SQL servers and also makes failover to a mirror SQL easier.

If you want to use aliases for the service databases, you need to configure them before starting installation.

The utility you use on the SQL client is `cliconfg`, and adding an alias looks similar to the following screenshot:

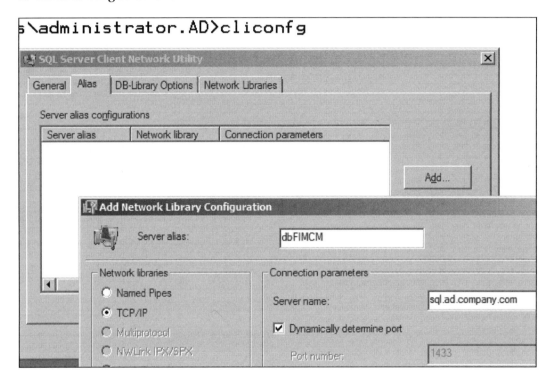

Be careful and specify the port, if the local. Windows firewall on your SQL server only allows connection to TCP 1433, or whatever port your instance is using.

The Company will use this approach for all production servers and for all SQL **Management Agents (MAs)**. Using SQL aliases on SQL Management Agents makes it easier to move a configuration from test to production, allowing the *same* SQL alias to point to different SQL instances and making the FIM-Dev server use the test instances of the databases, while the production FIM-Sync server uses the production instances.

Depending on the software using the alias, you might need to install the SQL Client Connectivity component. It is, for example, required when using SharePoint Foundation.

If you use SQL aliases in your SharePoint Foundation farm, to connect to the SQL Server, you must install the SQL client connectivity components on your farm servers, in order to use the SPF-VSS writer for backup/restore. The components include SQL WMI provider for configuration management, which the SPF-VSS writer needs to resolve SQL aliases to the correct SQL Server. It is not necessary to install any of the management tools, such as SQL Management Studio. You must use the same installation source (for example, a data DVD) that you would use to install the full SQL Server product. Choose to make a custom installation and choose only the client components to install.

Do not use the separate, standalone version of the client components. That version does not include the SQL WMI provider.

The Company has identified that the SQL aliases in the following table are required for the FIM Implementation:

SQL Alias	SQL Client	SQL Server
dbSharePoint	FIM-Dev	FIM-Dev
dbSharePoint	FIM-Service	SQL
dbFIMSync	FIM-Dev	FIM-Dev
dbFIMSync	FIM-Sync	SQL
dbFIMService	FIM-Dev	FIM-Dev
dbFIMService	FIM-Service	SQL
dbFIMService	FIM-Sync	SQL
dbFIMCM	FIM-CM	SQL

As you might have noticed, I am not using aliases for the SCSM databases. This is because the SCSM setup suggests the local SQL server to host the databases used by the SCSM Management and the SCSM Data Warehouse features. On the SCSM 2010 TechNet site (http://technet.microsoft.com/en-us/library/ff461010), there is no information, at the time of writing, on whether SCSM 2010 supports aliases or not.

FIM-Dev

The SQL installation on the FIM-Dev server has a few non-standard steps. The reason is that, on this server, we will also install Visual Studio 2008, in order to be able to not only create custom FIM add-ons such as workflows but also develop SSIS packages. This means we need to coordinate the SQL installation with the Visual Studio installation.

I will not give you a complete step-by-step guide for this; I will just point out the critical parts as follows:

1. Install SQL Server 2008 R2 with the following components:
    i. Feature Selection
       Database Engine Services
       Full-Text Search
       Integration Services
       Client Tools Connectivity
       Management Tools – Basic
       Management Tools – Complete
    ii. Server Configuration
       SQL Server Agent: Startup Type: Automatic
2. Install SQL Server 2008 R2 SP1.
3. Install Visual Studio 2008.
4. Install Visual Studio 2008 SP1.
5. Modify the SQL Server 2008 R2 installation and add the feature Business Intelligence Development Studio.
6. Reapply SQL Server 2008 R2 SP1.
7. Apply updates from Windows Update to VS and SQL.

SQL

The installation of a central SQL server or adding of instances to an existing SQL server or SQL server cluster is usually not part of the FIM installation but rather something you order from your database administrators.

The SQL feature requirements for each service database are as follows:

- FIM Synchronization Service: Database Engine Service
- FIM Service: Database Engine Service and Full-Text Search
- FIM CM: Database Engine Service

In many solutions where FIM is used, SQL Server Integration Services (SSIS) is also used. This is not a requirement, but with SSIS we will be able to add some data transformation to our solution. This will be described a little bit more in *Chapter 11, Customizing Data Transformations*.

> Remember to make sure the local Windows firewall is allowing inbound connections to SQL services (TCP 1433), in order for it to be used by the different FIM services hosting their databases on it.

In order for the servers to use a remote SQL server, you need to install the SQL Server Native Client on these servers. This can be downloaded separately, or you can install it from the SQL Server media (Client Tools Connectivity). As we have already discussed in this chapter, I prefer to always use Client Tools Connectivity from the SQL Server media.

For troubleshooting purposes, you might also want the SQL Management tools installed on the FIM servers.

SCSM

The Company will have separate servers hosting SCSM and the databases required by SCSM. This is because they are, at the moment, not sure about how to use the Reporting feature, and the FIM Reporting implementation is considered a kind of FIM Reporting test. If this feature is required full scale in a large organization, you need to take a very close look at how to design the SCSM infrastructure to cope with the possibly very large amount of data the data warehouse might be required to handle.

SCSM requires that:

- The System Center Service Manager Management Server be deployed to a standalone machine—a separate SQL server instance is recommended
- The System Center Service Manager Data Warehouse and associated database be deployed to a standalone machine—a separate SQL server instance is recommended

Installation

So basically, the SCSM installation will use two SQL servers, one on the SCSM-MGMT server and one on the SCSM-DW server.

The Company will use the two-server deployment scenario of SCSM, as described at Microsoft TechNet (http://aka.ms/SCSM2010Deployment); a summary is shown in the following figure:

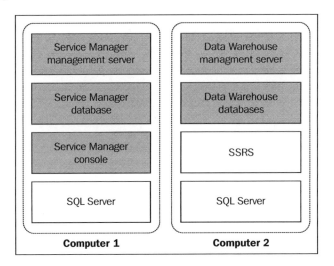

At The Company, **Computer 1** is the SCSM-MGMT server and **Computer 2** is the SCSM-DW server.

In the SCSM documentation (http://aka.ms/SCSM2010Deployment), there is a mention of the requirement of an Authorization Manager hotfix (http://support.microsoft.com/kb/975332). This hotfix, however, is included in Windows Server 2008 R2 SP1.

The SQL feature requirements for SCSM-MGMT are as follows:

- Database Engine Services: Full-Text Search

The SQL feature requirements for SCSM-DW are as follows:

- Database Engine Services: Full-Text Search
- Reporting Services: On the Reporting Services Configuration page, you should select the option to **Install the native mode default configuration**

Web servers

There are a number of web servers involved when installing FIM 2010 R2. Depending on load and/or Service Level Agreement (SLA), you might require some kind of load balancing deployment. The goal of the setup at The Company is to make the FIM 2010 R2 deployment as easy as possible to scale out, in case it is needed later on.

One way of making scaling out easier is to use aliases for the websites and run all application pools as user accounts. That way, it will be easy for The Company to extend the websites into farms, if required in the future.

FIM Portal

The FIM Portal is the interface for administrating the FIM Service and also for user self-service.

FIM Portal will be installed on two different servers at The Company, as follows:

- FIM-Dev: For test and development
- FIM-Service: For production

The FIM Portal is based on SharePoint and requires that Windows SharePoint Services 3.0 (WSS) or Microsoft SharePoint Foundation 2010 be installed.

By default, WSS and SharePoint Foundation use a local Windows Internal Database, and if you would like to use a central database instead, you need to modify the default setup.

The Company is using Microsoft SharePoint Foundation 2010 SP1. The setup of SharePoint Foundation on the FIM-Dev server is using the local SQL server and the setup on the FIM-Service server will use the central SQL server for the SharePoint databases.

As with SQL Servers, web servers might also move from one server to another or need to be scaled out into a farm. In those cases, it is useful to implement some alias for the websites. It is simple to add a new DNS record, so that users can type something else in their browser and still end up on the web server you would like them to.

Installation

But since we are dealing with SharePoint and also use Kerberos and SSL, it's a little more complex. For every alias you need to:

- Add a so-called Alternate Access Mapping in SharePoint
- Add a **Subject Alternative Name (SAN)** in a certificate
- Register a new SPN (Service Principle Name)

The URLs used by the The Company to access the two instances of the FIM Portal will be `https://Dev-FIMPortal` and `https://FIMPortal`, where `Dev-FIMPortal` is an alias for the FIM-Dev server and `FIMPortal` is an alias for the FIM-Service server.

FIM Password Reset

The FIM Password Registration and Reset portals at The Company will be installed on a separate server, FIM-PW.

The requirement of the web server is that it support ASP.NET and the Authentication Method (usually Windows Authentication) that you are planning to use in the Password Registration Portal.

Add the web server (IIS) role and add the following components to the default ones:

- ASP.NET (will add some additional components automatically)
- Windows Authentication
- IIS 6 Management Compatibility (including all subcomponents)

It is a best practice to use SSL when users access the Password Registration and Reset portals. If you, as The Company, are hosting both portals on the same server, you might also need to consider adding DNS aliases as well as additional IP addresses, if you would like to use the default port TCP 443 for SSL.

The Company is using two different aliases for the two portals, `FIM-PW-Reg` and `FIM-PW-Reset`.

The preparation on the IIS server will include the following steps:

1. Install a certificate with the correct SAN entries.

    As you can see in the following Certificate Request, The Company will use the same SAN certificate for both websites:

Chapter 3

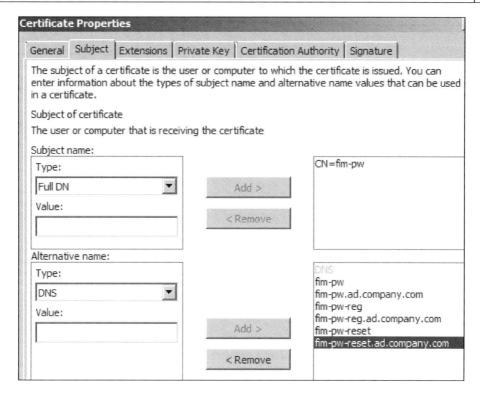

2. Add extra IP addresses to host the different sites.

   The Company adds two extra IP addresses to be used by the FIM Password portals, as you can see in the following screenshot:

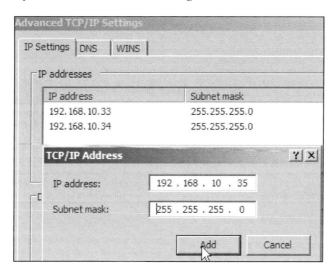

Installation

3. Create the DNS records required for clients to find the two portals.

FIM-PW	Host (A)	192.168.10.33	static
FIM-PW-Reg	Host (A)	192.168.10.34	static
FIM-PW-Reset	Host (A)	192.168.10.35	static

4. After installing the FIM Password portals IIS will be configured to bind these portals to the new IP addresses, using SSL on standard port 443.

FIM Certificate Management

The FIM CM server is basically a web application. The setup will not install the required web server roles. The requirements on the FIM CM server before installing the FIM CM are as follows:

- Add the web server (IIS) role and add the following components to the default ones:
    - HTTP Redirection
    - ASP.NET (will add some additional components automatically)
    - Windows Authentication
    - Dynamic Content Compression
    - IIS 6 Management Compatibility (including all subcomponents)
- FIM CM also requires the feature .NET Framework 3.5.1 to be installed.

> Make sure you only add the subcomponent .NET Framework 3.5.1. If you happen to select the parent component .NET Framework 3.5.1 Features, you will also get the WCF Activation component, which we do not want in this case.

The FIM CM portal requires you to use SSL, so the web server needs to have an SSL certificate containing the hostnames used to access the website. The Company will use the alias of cm.ad.company.com, to access the FIM CM portal. To also enable the use of the actual server name, the certificate used will be requested using the following name information:

- Subject name:
    - CN=cm.ad.company.com

- Alternative name:
    - `DNS=cm.ad.company.com`
    - `DNS=cm`
    - `DNS=fim-cm.ad.company.com`
    - `DNS=fim-cm`

Service accounts

Before we start the installation, we need to create a few service accounts used when installing the FIM environment. The Company uses a separate set of service accounts to be used by the development environment running on FIM-Dev.

It is crucial that you know your service accounts and use a good naming standard, so that it is easy to understand where and how it is used.

The only service account that is a bit *special* is the service account used by FIM Service. In order for FIM Service to actively take part in (both send and receive) e-mail-based workflows, it needs to be an account that has Microsoft Exchange Mailbox. If you do not have Exchange as your e-mail system, FIM Service can only send e-mails but not receive them.

The accounts created by The Company are listed in the following table:

Account name	Usage	Notes
`Dev-FIMMA`	Used on the FIM-Dev server by FIM Synchronization Service to access FIM Service and other CDSs.	The Company uses this account for other Management Agents (MAs). Whether to use fewer accounts and use the same account for multiple MAs, or have a separate account for each MA depends on your internal policies.
		During setup of FIM Service, on the FIM-Dev server, this account is assigned to the Built-in Synchronization account.
		This account requires that you add it to the following User Rights Assignments, either using group policy or using the local security policy: • Allow log on locally

Installation

Account name	Usage	Notes
`Dev-FIMService`	Used on the FIM-Dev server. User account for the FIM Service service.	A mailbox user account so that the FIM Service can both send and receive e-mails during workflows. E-mail address at The Company is `dev-fimservice@ad.company.com`.
		To secure this account, it is recommended that you add it to the following User Rights Assignments either using group policy or using the local security policy: • Deny log on as a batch job • Deny log on locally • Deny access to this computer from the network
`Dev-FIMSync`	Used on the FIM-Dev server. User account for the FIM Synchronization service.	To secure this account, it is recommended that you add it to the following User Rights Assignments, either using group policy or using the local security policy: • Deny log on as a batch job • Deny log on locally • Deny access to this computer from the network
`Dev-FIMSPPool`	Used on the FIM-Dev server. User account for the SharePoint Application Pool.	
`svcFIMMA`	Used on the FIM-Sync server by FIM Synchronization Service to access FIM Service and other CDSs.	The Company uses this account for other Management Agents. Whether to use fewer accounts and use the same account for multiple MAs, or have a separate account for each MA depends on your internal policies.
		During setup of FIM Service, this account is assigned to the Built-In-Synchronization account.
		This account needs that you add it to the following User Rights Assignments, either using group policy or using the local security policy: • Allow log on locally

Account name	Usage	Notes
`svcFIMService`	Used on the FIM-Service server. User account for the FIM Service service.	A mailbox user account so that the FIM Service can both send and receive e-mails during workflows. E-mail address at The Company is `fimservice@ad.company.com`.
		To secure this account, it is recommended that you add it to the following User Rights Assignments, either using group policy or using the local security policy: • Deny log on as a batch job • Deny log on locally • Deny access to this computer from the network
`svcFIMSync`	Used on the FIM-Sync server. User account for the FIM Synchronization service.	To secure this account, it is recommended that you add it to the following User Rights Assignments either using group policy or using the local security policy: • Deny log on as a batch job • Deny log on locally • Deny access to this computer from the network
`svcFIMSPPool`	Used on the FIM-Service server. User account for the SharePoint Application Pool.	
`svcFIMPWService`	Used on FIM-PW, as the account used by FIM Password Registration and Reset portal.	
`svcFIMCMPool`	Used on the FIM CM server. User account for the Web Application Pool.	In *Chapter 12, Issuing Smart Cards*, we will look at some other service accounts used by FIM CM.
`svcSCSMAdmin`	Used on SCSM-MGMT and SCSM-DW, as the Management Group Administrator.	

Installation

Account name	Usage	Notes
svcSCSMService	Used on SCSM-MGMT and SCSM-DW, as the Service account for the Management Service.	Needs to be local administrator on the SCSM-MGMT and SCSM-DW servers.
svcSCSMWF	Used on SCSM-MGMT, for workflows.	Must have permissions to send e-mail and must have a mailbox on the SMTP server (required for the E-mail Incident feature).
svcSCSMReport	Used on SCSM-DW for Reporting.	Used by SQL Server Reporting Services to access the DWDataMart database to get data for reporting.

As you can see, there are quite a number of service accounts required for a complete FIM deployment. Before you go ahead and create all of them, make sure you are actually planning to use the feature requiring the specific service account.

Kerberos configuration

Everything in FIM is based on Kerberos authentication! FIM Service only accepts Kerberos authentication. Furthermore, there are many occasions when FIM service accounts need to act on behalf of the user, using what is called Kerberos Delegation. Sometimes Kerberos Delegation is limited to only specific services and we usually call that **Kerberos Constrained Delegation (KCD)**.

The primary reason for not getting your FIM deployment working is some mistakes in the Kerberos configuration. Once in place, it will just work, but changes in the environment, such as usage of new aliases, will make it necessary to make adjustments over time.

Let me give you one example to clarify this a little more.

A user accesses the FIM Portal, `http://fimportal`; FIM Portal acts on behalf of the user to access FIM Service on the server FIM-Service, so that the FIM Service *thinks* it is the original user that is making the request.

To make this a little more complex, Kerberos introduces what is called a **Service Principal Name (SPN)**. The SPN is used by the client to retrieve the so-called Service Ticket used to perform Kerberos authentication against a service. The SPN is a way to tell Active Directory which account is responsible for that service.

In order for an account to act on behalf of others, it needs to be configured in Active Directory to be trusted for delegation.

Let's say that the http service for the name fimportal is owned by the account svcFIMSPPool, and that the FIMService service is owned by the account svcFIMService.

We then first tell AD who owns which service, by using the setspn command. In the example, it would be setspn -S http/fimportal svcFIMSPPool and setspn -S FIMService/FIM-Service svcFIMService. We would then need to configure the svcFIMSPPool account to be trusted for delegation to the FIMService service owned by the svcFIMService account.

But that was just an overview. Let's look at the exact commands used by The Company to configure the Kerberos settings in their environment.

First of all, we need to make sure that IIS is using the application pool account and not the local system account when performing Kerberos authentication. In IIS 7, a new performance enhancement was added that gave IIS the possibility to use what is called Kernel Mode authentication. This however means that IIS 7 defaults to using its system account, even if you configure the use of a different application pool account.

In FIM, we will use a lot of application pool accounts and will therefore need to modify the behavior in IIS on all portal servers.

There are multiple ways of doing this; I usually configure IIS to continue to use the enhanced performance in Kernel Mode authentication and also use the application pool identity whenever possible.

SharePoint, however—at the time of writing—does not support Kernel Mode authentication. On the SharePoint-based FIM Portal servers, the solution is therefore to turn off Kernel Mode authentication. Chun Liu has written a blog post describing why we should do that (http://blogs.msdn.com/b/chunliu/archive/2010/03/24/why-SharePoint-2010-not-use-kernel-mode-authentication-in-iis7.aspx). Supported or not, I have been using Kernel Mode authentication in almost all my FIM Portal deployments, without any errors. If you do, be prepared to turn it off in case you run into any errors that might be related to it.

To configure IIS to use both Kernel Mode and the application pool identity, we need to do a little configuration file editing:

1. On the web server, open an elevated (run as administrator) command prompt and navigate to C:\Windows\System32\inetsrv\config.
2. Type Notepad applicationHost.config; this will open up the configuration file we need to modify. If you have some kind of XML editor instead, you can use that instead of Notepad. It would also be a best practice to make a backup copy of the applicationHost.config file before starting to edit it.

Installation

3. In the `applicationHost.config` file, navigate to the section `<system.webServer>` (in one of my example files it is on line 280, but depending on what you installed, it might be somewhere else).

4. In the `<system.webServer>` section, find the `<security>` section.

5. In the `<security>` section, locate the `<windowsAuthentication>` section.

6. Modify the line `<windowsAuthentication enabled="false">`, so that it reads `<windowsAuthentication enabled="false" useAppPoolCredentials="true">`.

7. Save the file and run `iisreset`, to have IIS accept the new settings.

In the latest versions of IIS, Internet Information Services Manager can be used to modify this value by using the **Configuration Editor** tool found in the **Management** section in IIS Manager. If you start the Configuration Editor, you can navigate to **system.webServer | security | authentication | windowsAuthentication** and set the **useAppPoolCredentials** value to **True**.

SETSPN

The `SETSPN` utility is what you use to configure and verify all the SPNs used by FIM.

If you type `SETSPN /?`, you will get a list of parameters to use. These vary a little from one version of Windows to another. In my examples, I am using Windows Server 2008 R2 SP1.

The most common switches for SETSPN are as follows:

- `SETSPN -S`: Add SPN after verifying that no duplicates exist (`-A` is available in older versions of Windows only; it adds SPN but does not check for duplicates)
- `SETSPN -Q`: Query for existence of SPN
- `SETSPN -L`: List SPNs registered to an account

There are multiple registrations made by The Company.

For the FIM-Dev environment, the following is registered:

```
SETSPN -S http/FIM-Dev Dev-FIMSPPool
SETSPN -S http/FIM-Dev.ad.company.com Dev-FIMSPPool
SETSPN -S http/Dev-FIMPortal Dev-FIMSPPool
SETSPN -S http/Dev-FIMPortal.ad.company.com Dev-FIMSPPool
SETSPN -S FIMService/FIM-Dev Dev-FIMService
SETSPN -S FIMService/FIM-Dev.ad.company.com Dev-FIMService
```

> **Downloading the example code**
> You can download the example code files for all Packt books you have purchased from your account at http://www.packtpub.com. If you purchased this book elsewhere, you can visit http://www.packtpub.com/support and register to have the files e-mailed directly to you.

By using `SETSPN -L`, you should get the results shown in the following screenshot, so that you can verify that the correct SPNs have been registered to the `Dev-FIMSPPool` and `Dev-FIMService` accounts:

```
C:\Users\Administrator>SETSPN -L Dev-FIMSPPool
Registered ServicePrincipalNames for CN=Dev-FIMSPPool,OU=FIM Service Accounts,DC=ad,DC=company,DC=com:
        http/Dev-FIMPortal.ad.company.com
        http/Dev-FIMPortal
        http/fim-dev.ad.company.com
        http/fim-dev

C:\Users\Administrator>SETSPN -L Dev-FIMService
Registered ServicePrincipalNames for CN=Dev-FIMService,OU=FIM Service Accounts,DC=ad,DC=company,DC=com:
        FIMService/FIM-Dev.ad.company.com
        FIMService/FIM-Dev
```

For the FIM production environment, there are a few more accounts involved, since this also involves the FIM Certificate Management, FIM Password, and FIM Reporting environments.

For the FIM Service and FIM Portal in the production environment to work, the following is registered:

```
SETSPN -S http/FIM-Service svcFIMSPPool
SETSPN -S http/FIM-Service.ad.company.com svcFIMSPPool
SETSPN -S http/FIMPortal svcFIMSPPool
SETSPN -S http/FIMPortal.ad.company.com svcFIMSPPool
SETSPN -S FIMService/FIM-Service svcFIMService
```

For the FIM Password Registration portal, you do not need any SPN if the URL used is the actual server name, but since The Company uses `FIM-PW-Reg` as an alias, the following is registered:

```
SETSPN -S http/FIM-PW-Reg svcFIMPWService
SETSPN -S http/FIM-PW-Reg.ad.company.com svcFIMPWService
```

Installation

The FIM CM server will be using an application pool identity. `svcFIMCMPool` is the account name used by The Company. This account will be used by the `http` service of the FIM CM server. The FIM CM configuration wizard will do the registration for some of these SPNs for us, but if we plan to use some alias, like The Company uses `cm.ad.company.com`, we need to add them manually. So, The Company needs to add the following registrations:

```
SETSPN -S http/cm.ad.company.com svcFIMCMPool
SETSPN -S http/cm svcFIMCMPool
```

Delegation

Delegation is configured when one account needs to act on behalf of another account.

There are many occasions when this occurs within an FIM deployment. The most common one is when a user accesses FIM Portal, and the Web Application Pool Identity needs to perform Kerberos Delegation to the FIM Service.

Delegation configuration is performed in Active Directory using the **Delegation** tab of the account that needs to perform delegation.

The delegations configured within The Company for different scenarios are as follows:

Account name	Delegation to…	Scenario
`Dev-FIMSPPool`	FIMService/Dev-FIMService	The FIM Portal on the FIM-Dev server needs to access the FIM Service on the FIM-Dev server.
`Dev-FIMService`	FIMService/Dev-FIMService	In case a workflow running in the FIM Service needs to access the FIM Service.
`svcFIMSPPool`	FIMService/svcFIMService	The FIM Portal on the FIM-Service server needs to access the FIM Service on the FIM-Service server.
`svcFIMService`	FIMService/svcFIMService	In case a workflow running in the FIM Service needs to access the FIM Service.
`svcFIMPWService`	FIMService/svcFIMService	Password Registration and Reset Portal needs to access the FIM Service on the FIM-Service server.
`svcFIMCMPool`	HOST/ca.ad.company.com	The FIM CM application pool account needs to access the CA server.

System Center Service Manager Console

If you are going to use the Reporting Feature of FIM 2010 R2, you need to install the System Center Service Manager Console on the server(s) running the feature.

Installing the SCSM console is, at the moment, a three-step installation. You will need to install the following components, in order:

1. SCSM 2010 SP1 Service Manager console.

    On the splash screen of SCSM 2010 SP1, select **Install a Service Manager console**.

    During the installation of the console, you will get the opportunity to install Microsoft Report Viewer Redistributable if you haven't already.

2. Cumulative Update 2, KB2542118.
3. Hotfix, KB2561430.

Installation

The installation of the different components is quite straightforward, once the prerequisites are in place.

FIM Synchronization Service

The Company will have two separate instances of FIM Synchronization Service, one on the FIM-Dev server and one on the FIM-Sync server.

The FIM Synchronization Service setup creates five security groups. The first three groups correspond with the FIM Synchronization Service user roles — Administrator, Operator, and Joiner. The other two groups are used for granting access to the Windows Management Instrumentation (WMI) interfaces — Connector Browse and Password Set.

By default, the FIM Synchronization Service creates the five security groups as local computer groups instead of domain global groups. If you plan to use domain global groups, you must create the groups before you install FIM Synchronization Service.

The account doing the installation needs to be a local administrator on the server and also needs to have enough permission on the SQL server to create the database.

The setup itself is quite straightforward. The following guide does not cover every step of the wizard, just the ones where you need to pay attention:

1. To start the setup for FIM Synchronization Service, open up the FIM 2010 R2 DVD and run `Setup.exe` in the `Synchronization Service` folder. I make it a habit to right-click and choose **Run as administrator**.

Installation

2. FIM Synchronization Service will create a few *data* folders where it will store temporary data. If you have a strict policy against storing data in C:, you might consider installing on some other drive.

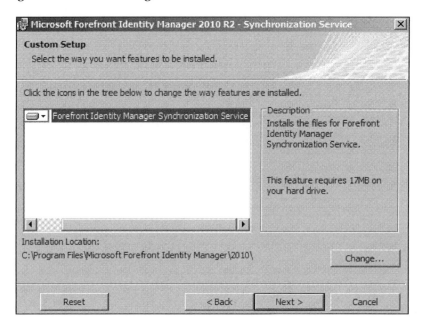

3. Since we are using a SQL alias, **dbFIMSync**, we configure the SQL server as a remote machine even on FIM-Dev, where the SQL server is local.

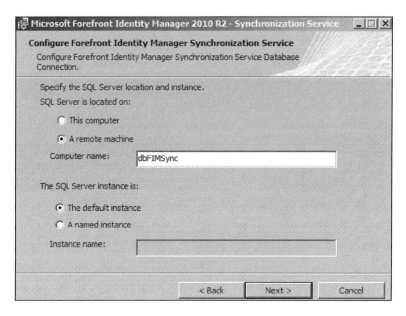

[54]

Chapter 3

4. You might receive the error shown in the following screenshot when doing the installation on the FIM-Sync server, where the SQL alias is pointing to the remote server `sql.ad.company.com`. Two things you need to check here are as follows:
    - Is the local windows firewall on the SQL server allowing the connection?
    - Have you installed the SQL Server Native Client software on the FIM server?

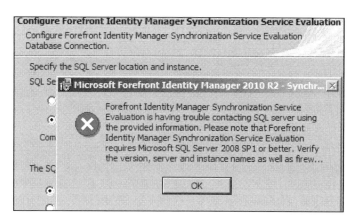

5. Remember to use the correct service account for the specific instance of the FIM Synchronization service. On FIM-Dev, it is **Dev-FIMSync**, and on FIM-Sync it is **svcFIMSync**.

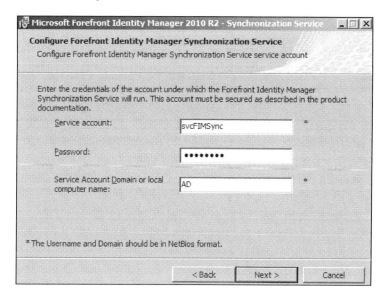

Installation

6. By default, setup will create local groups for the different roles in FIM Synchronization service. If you have created domain groups instead, specify these as `domain\groupname`.

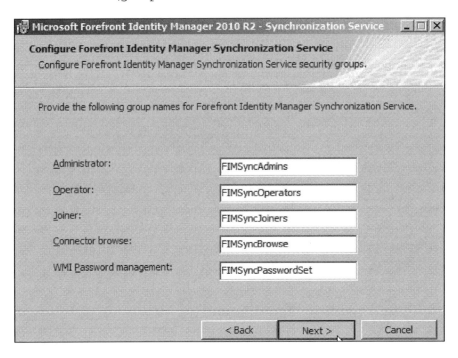

7. You should allow setup to open up the local windows firewall to allow FIM Service to do, say, password resets. If the local firewall is managed using group policies, make sure to add the appropriate rules to the policy configuration.

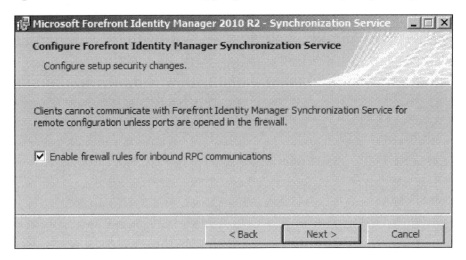

Chapter 3

8. If you have not secured the service account as suggested, you will get a warning. To secure this account, it is recommended that you add it to the following User Rights Assignments, either using group policy or using the local security policy:
   - Deny log on as a batch job
   - Deny log on locally
   - Deny access to this computer from the network

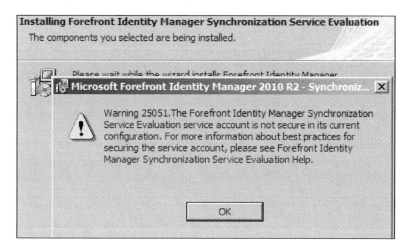

9. At the end of the installation, you will get a prompt about backing up the encryption keys.

Make sure you keep track of the location where the encryption key is saved.

The encryption key generated should be saved in a secure location.

[57]

Installation

10. After finishing the setup, you are prompted to log off and log on again. The account used during installation is automatically added to the `FIMSyncAdmins` group. The log off/log on is to make sure that group membership takes effect.

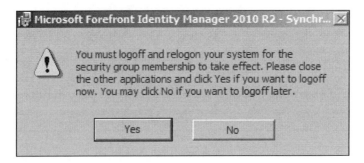

FIM Service and FIM Portal

As with the Synchronization service, The Company will have two separate instances of FIM Service and FIM Portal.

The Company is initially co-locating FIM Service and FIM Portal on the same boxes. Depending on load and other parameters, they might in future decide to separate the two and also scale out into a farm of servers.

To install FIM Service and FIM Portal, the user running the installation needs to:

- Be a local administrator
- Be an administrator in the SharePoint site that will host the FIM Portal
- Have permission to create the database on the database server

The account performing the installation will be given the administrator role within FIM Service. This account is the only account initially able to do anything within FIM Portal and FIM Service. In this book, I am using the `AD\Administrator` account, but I need to point out that it is considered a best practice to create a separate account to perform the installation and become the FIM Service administrator.

Chapter 3

To start the setup of FIM Service and FIM Portal, open up the FIM 2010 R2 DVD and run `Setup.exe` in the `Service and Portal` folder. I make it a habit to right-click and choose **Run as administrator**. Install FIM Service and FIM Portal following the ensuing steps:

1. The FIM Service and FIM Portal setup is used to install many features. Be careful to select the features you want on the current server. If you are not sure, you can leave them out and go back later and add them. On the FIM-Dev server, only the FIM Service and FIM Portal are installed. On the FIM-Service server, we will also install the FIM Reporting feature. In order for FIM Reporting to be installed, the SCSM infrastructure needs to be in place. The Reporting feature will also require the SCSM Console to be installed, as discussed in the *Prerequisites* section of this chapter.

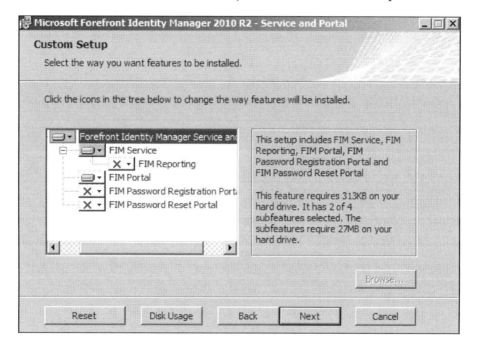

Installation

2. Since we are using SQL aliases, the Database Server is **dbFIMService**, for both FIM-Dev and FIM-Service setups.

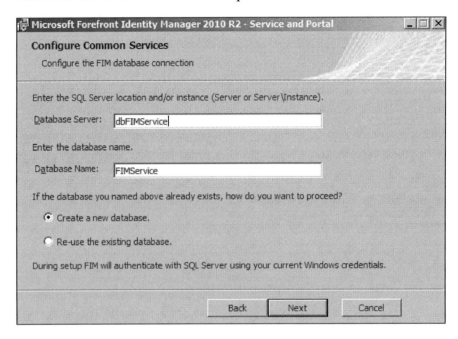

3. If you are running Exchange 2007 or later and the FIM Service service account has been assigned a mailbox, you can check all boxes on the **Configure Mail Server Connection** page. If you do not run Exchange, FIM Service will not be able to receive mail, but it will be able to send mail. Just enter the SMTP server address as **Mail Server** and uncheck all the checkboxes.

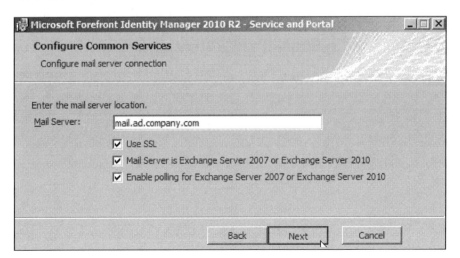

Chapter 3

4. If FIM Reporting is to be installed, a question on the **Management Server** appears. Write the name of the SCSM Management server and *not* the name of the SCSM Data Warehouse server.

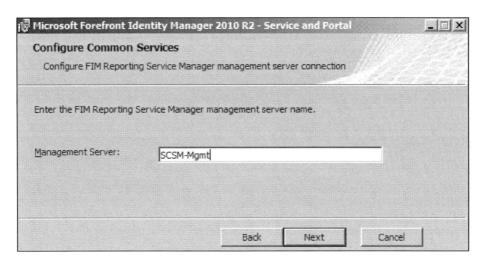

5. If you get this error about missing all or part of the **Service Manager Console**, you need to abort the setup and install the required software and patches before retrying the installation.

Installation

6. I recommend that you allow the FIM setup to generate the certificate used by FIM Service. Note that this is not the SSL certificate used by IIS. If you would like to generate your own certificate to be used, you need to make sure that CN=ForefrontIdentityManager is in the certificate, otherwise FIM Service will not be able to use the certificate.

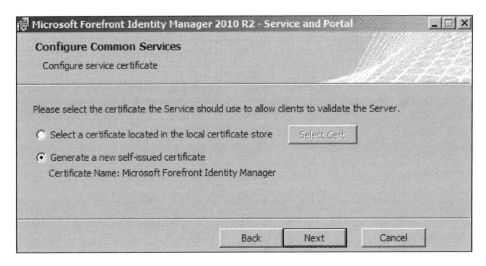

7. Make sure you configure the correct FIM Service service account and the correct e-mail address of the account.

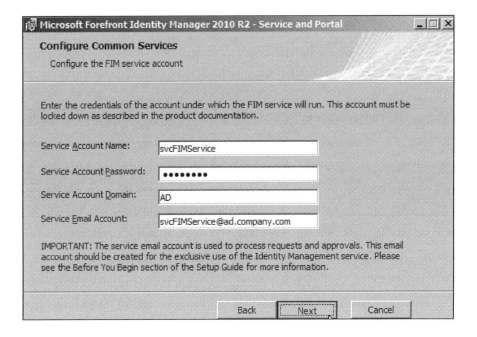

8. If you have not followed the instructions on how to secure the service account, you will get a warning message. To secure this account, it is recommended that you add it to the following User Rights Assignments, either using group policy or using the local security policy:
    - Deny log on as a batch job
    - Deny log on locally
    - Deny access to this computer from the network

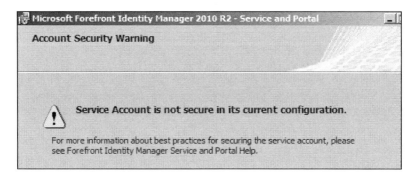

9. Make sure the correct FIM Synchronization server and the corresponding FIM MA account are configured. The **FIM Management Agent Account** specified will have to be used when we later create the FIM Service Management Agent.

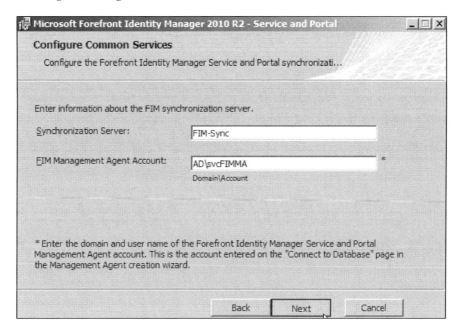

Installation

10. If you are not using the server name as **FIM Service Server address**, make sure you have the correct SPN as well as the correct DNS records registered. In a scaled-out solution with clustered FIM Service servers, this would point to the cluster name.

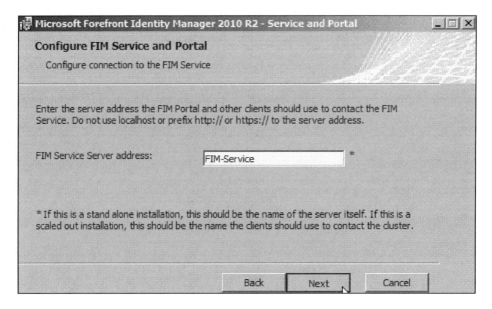

11. If you have configured the SharePoint site to use SSL and an alias as the default name, this alias should be used. At The Company, the URLs used to access the SharePoint sites are `https://fim-dev`, for the FIM-Dev environment, and `https://fimportal`, for the FIM production environment.

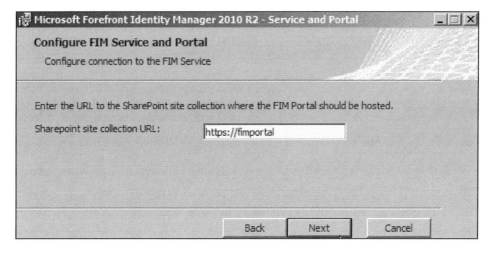

12. The FIM Portal will have a link pointing to the Password Registration Portal.

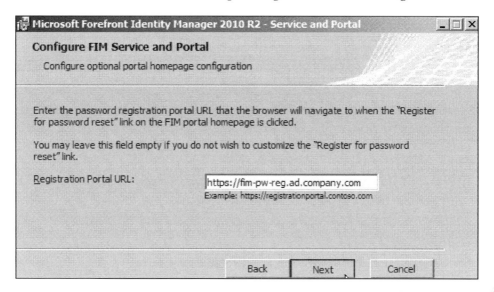

13. Don't forget to check both boxes to allow access to FIM Service and FIM Portal on the **Configure security changes configured by setup** page. Even if you initially do not plan to use any external clients to connect to FIM Service, I recommend that you open up the firewall. You are likely going to have external clients sooner than you imagined.

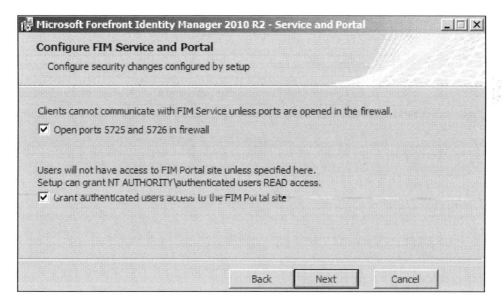

Installation

14. The Company does not have a Password Reset feature in the FIM-Dev environment—it only has it in the Production environment. If, as is the case at The Company, the FIM Password portals are running on separate servers, the account used by IIS to run the application pools should be configured on the **Enter information for FIM Password Portals** page.

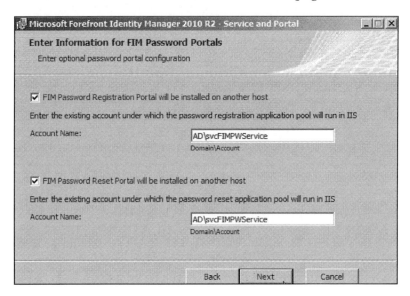

15. By now, I guess you realize that there are a number of reasons that you might not have a successful installation. If for any reason any errors occur, review the prerequisites and restart the installation.

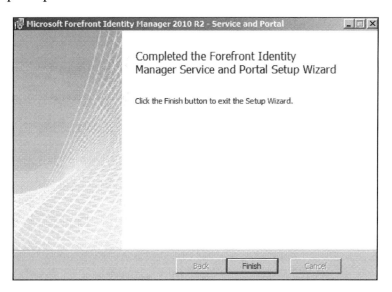

Chapter 3

16. If you think you might have made some errors in the configuration, mistyping something for example, just go to the **Programs and Features** section in the **Control Panel** and select to make a **Change** of the **FIM Service and Portal installation** as seen in the following screenshot:

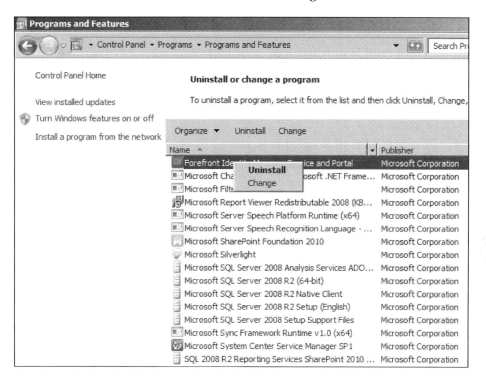

FIM Password Reset portal

The FIM Password Registration and Reset portals are, in the example of The Company, installed on a separate server, the FIM-PW server.

In FIM 2010 R2, we can have two different scopes for the Password Reset and Registration—**Intranet** or **Extranet**. If we'd like to have some differentiation between the two, we need two instances of the Password Reset and Registration portals. The Company will initially have one scope—Intranet.

The FIM Password Registration portal and the Password Reset portal will be installed as two separate websites in IIS. If the web server hosting these portals also contains other websites, you need to consider which ports and/or hostnames are available for use by FIM Password Reset portals.

Installation

To start the setup of the FIM Registration and Reset portals, open up the FIM 2010 R2 DVD and run `Setup.exe` in the `Service and Portal` folder. I make it a habit to right-click and choose **Run as administrator**. Install the FIM Registration and Reset Portal following the ensuing steps:

1. The FIM Password Registration and FIM Password Reset portals can be installed on separate machines or on the same machine. These portals do not use SharePoint, as you can see in the *Prerequisites* section in this chapter.

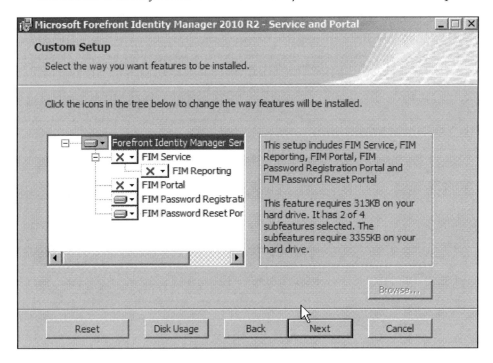

2. The Company is using the same account to run the application pool for both password portals. The hostname and port need to be unique on the IIS used. During setup, you cannot configure SSL, so I recommend that you use a unique hostname and port 80, and then afterwards change the binding in IIS to use SSL.

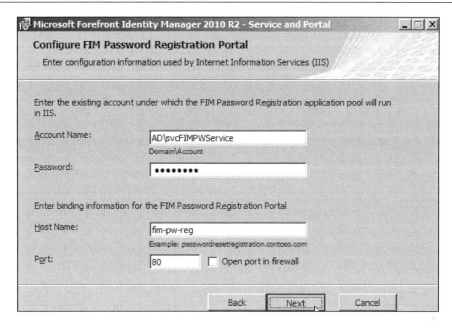

3. Enter the name of the FIM Service that the Password Registration and Reset Portal should use. At The Company, they only have one set of Password Portals, so they configure it for **Intranet** usage. The implications of choosing extranet and/or intranet will be explained in *Chapter 7*, *Self-service Password Reset*, where self-service password reset is described in more detail.

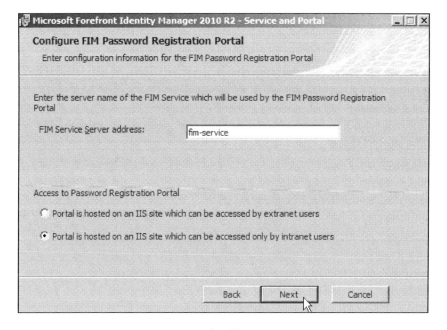

Installation

Setup will not configure the **FIM Password Registration Site** to use the application pool credentials. Authentication using Kerberos will therefore fail, since we registered the SPN for the `AD\svcFIMPWService` account.

You have to manually modify the **useAppPoolCredentials** value to **True**, in the `system.webServer.security.authentication.windowsAuthentication` section in the **Configuration Editor**.

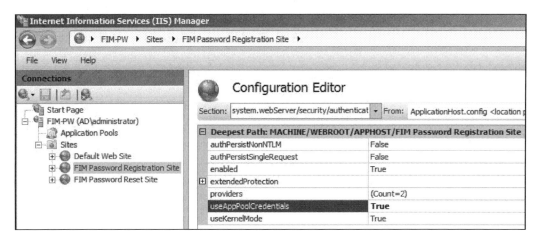

FIM Certificate Management

The installation of the FIM CM service is actually a few different installations.

One is the installation of the web application, and the other is the installation of the so-called modules on the Certificate Authority server.

The web application is in itself a two-step process, where you first install and then run the FIM CM Configuration Wizard, to actually tell the FIM CM how to operate.

After making sure the web server prerequisites are in place, you can start the FIM CM installation.

To start the setup of the FIM CM service and portal, open up the FIM 2010 R2 DVD and run `Setup.exe` in the `Certificate Management\x64` folder. I make it a habit to right-click and choose **Run as administrator**.

On the FIM CM server, you usually do not also have the **Certification Authority (CA)** server, so only **FIM CM Portal** and **FIM CM Update Service** should be installed. The only question you will be asked during the installation is what name you would like to use on the Virtual Directory in IIS, the default being `CertificateManagement`.

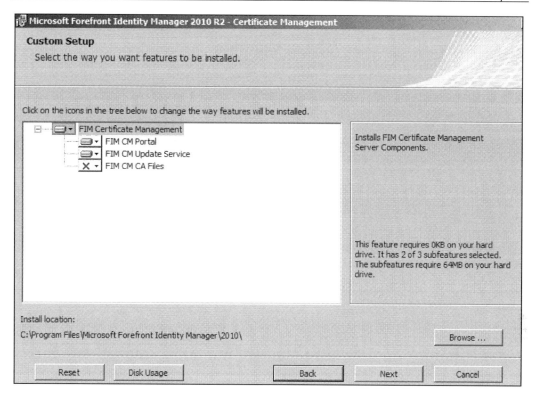

The next step will then be to run the Certificate Management Configuration Wizard to tell FIM CM how to operate. This will be covered in *Chapter 12, Issuing Smart Cards*, dedicated to the FIM CM service.

We will also need to install the FIM CM CA files on the CA server, but that is done after configuring the CM server and will also be covered in *Chapter 12, Issuing Smart Cards*.

SCSM management

The SCSM setup contains a version of the Microsoft Report Viewer 2008 Redistributable Package, but I recommend that you download and install the Microsoft Report Viewer 2008 SP1 Redistributable Package before you begin installing the SCSM software. This way, you ensure that you have the latest version of the Report Viewer.

Installation

On the System Service Manager 2010 SP1 media, navigate to the `amd64` folder and run `Setup`. On the splash screen, select **Install a Service Manager management server**. Follow the ensuing steps during setup:

1. During setup, a check is made to verify that prerequisites are met. If you are running 2008 R2 SP1 as the operating system you get the warning about **Authorization Manager hotfix**, mentioned in the *Prerequisites*, even though it is not required.

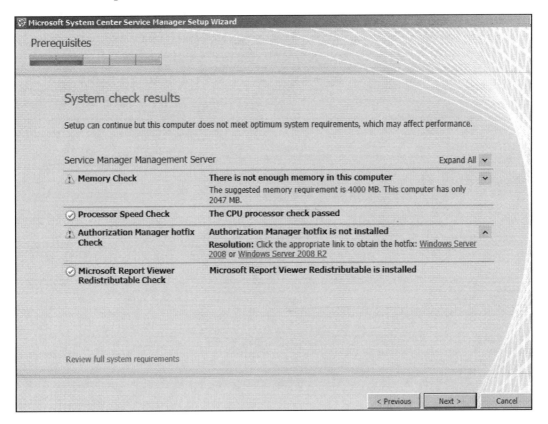

2. A warning message appears, if you are using the default collation (**SQL_Latin1_General_CP1_CI_AS**). Support for multiple languages in Service Manager is not possible when you are using the default collation. If you later decide to support multiple languages using a different collation, you have to re-install SQL Server. For more information on this, go to `http://aka.ms/SCSMCollations` and `http://aka.ms/SQLCollations`.

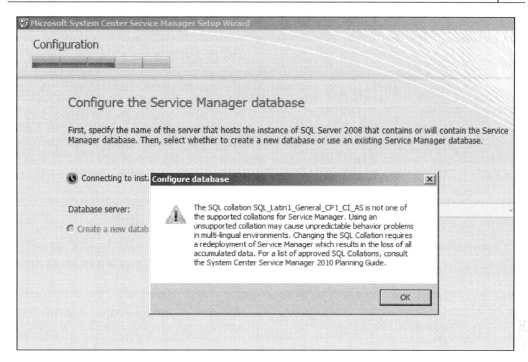

3. If setup detects a local SQL instance, it will suggest using that one and creating a new database in the default instance.

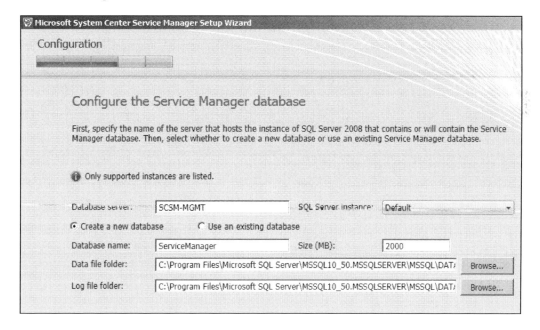

Installation

4. Management group names must be unique. Do not use the same management group name when you deploy a Service Manager management server and a Service Manager data warehouse management server. Furthermore, do not use the management group name that is used for Operations Manager.

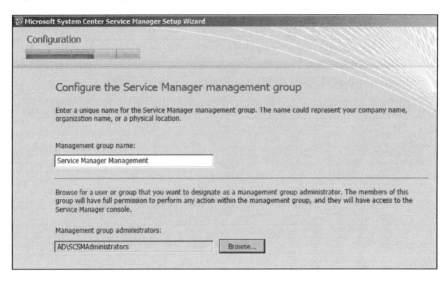

5. Remember to make the service account you use a member of the local administrators group. The Company uses the svcSCSMService account in their setup.

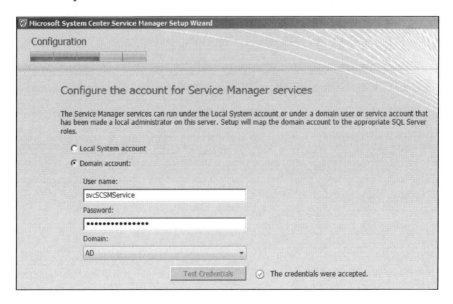

Chapter 3

6. The Company uses the `svcSCSMWF` account as the workflow account.

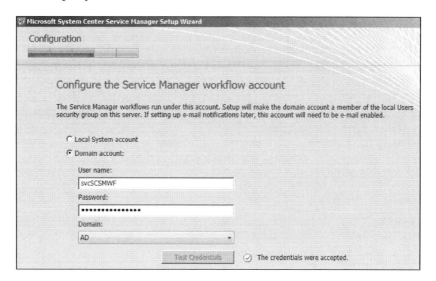

7. After the setup is finished, you should make sure that the checkbox for **Open the Encryption Backup or Restore Wizard after Setup closes. You are advised to complete that process to be prepared in the event of future disaster recovery needs.** is checked, so that you can make a backup of the encryption keys used by SCSM.

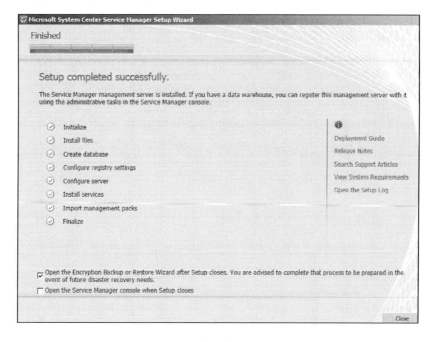

Installation

SCSM Data Warehouse

The SCSM setup contains a version of the Microsoft Report Viewer 2008 Redistributable Package, but I recommend that you download and install the Microsoft Report Viewer 2008 SP1 Redistributable Package before you begin installing the SCSM software. This way you ensure that you have the latest version of Report Viewer.

On the System Service Manager 2010 SP1 media, navigate to the `amd64` folder and run `Setup`.

On the splash screen, select **Install a Service Manager data warehouse management server**. Follow the ensuing steps during setup:

1. During setup, a check is made to verify that prerequisites are met. If you are running 2008 R2 SP1 as the operating system, you get the warning about **Authorization Manager hotfix**, mentioned in **Prerequisites**, even though it is not required. You will also see a warning about not having enough memory, if the server has less than 8GB of RAM.

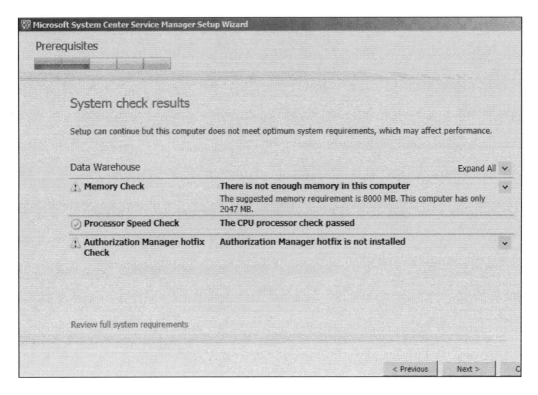

Chapter 3

2. If setup detects a local SQL instance, it will suggest using that one and creating a new database in the default instance.

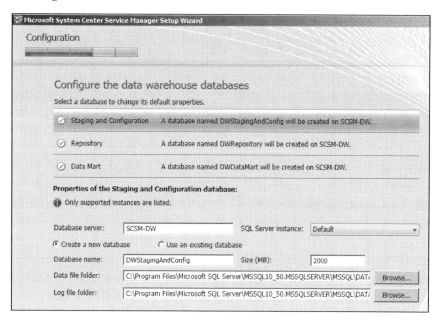

3. Management group names must be unique. Do not use the same management group name when you deploy a Service Manager management server and a Service Manager data warehouse management server. Furthermore, do not use the management group name that is used for Operations Manager.

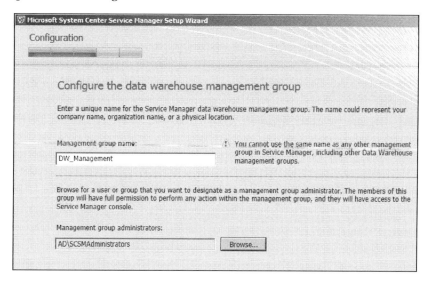

Installation

4. Service Manager will use the existing computer as a reporting server, if SQL Server Reporting Services is present.

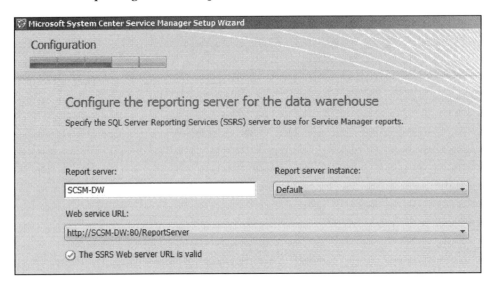

5. Remember to make the service account you use a member of the local administrators group. The Company is using the same service account, svcSCSMService, for both the SCSM-MGMT and SCSM-DW servers in their SCSM setup.

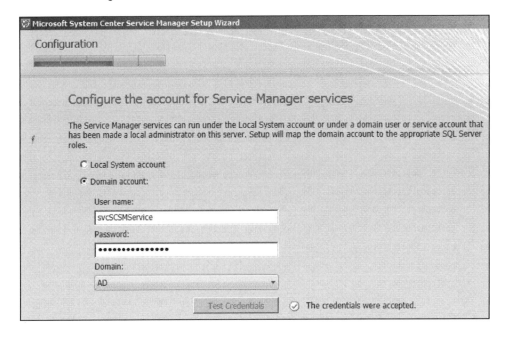

6. The Company is using `svcSCSMReport` as the reporting account.

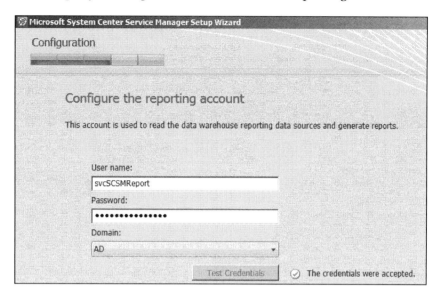

7. After the setup is finished, you should make sure that the checkbox for **Open the Encryption Backup or Restore Wizard after Setup closes. You are advised to complete that process to be prepared in the event of future disaster recovery needs.** is checked, so that you can make a backup of the encryption keys used by SCSM.

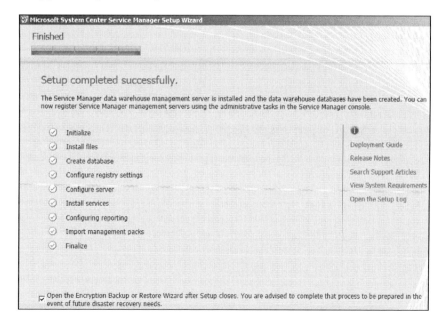

Post-installation configuration

Before we can start to use our new FIM environment, we need to perform some post-installation tasks.

Granting FIM Service access to FIM Sync

In order for the FIM Service to manage the FIM Synchronization Service, we need to add the FIM Service service account to the `FIMSyncAdmins` group. If you are implementing Password Reset, you also need to add the FIM Service service account to the `FIMSyncPasswordSet` group.

After adding the FIM Service service account to the new groups, you need to restart the FIM Service service in order for the new group membership to take effect.

In the example of The Company, this means that the FIM Service account on the Dev-FIM server should be a member of the `FIMSyncAdmins` group on the Dev-FIM server and the FIM Service account on the FIM-Service server should be a member of `FIMSyncAdmins` on the FIM-Sync server.

Securing the FIM Service mailbox

It is not required but it is a best practice to take a look at the mailbox used by the FIM Service (if you're running Exchange). A few things you might consider are as follows:

- Secure the mailbox, making sure only internal users can send mail to it.
- Configure the mailbox quota to make sure the FIM Service mailbox does not get blocked by default quota settings.
- Configure maximum mail sizes to make sure no one can send large e-mails to the FIM Service. Usually, you can limit this to 1 MB.

Disabling indexing in SharePoint

If SharePoint is used only for the FIM Portal, you will gain performance if you disable the indexing within SharePoint, since you will not be using the search capabilities of SharePoint. This is done a little differently in WSS 3.0 and SharePoint Foundation 2010, so please look in the documentation to see how to turn this off.

Redirecting to IdentityManagement

If you want to redirect the FIM Portal URL, say to let the user type `http://servername` and be redirected to `http://servername/identitymanagement`, follow the ensuing steps:

1. Navigate to the website installation directory. By default, this path is `c:\inetpub\wwwroot\wss\VirtualDirectories\80`.
2. Make sure the file system is showing file extensions.
3. Create a new text file named `default.aspx`.
4. Edit `default.aspx` as follows:
   ```
   <%@ Page Language="C#" %>
   <script runat="server">
   protected override void OnLoad(EventArgs e)
   {
     base.OnLoad(e);
     Response.Redirect("~/IdentityManagement/default.aspx");
   }
   </script>
   ```
5. Save the file, and run `iisreset`.

Enforcing Kerberos

If you have set all the prerequisites correctly, your clients should be able to authenticate to your FIM Portal using Kerberos. However, they might try say to connect using a client/browser that does not support Kerberos and end up with NTLM instead.

We can configure the FIM Portal to require Kerberos, if we like.

This is done by modifying the `web.config` file used by the SharePoint website. Follow the ensuing steps to modify the `web.config` file:

1. The `web.config` file is located at `C:\inetpub\wwwroot\wss\VirtualDirectories\80`.

   Before modifying the file, make sure you make a backup copy.

2. In order to be able to save the file, you need to run your editor (Notepad, maybe) in elevated mode (run as administrator).
3. Open the file and locate the section `<resourceManagementClient .../>`.

Installation

4. Add `requireKerberos="true"`, so that it reads
   `<resourceManagementClient requireKerberos="true" . . . />`.

5. After saving the file, run `iisreset`.

Editing binding in IIS for FIM Password sites

After installing the FIM Password Registration and Reset Portals, you might need to change the binding of the websites created by the FIM Password Portal setup.

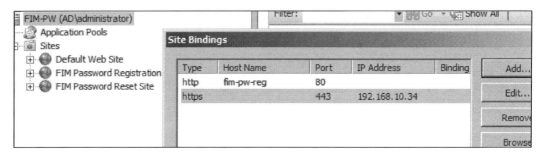

If you, as in the example used in this book, used a separate host header name during installation, you would then need to add the binding of **https**, using the correct certificate and the correct IP. You may then also configure IIS to force the use of SSL for the FIM Password websites, if you like.

Registering SCSM Manager in Data Warehouse

After you have deployed the Service Manager and Data Warehouse management servers, you must run the Data Warehouse Registration wizard. This wizard registers the Service Manager management group with the data warehouse management group and deploys management packs from the Service Manager management server to the data warehouse management server. The management pack deployment process can take several hours to complete. It is a best practice not to turn off any Service Manager computers or stop any Service Manager services during this time. During this registration process, you can continue to use the Service Manager console to perform any Service Manager functions that you want.

To ensure that reporting data will be available, use the following procedure to register the data warehouse and deploy the management packs:

1. By using an account that is a member of the Service Manager and data warehouse management administrators group, log on to the computer that hosts the **Service Manager Console**. In our example, this is the SCSM-MGMT server.

2. In the **Service Manager Console**, select **Administration**.
3. In the **Administration** pane, expand **Administration**.
4. In the **Administration** view, in the **Register with Service Manager's Data Warehouse** area, click on **Register with Service Manager Data Warehouse**.

5. In the Data Warehouse Registration wizard, on the **Before You Begin** page, click on **Next**.
6. On the **Data Warehouse** page, in the **Server name** box, type the name of the computer hosting the data warehouse management server, and then click on **Test Connection**. If the test is successful, click on **Next**. In our example, the server name is **SCSM-DW**.

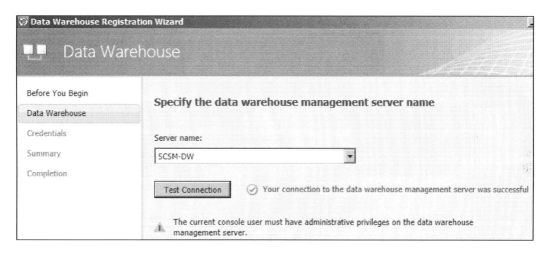

7. On the **Credentials** page, you can accept the default entry in the **Run as account** list, and then click on **Next**, or you can enter credentials from a user or group of your own choosing.
8. On the **Summary** page, click on **Create**.
9. On the **Completion** page, when the data warehouse registration succeeded is displayed, click on **Close**.

Installation

10. A dialog box states that the report deployment process has not finished. This is to be expected. On the **System Center Service Manager** dialog box, click on **OK**.

11. In a few minutes, after closing the Data Warehouse Registration wizard, the **Data Warehouse** button will be added to the Service Manager console.

You could get an error message that the Service Manager Data Warehouse SQL Reporting Services server is currently unavailable.

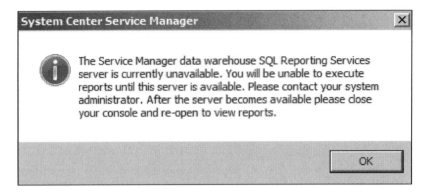

This might be due to the fact that the local firewall on the Reporting Services (SCSM-DW, in our example) server does not allow inbound connections to the ports used by Reporting Services. This is also true for SQL ports such as TCP 1433. In order for connections to work, you need to open up the ports in the firewall or disable the firewall.

To open port 80 on the SCSM-DW server, for Reporting Services to work, follow the ensuing steps:

1. From the Start menu, click on **Control Panel**, then click on **System and Security**, and then click on **Windows Firewall**. If **Control Panel** is not configured for *Category* view, you only need to select **Windows Firewall**.

2. Click on **Advanced Settings**.

3. Click on **Inbound Rules**.

4. Click on **New Rule**, in the **Actions** window.

5. Select **Port** on the **Rule Type** page.

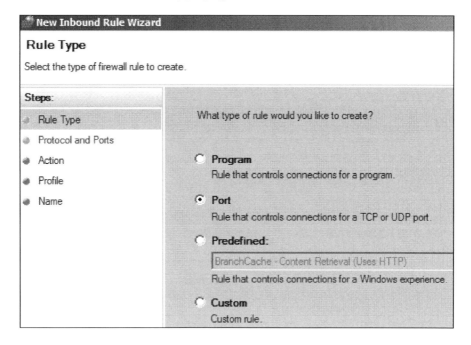

6. Click on **Next**.
7. On the **Protocol and Ports** page, click on **TCP**.
8. Select **Specific Local Ports** and type a value of 80.

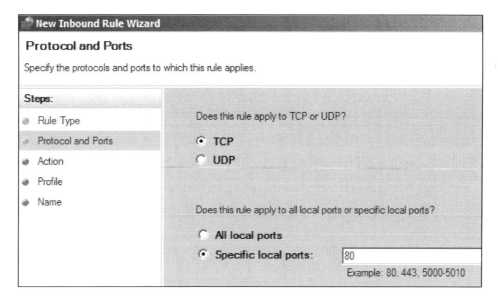

Installation

9. Click on **Next**.
10. On the **Action** page, click on **Allow the connection**.
11. Click on **Next**.
12. On the **Profile** page, click on the appropriate options for your environment.
13. Click on **Next**.
14. On the **Name** page, enter the name **ReportServer (TCP on port 80)**.

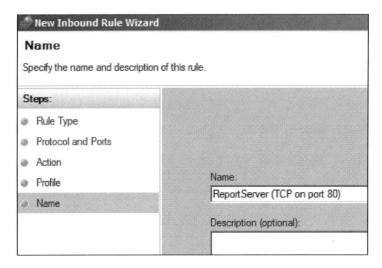

15. Click on **Finish**.
16. Restart the computer.

Repeat the previous steps for TCP 1433, if you need to remotely manage or connect to the Database Engine.

In order for Reporting to work, we also need to allow the SCSM Data Warehouse server where SQL reporting is running, to access the SQL server used by SCSM Management. In our example, that means we also need to open up the firewall on the SCSM-MGMT server to allow inbound connections to TCP1433.

For a complete list of ports required by SCSM 2010, please take a look at `http://aka.ms/SCSM2010Ports`.

FIM post-install scripts for Data Warehouse

If you are installing and planning to use Reporting, you will have to run some scripts on the SCSM Data Warehouse server that will (among other things) grant the FIM Service account permissions to the SCSM databases.

The scripts can be found on FIM 2010 R2 DVD, in the `Data Warehouse Support Scripts` folder. I have made them available for download at my blog as well (http://blog.konab.com/fim-2010-r2-book/reporting).

Copy the folder containing the scripts to your SCSM 2010 Data Warehouse server and execute the PowerShell script, `FIMPostInstallScriptsForDataWarehouse.ps1`.

Summary

Installing the prerequisites is, as you can see, the toughest part, while installing the products involved in the FIM family is quite straightforward.

In this chapter, I have shown what it would look like if you installed all FIM 2010 R2 components using the setup that my example company, The Company, is using.

In my opinion, the *key* to a successful FIM 2010 R2 installation is to really understand the prerequisites, making sure you understand all your service accounts, aliases, and Kerberos settings.

Please remember that if you are not planning to use parts of the product, you might be able to reduce the number of machines involved. If you, for example, are not interested in FIM Reporting, the whole setup of the SCSM infrastructure is not required.

Now that we have our installation in place, it is time to start using our FIM 2010 R2 infrastructure. In the next chapter, we will start off by looking at the initial configuration of the FIM Synchronization, FIM Service, and FIM Portal components.

4
Basic Configuration

If you have followed this book, you will now have a freshly installed FIM 2010 R2 environment. In this chapter, we will discuss some of the basic configurations we need to look at, no matter how our environment looks or how we plan to use FIM 2010 R2.

If you have an environment already set up, I hope that this chapter can act as a guide for you to verify that you have not missed any important steps causing your FIM environment to not work properly.

In this chapter we will focus on the initial configuration of FIM Synchronization Service and FIM Service. Specifically, we will cover the following topics:

- Creating Management Agents
- Schema management
- FIM Service MA
- Initial load versus scheduled runs
- Moving configuration from development to production

All the configurations are made on the FIM-Dev system, and as you will see at the end of this chapter, we will move that configuration from the development to the production servers.

Basic Configuration

Creating Management Agents

Before we even start to use our FIM implementation to manage identities, we need to decide where the information about the identities will come from and where the information will go.

It is also very important that we start off with the essential connections and then add other connections after verifying that the basics are working.

A very typical scenario is the one we have—The Company has an HR (Human Resource) system that will, for the most part, work as the source of identity information. Then it has Active Directory, which is the primary system to receive identity information.

The basic flow will be HR - FIM - AD.

But that is only the basic flow, and as you will see later in this book, there are other sources of information and also other targets.

Active Directory

Almost 100 percent of the FIM implementations have at least one Management Agent connected to an Active Directory.

There are a few things to consider before creating this Management Agent. I suggest you use an approach where you start off simple and then add functionalities along the way.

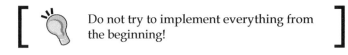
Do not try to implement everything from the beginning!

If, for example, your plan is to have FIM manage both users and groups in AD, start off by implementing the management of users and then add groups when the user part is working.

Are we interested in the whole AD or only parts?

- A typical Active Directory has parts that we are not interested in having FIM mess with

Test OU?

- If possible, it is nice to have some kind of test OU that can be used to do initial testing without risking messing up the whole AD

[90]

Least privileged

The Management Agent will use an account to talk to Active Directory. The Company is using the approach to have as few MA accounts as possible rather than having one account for each connected system.

In the case of The Company, the `svcFIMMA` account (`Dev-FIMMA` on the FIM-Dev server) will be the account that we will use to connect to Active Directory. What we need to do is to give this account the required permissions needed, to manage relevant objects in the AD.

You would always want to apply a *least privileged* approach, when assigning permissions to the MA account. But don't go crazy. If you try to implement the permissions on an attribute level, you will have a lot of change management to deal with, as we make FIM manage more and more.

I usually use the following approach:

1. I create a new OU dedicated to be managed by FIM.

   The idea is that Active Directory administrators should not manage the objects directly in the AD, if the objects are meant to be managed by FIM. Creating a dedicated OU and naming it as `Managed`, for example, makes it easy to separate duties. I usually create this OU in the root of the AD, to minimize the risk of unexpected inheritance of policies and permissions. As you will see later in this chapter, this high-level, dedicated OU will also make it easier when defining the **Distinguished Name (DN)** for objects, which FIM should manage, in the AD. In some cases, customers decide to use an existing OU; this might require some more planning as this also means there are existing objects and permissions to consider.

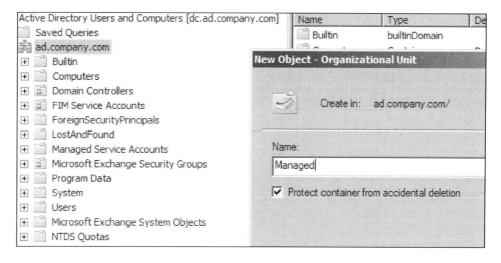

Basic Configuration

2. We then need to give FIM the required permissions to manage the objects. Right-click on the OU and run the delegate control wizard. Give the FIM MA account (`svcFIMMA`) management permissions on user (and maybe group) objects.

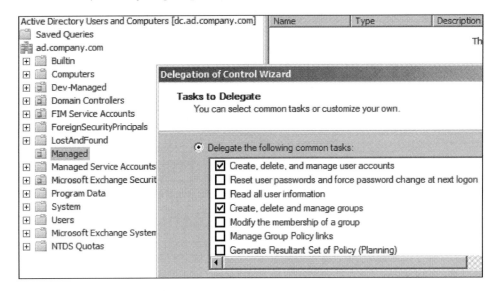

3. In some cases, the aforementioned wizard might give the FIM MA account more permissions than needed. If, for example, FIM should only be able to *create* and *manage* the objects but not *delete* them, we need to adjust the permissions in order to use the least privileged approach.

Using the same AD for dev/test makes it very important that we use a different account for our FIM-Dev machine and also assign dedicated permissions to the `Dev-FIMMA` account. In The Company, I create another OU called `Dev-Managed`. On this OU, I give the `Dev-FIMMA` account permission to manage the users and groups.

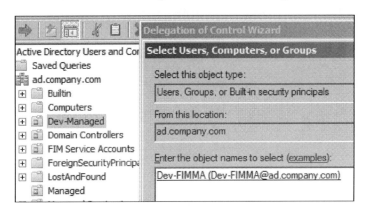

Directory replication

When importing (reading) information from AD, it is possible to use what is called **delta**. Delta means we only get the changes since the last time we checked. In order for the FIM Active Directory Management Agent to read only the changes—the delta information in AD, it needs a special permission called **Replicating Directory Changes** at the domain level. You can read more about this at http://support.microsoft.com/kb/303972.

1. Open up the **Security** tab in the domain (ad.company.com for example).
2. You either create a group, if that is how you always do it, or you assign permission to the FIM MA account(s). You need to check the **Allow** option for the **Replicating Directory Changes** permission:

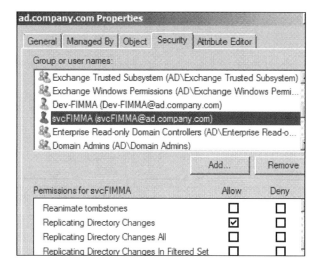

Password reset

If you are implementing password synchronization and/or the Self-service Password Reset feature, you will need to assign permissions for that; details about this are given in *Chapter 7, Self Service Password Reset*.

Creating AD MA

In this segment, I walk you through the steps for creating the AD MA. This is the first time in this book we will talk about this, and some new terms will be used. Some of these terms will be explained later on in this book, as we start to use more advanced features. So I ask you to be patient. This wizard is to show you how to get a very basic AD MA up and running. We will later on modify many of its settings, and at that point I will explain it in more detail.

Basic Configuration

If you are curious to know about some terms right away, I urge you to click the **Help** button available on all the pages in the wizard.

To begin with, you need to log in to the FIM-Dev server using an account that is a member of the `FIMSyncAdmins` group.

1. Start FIM **Synchronization Service Manager on FIM-DEV**.
2. Select the **Management Agents** tool, and click **Create Management Agent** in the **Actions** pane.
3. Select **Active Directory Domain Services** in the **Management agent for:** drop-down list:

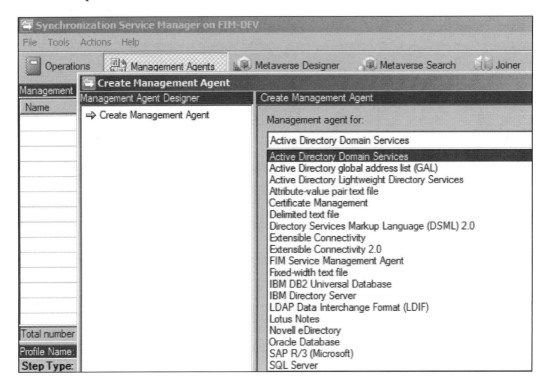

Chapter 4

4. Give the MA a descriptive name; at The Company we simply call it **AD**:

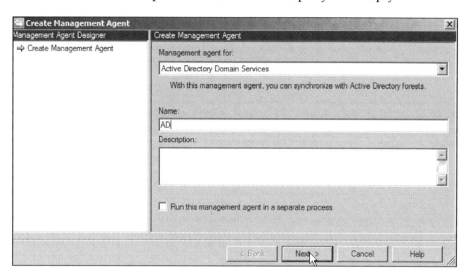

5. The AD MA connects to the Active Directory forest, and not to a specific domain in the forest. We decide later on which domain in the forest to connect to. When connecting to the AD forest, we configure the account used for the connection. As this is on the FIM-Dev server, we use the `Dev-FIMMA` account. By clicking on the **Options...** button, we can choose to not encrypt the traffic. It is recommended that you leave the default **Sign and Encrypt LDAP Traffic** option as it is:

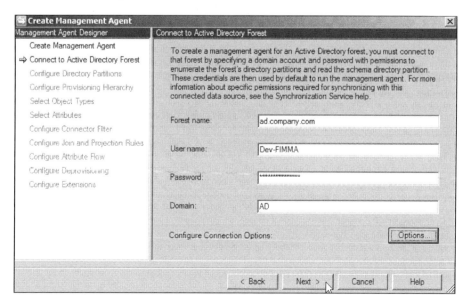

Basic Configuration

6. In the **Configure Directory Partitions** section, select the domain partition **DC=ad,DC=company,DC=com**. If you want FIM to use a preferred set of domain controllers, check **Only use preferred domain controllers** and click the **Configure...** button to choose the ones you want FIM to use. The default is to work with the whole domain; but we do not want that, so let's click the **Containers...** button:

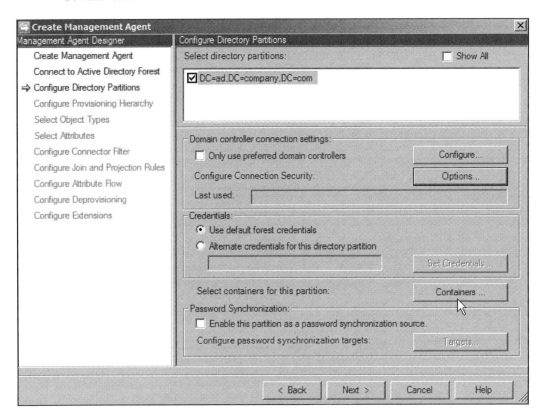

7. In the **Select Containers** dialog, uncheck the domain (top) level, thereby unselecting all the options.

Chapter 4

8. Then select the containers you want FIM to manage. In our example, we select the **Dev-Managed** OU. As this is the development environment and we are talking to the production AD, it is vital that we do not make any mistakes in choosing the accounts or OUs. It is most likely that we might need to change this selection later on, if our AD design is changed:

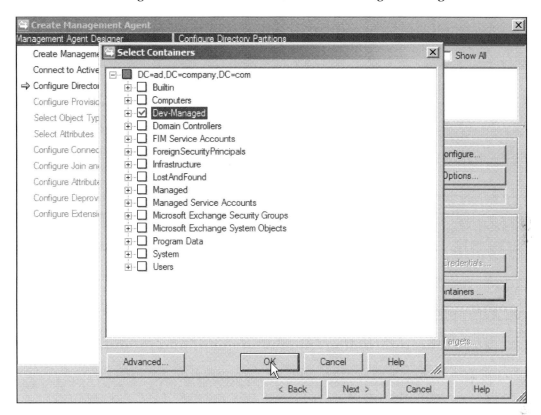

Basic Configuration

9. On the **Configure Provision Hierarchy** page, we do not need to change anything; just click **Next**:

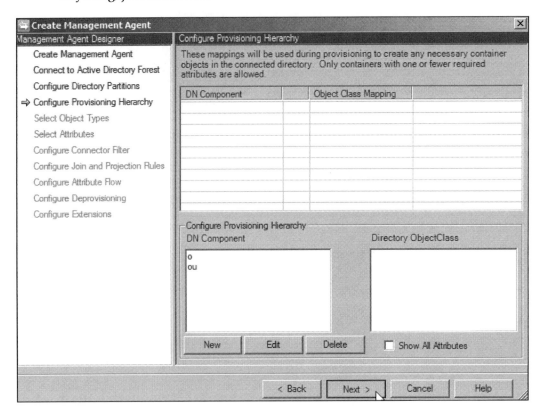

In some cases, we would like FIM to automatically create the OU structure, if it is missing when we try to create a user or group in AD, for example. We call this Hierarchical Provisioning, and on this page of the MA, you can configure this if you want it. You can read more about this at http://blogs.technet.com/b/doittoit/archive/2009/05/20/introducing-hierarchal-provisioning.aspx.

Chapter 4

10. In the **Select Object Types** page, select the object types, which you know FIM needs to manage. Do not deselect the default **Container**, **domainDNS** and **organizationalUnit** object types; these are required for FIM to know *where* in AD the objects reside. Also, do not select object types you have no need for. Initially, The Company has no need for the **contact** object type so we do not select it. This might change, however, if requirements on what FIM should do change.

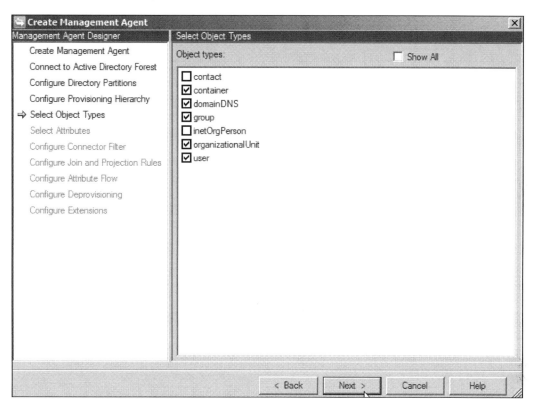

Basic Configuration

11. Select the attributes that you know you need. Needs will be discussed in the following chapters, and we will make frequent changes to this configuration. If you check **Show All**, it will display the complete schema of your AD. A special case is the **objectSid** and **sAMAccountName** attributes. These will be required if we want users to access FIM.

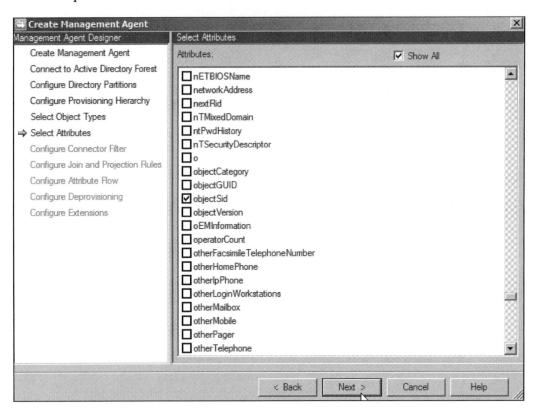

12. If for some reason we have configured the containers and object types in a way that we can reach objects we are not supposed to manage, we can make a connector filter to make sure these objects are out of scope. We will, in this book, configure a connector filter in our FIM Service, so my recommendation is that you leave this as it is.

Chapter 4

There are however, special cases when we need to limit the objects that are imported into the connector space. The AD MA contains a feature that allows us to do pre-import filtering. Read more about this at http://aka.ms/FIMPreImportFilter. I have found this feature very useful when connecting to an existing AD, where the objects FIM is interested in are mixed with other objects.

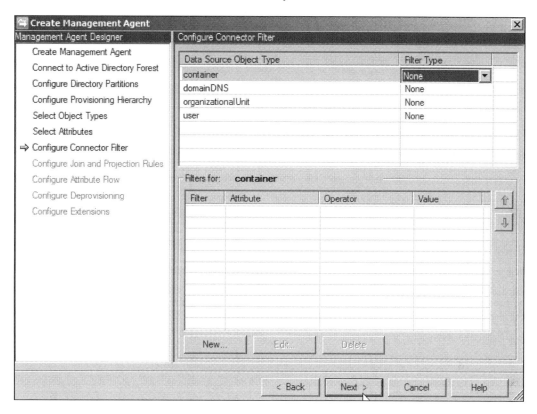

Basic Configuration

13. The Join and Projection rules will be configured using FIM Service in our environment. So, click **Next**.

    If you are running only Synchronization Service or for some other reason using non-declarative (classic) synchronization, this is where you will configure your Join and Projection rules for the AD MA:

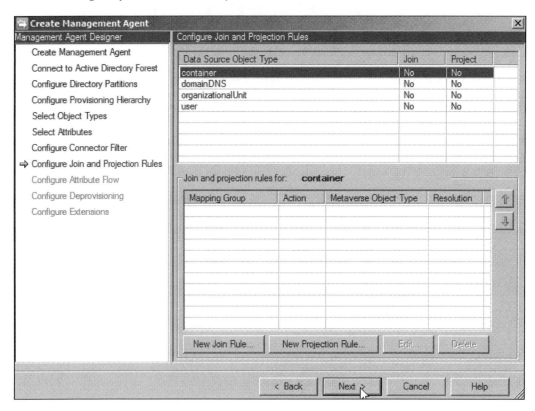

Chapter 4

14. Attribute flow will be configured using FIM Service in our environment. So, click **Next**.

    If you are running only Synchronization Service or for some other reason using non-declarative (classic) synchronization, this is where you will configure your attribute flow rules for the AD MA. FIM supports the usage of both declarative and non-declarative attribute flows in your MAs. In *Chapter 11, Customizing Data Transformations*, I will show one example of such a case.

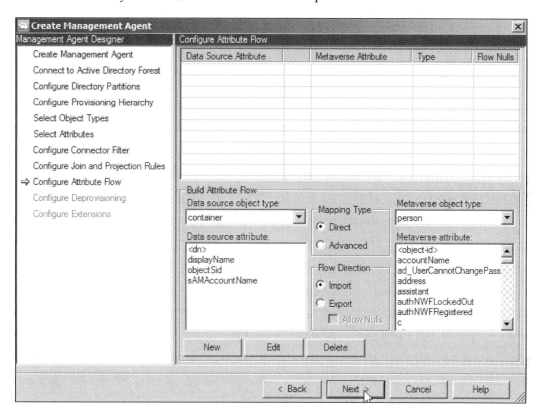

15. On the **Configure Deprovisioning** page, there are a few things we need to consider:

    i. **Deprovisioning** is what happens when an object in the connector space is disconnected from its Metaverse object. We will look into how we can control this, later in this book. If you are uncertain, leave the default value as **Make them disconnectors**.

Basic Configuration

ii. **Stage a delete on the object for the next export run** is what you will select if you want FIM to delete objects in AD when they are disconnected from the MV. To actually have deletes of users and groups in AD could cause a lot of problems, if they occur when they shouldn't. In all cases, when we allow FIM to perform the deletes of objects in a CDS, we need to be very careful.

iii. The **Do not recall attributes contributed by objects from this management agent when disconnected** checkbox might sometimes be useful if, for example, you are replacing a Management Agent with a new one and do not want the MV attributes to be deleted in the process.

Carol Wapshere has written a great article explaining our options for deprovisioning. Go to http://aka.ms/FIMDeprovisioning, and read it before you start using the options for deprovisioning.

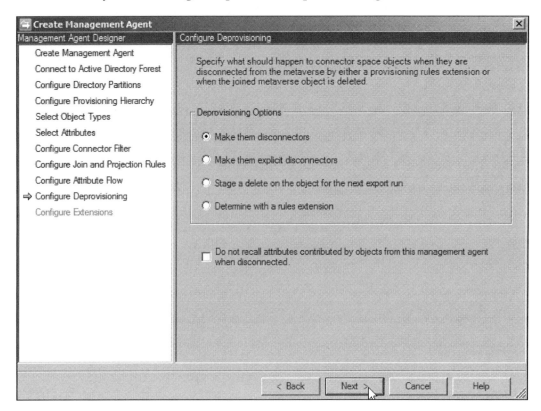

16. If you are doing a non-declarative (classic) synchronization using only Synchronization Engine and are using code to solve some problems, this is where you will configure which DLL contains your code. This is also where you will select the version of Exchange that you will use, if FIM is to provision users for Exchange. For now, we will leave this as **No provisioning**; we will later change this to **Exchange 2010**, when we start to configure our FIM environment for Exchange management:

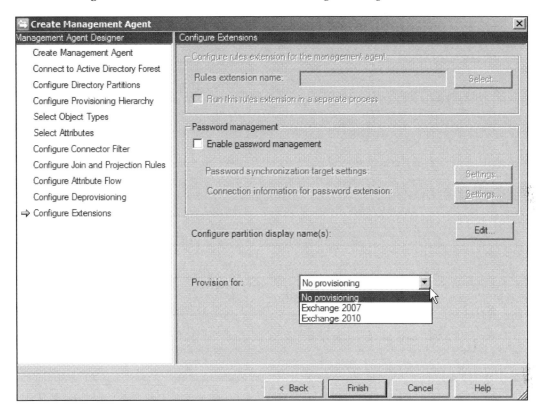

HR (SQL Server)

If almost all the implementations of FIM have a connection with AD, I would say that the second most common connector is SQL Server. Even if you don't have an existing system using SQL, there are occasions when creating a few SQL tables will help in overall FIM deployment. This is because SQL is, after all, very good with data and functions such as **SQL Server Integration Services (SSIS)**, which are sometimes useful for data transformations. I will discuss this further in *Chapter 11, Customizing Data Transformations*.

Basic Configuration

At The Company, the HR system uses SQL Server as a database and we will interact with HR using a typical SQL MA. As with Active Directory, we should implement a least privileged approach when assigning permissions to the account that FIM is using to connect to SQL.

As the HR database (at present) is not supposed to receive any data, just send the data to FIM; we can assign the db_datareader permissions to the Dev-FIMMA account (or its equivalent):

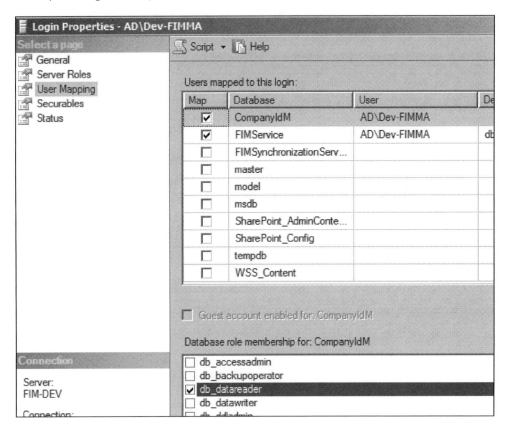

At The Company, the HR data is in a database named **CompanyIdM**.

If you want to filter what information is available to FIM in SQL, you can easily do that by creating a SQL view and configuring FIM to read from that view. Just remember that when FIM is using a SQL view to talk to SQL, updates become a little trickier. If you create a complex view for FIM to read and later on realize that FIM should also be able to update some column in some table, it may not be possible without redesigning the view.

Before we can configure our MA, we need to understand the data source we are connecting to. So, let's take a quick look at how the HR database is built up.

In the HR table (named **HRData**), there is information about our users and organizational units. Note the relations we have, where the columns **manager** and **parentOrg** are actually referencing other objects in the table.

If the SQL data has this kind of reference information, we will be able to use this to synchronize these to attributes in other CDSs, which also use reference attributes. For example, as the **manager** column in our HR data is a reference value, FIM can easily populate the **manager** attribute in AD, and also reference an attribute pointing to another object in the AD.

There is also another view (named **vwHRMVData**), where at the moment, the **parentOrg** column is used to show who a **member** of a specific orgUnit is:

	objectID	attributeName	memberID
1	78CF825D-0440-4073-BE3…	member	AD3CBDA7-9393-4D26-9B…
2	78CF825D-0440-4073-BE3…	member	66CF7C82-4697-45E2-8A0…
3	78CF825D-0440-4073-BE3…	member	76A78F2F-0C30-4E15-875…

You might realize that this is not what a typical HR database looks like; this is actually a FIM-optimized HR table. In *Chapter 11, Customizing Data Transformations*, we will take a look at some of the ways of creating this.

Creating SQL MA

In this section, I will walk you through the process of creating the SQL MA for the HR system:

1. Start FIM **Synchronization Service Manager**.
2. Select the **Management Agents** tool and click **Create Management Agent** in the **Actions** pane.

Basic Configuration

3. Select the **SQL Server** option in the **Management agent for:** drop-down list:

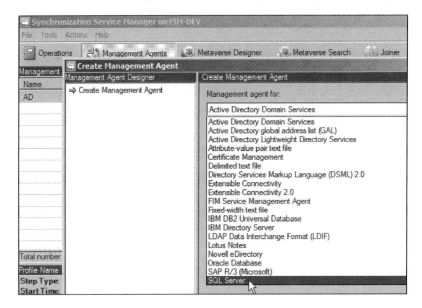

4. Give the MA a descriptive name. At The Company, we simply call it **HR**:

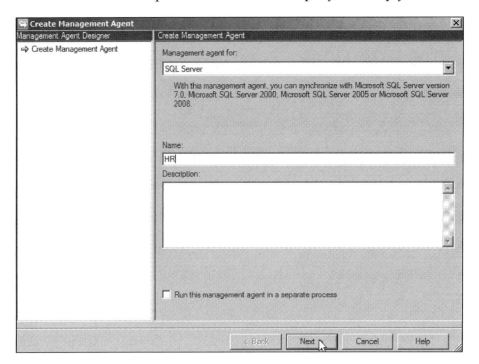

Chapter 4

5. As we are using SQL aliases, we use the alias server name **dbHR**. The *base* table is **HRData** and the **Multivalue Table**, which is the view, is **vwHRMVData**, described earlier:

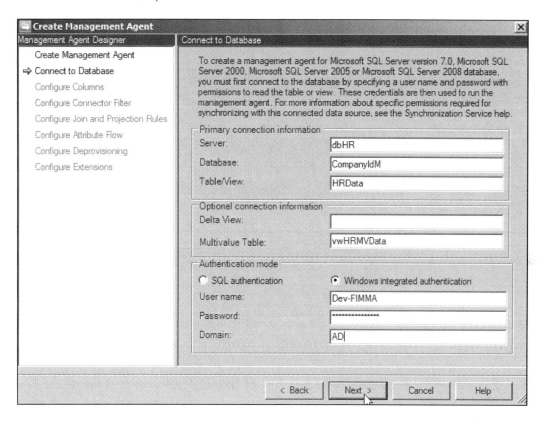

Basic Configuration

6. The SQL MA has retrieved the schema, the **Columns**, and the **Database Types** from the SQL database, but we need to make some adjustments. First, let's click on the **Set Anchor...** button, and set the anchor attributes:

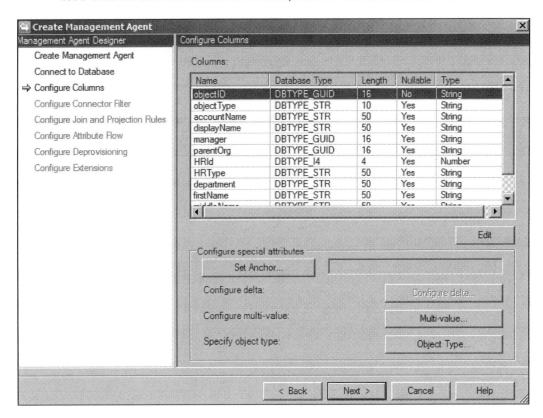

7. The anchor attribute consists of the column in the database that contains the unique value of each object, which does not change. Which attribute to be used as an anchor attribute in each of the CDSs is an important decision to make. The anchor attribute should never change for a specific object. If it changes, it will be detected as a *delete* of the old object and an *addition* of a new object by FIM, when importing information from the CDS. The **HRData** table at The Company uses the column **objectID**, using the DBTYPE_GUID data type as the anchor attribute.

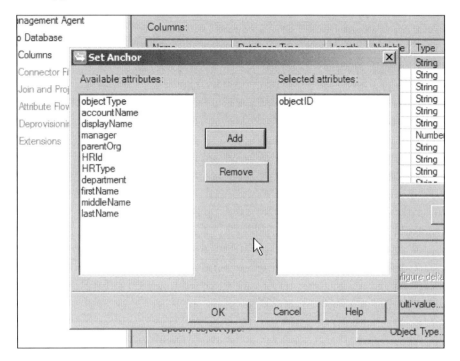

Basic Configuration

8. In **Multi-value settings**, we need to tell FIM how the multi-value view or table is built. In our **vwHRMVData** view, the attribute name is defined in the **attributeName** column, and the reference is in the **memberID** column. So far, we only know of one multi-value attribute and that is **member**, which is of the **Reference (DN)** type. The Reference means it contains the value of the anchor attribute of some other object in the **HRData** table. If later on our multi-value view is to contain other values such as e-mail addresses or direct reports, we will need to add these to this setting.

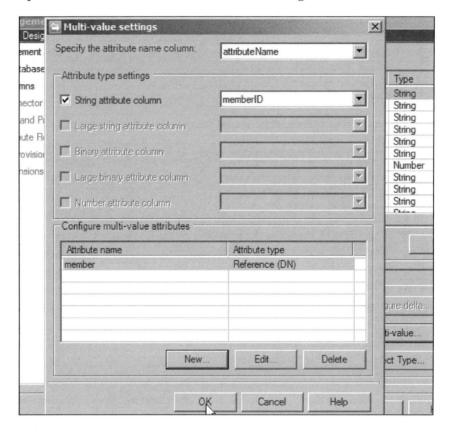

[112]

Chapter 4

9. Clicking the **Object Type...** button allows you to define if the SQL MA only contains one fixed object type or if the information about object type is stored in a column. If you can get this information as a column in the view or table, that would be better. This particular setting can only be configured during the creation of the MA; if you would like to change this later on, you will need to recreate the MA. In our **HRData** table, we have the object types in the column **objectType**. In order for FIM to detect the possible object types available, the table or view we look at must contain sample data with the possible object-type values.

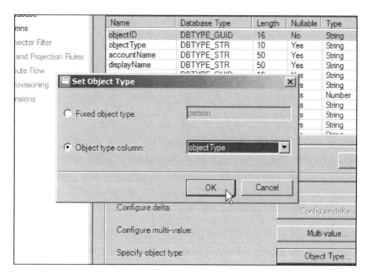

10. There are two attributes in the list that need to be edited, as we need to tell FIM that they are of the **Reference (DN)** type. This tells FIM that the data in the column contains the **objectID** value of some other object. Select **manager**, click the **Edit...** button, and check the **Reference (DN)** checkbox. Do the same for the **parentOrg** attribute:

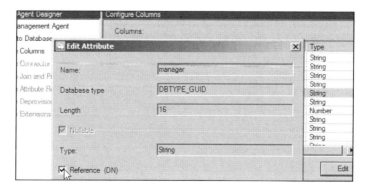

[113]

Basic Configuration

11. If for some reason we have configured the table or view used by the MA in a way that we reach objects we are not supposed to manage, we can configure a connector filter to make sure these objects are out of scope. We will configure this in our FIM Service, so my recommendation is that you leave it as it is:

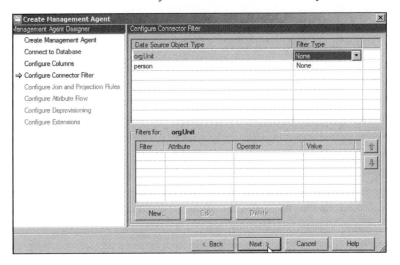

12. Attribute flows will be configured using FIM Service in our environment. So, click **Next**.

    If you are running only Synchronization Service or for some other reason using non-declarative (classic) synchronization, this is where you can configure your attribute flow rules for the HR MA:

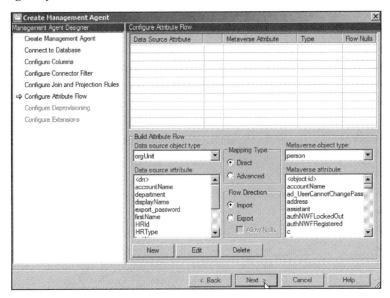

Chapter 4

13. On the **Configure Deprovisioning** page, there are a few things we need to consider, which have been explained in the *Creating AD MA* recipe. Also, Carol Wapshere has written a great article explaining our options around deprovisioning. You can go to http://aka.ms/FIMDeprovisioning and read it before you start using the option to deprovision.

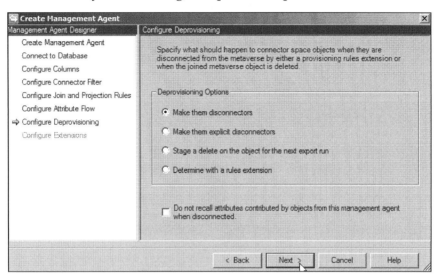

14. If you are doing a non-declarative (classic) synchronization using only Synchronization Engine and are using some code to solve some problems, this is where you can configure which DLL will contain your code:

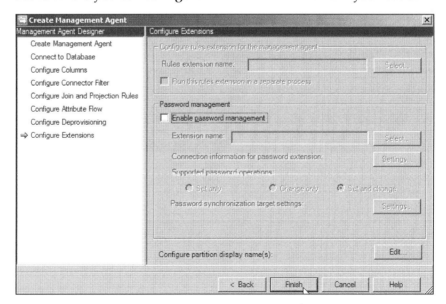

Run profiles

In order for Synchronization Engine to do anything useful we need to create **run profiles** for each Management Agent, depending on our needs. A run profile is used for telling the MA to import, synchronize, or export the data that it has in its connector space.

In the help section of Synchronization Service Manager, or on sites such as `http://aka.ms/FIMRunProfile`, the concept is fully explained.

As we need to create them for all MAs, you should use some kind of naming standard.

Single or Multi step

When you create run profiles you have the option to use multi-step profiles.

You can, for example, create a profile that does import and synchronization, rather than having one profile doing import and then another doing synchronization. Initially, I recommend that you only use single-step profiles, as that will give you maximum control to begin with. Using only single step profiles, you will also avoid the problem described in the following explanation.

If you look at `http://aka.ms/FIMRunProfile`, you will find the following explanation:

> *When you configure a run profile with a single step of the type "Delta Import and Delta Synchronization", a condition can occur in which existing disconnector objects from a previous run are not processed. This condition occurs because the existing objects in the connector space that have not changed since the last run are ignored.*

Schema management

Very early on in our FIM deployment, we ran into discussions regarding the need for schema changes in FIM.

The default schema is, in almost every case, not sufficient and needs to be modified.

I will only give a short overview in this chapter about this, and will try to explain more in the coming chapters, as we look into the details of FIM implementation at The Company.

FIM Sync versus FIM Service schema

One of the problems with the FIM Synchronization/FIM Service system is that it holds two schemas. We have one schema for the FIM Synchronization Service database and one for the FIM Service database.

Depending on our needs, we change one or both of these schemas. Whether the attributes or objects are required within FIM Service depends on whether or not they are managed using FIM Portal, or used in some policy. If not, we do not need them in the FIM Service schema.

On the other hand, if an attribute or object type is used in a policy within FIM Service, but is never supposed to be synchronized to other data sources, we do not need to change the FIM Synchronization Service schema.

Object deletion in MV

One type of schema configuration that we need to look at in our deployment is **Object Deletion Rules** in the FIM Synchronization Service database.

Open up the **Synchronization Service Manager** window, and select the **Metaverse Designer** tool; this is where you will configure the MV schema or, if you like, the FIM Synchronization Service database schema.

If you want to select an object type, you can select **Configure Object Deletion Rule** in the **Action** pane:

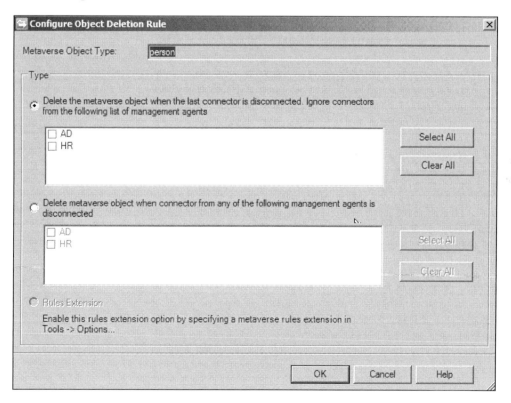

Basic Configuration

Here we can decide on what grounds the object should be deleted from the Metaverse.

The settings available in this dialog can be a bit confusing, but if you read the help section or look at http://social.technet.microsoft.com/wiki/contents/articles/understanding-deprovisioning-in-fim.aspx, you will find some explanation and ideas on when to use which method.

The default setting is that it will be deleted when the last connector is disconnected. It is vital to understand that an object cannot exist in the MV if it does not have a connector to an object in at least one connector space.

In many projects that I have been involved with, object deletion is not meant to happen at all. The idea is that once an object is created within FIM, it should live on and just change its status.

Modifying FIM Service schema

As I already explained, we will make some schema changes as we configure FIM to suit the needs of The Company. But there is one attribute that I have been forced to change in 99% of my FIM implementations—the EmployeeType attribute.

Before you start changing the FIM Service schema, you should have a look at http://aka.ms/FIMServiceSchema.

> In FIM Service, as in many other products, modifying the schema in the wrong way might stop it from working and require you to do a total rebuild of your FIM environment.

The EmployeeType attribute is commonly used to store information that governs many policies. There is usually a big difference between being a *Contractor* or an *Employee*, for example. And every company has its own *values*. If you look earlier on in this chapter, you will see that in the HR database at The Company, there are two different values in **HRType** for person objects. The values are **Employee** and **Contractor**.

If we look at a user in the FIM Portal and the values we can assign to the EmployeeType attribute (it is on the **Work Info** tab), we will see that you have three values to choose from—**Contractor**, **Intern**, and **Full Time Employee**. As you can see, this does not match with what The Company uses.

This is due to a validation setting on this attribute in the default FIM Service schema. In order to change this, we need to look in the FIM Portal and go to **Administration | Schema Management**:

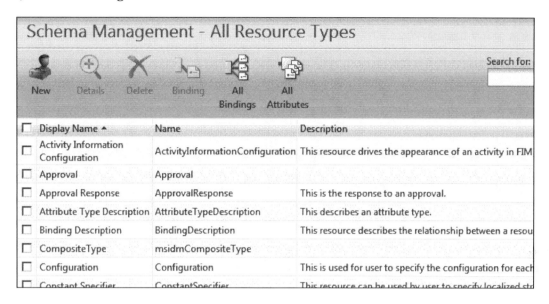

There are three things to manage here—**Resource Types** (often referred to as object types), **Attributes**, and **Bindings**. If you click **All Attributes** and search for **EmployeeType**, you will find the attribute we are interested in.

On the **Validation** tab, we will find the regular expression controlling the values we can store in this attribute:

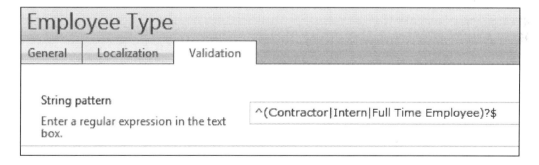

Basic Configuration

If I change this to `^(Contractor|Employee)?$`, it will match the needs of The Company.

Information about the syntax used for the regular expressions in FIM can be found at `http://aka.ms/FIMServiceSchema`.

This, however, is not enough because we can have one **Validation** on the attribute, but when binding an attribute to a resource type we can also define this; and for the `EmployeeType` binding to a **User** resource, this is the case.

In **Schema Management**, click **All Bindings** and search for `EmployeeType`. You will find the binding of the `EmployeeType` attribute to the **User** resource type. Once again change the **Validation** setting to `^(Contractor|Employee)?$`; this would actually have been enough, as the binding settings will override the base settings we have on the attribute type itself.

FIM Service MA

The AD and HR (SQL Server) MA only give the synchronization engine the possibility of talking to these data sources. But in order for FIM to apply its logic to the data flow, we need to have the very special MA connecting FIM Synchronization Service to FIM Service.

Even if you implement it like almost any other MA, you will soon find out that this is not a typical MA. In most cases, this will be the first MA we create.

Creating the FIM Service MA

I will walk you through the steps for creating the FIM Service MA, which are as follows:

1. Start FIM **Synchronization Service Manager**.
2. Select the **Management Agents** tool, and click **Create** in the **Actions** pane.

Chapter 4

3. Select the **FIM Service Management Agent** option in the **Management agent for:** drop-down list:

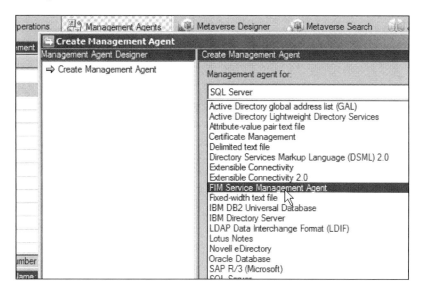

4. Give the MA a descriptive name; at The Company we simply call it **FIM Service**:

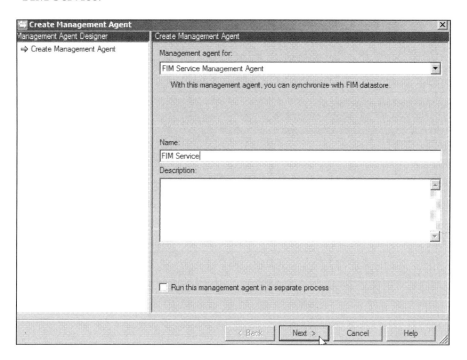

Basic Configuration

5. As we are using SQL Aliases, we will use the alias server name **dbFIMService**:

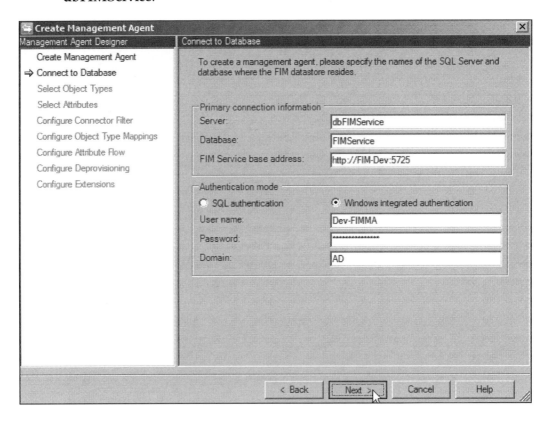

The FIM Service MA will not only connect to the FIM Service Database, but also make calls to the FIM web service interface. The default port for that service is 5725, so we connect to http://FIM-Dev:5725 as the FIM Service base address on the FIM-Dev server. This value will be changed from development to production during migration, as described later on in this chapter.

6. Select the object types you know FIM needs to manage:

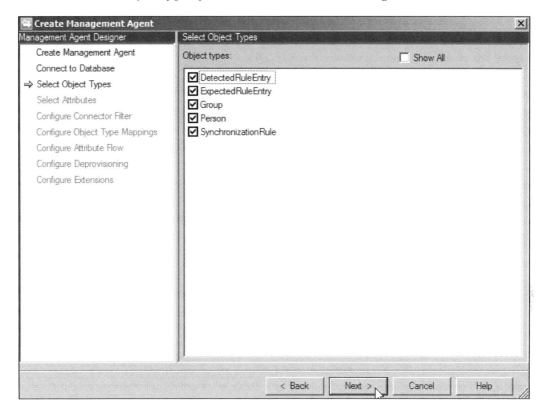

Do not deselect the default object types. These are required for FIM to do declarative synchronization. If we later on add new resource types (object) to the FIM Service schema, we might need to go back and add them to this configuration.

Basic Configuration

7. By default, all the predefined attributes are selected. But later on, if we add attributes to the FIM Service schema, we will need to get back here and select them. Giving FIM Synchronization Service access to new objects and attributes in FIM Service is not that straightforward, and will be explained later in this book, as the need arises:

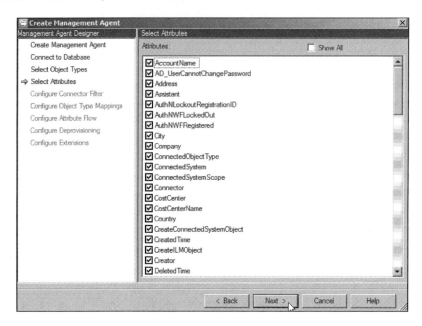

8. We will leave the connector filter as it is for the moment, but will return here later, to filter some accounts:

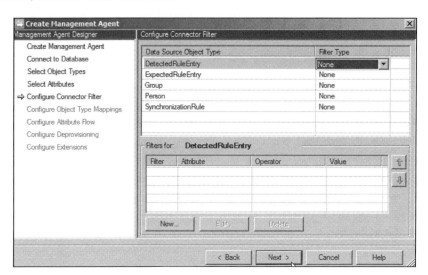

Chapter 4

9. We need to tell the MA how to map the object types in the FIM Service schema to the object types in the MV schema. If you have not made any customization to your schema, it should be **Group**: **group** and **Person**: **person**:

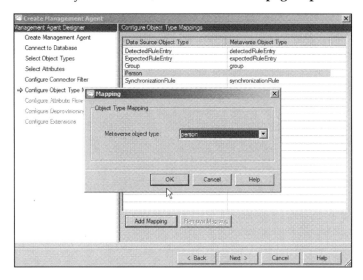

10. We will leave the attribute flow with the default values for the moment. But this is a setting you will frequently come back to and change, as new attributes are managed by FIM. Note that the **Advanced Mapping Type** option is not available in the FIM Service MA; we can only have **Direct** mappings:

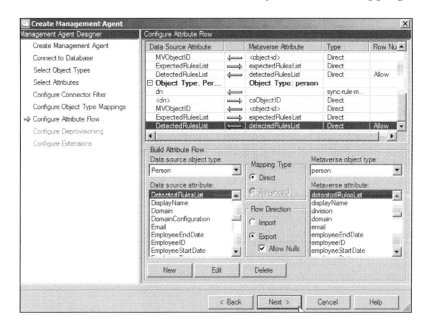

11. We have earlier discussed the concept of deprovisioning. Go to
    http://aka.ms/FIMDeprovisioning, and read it before you start using
    this option. I suggest you use the default setting to begin with. If you also
    have the default for Object Deletion in the MV schema, the result will be that
    once an object has made it into the MV/FIM Service database, it will not be
    deleted. This is because it will always have a connector between the MV and
    FIM Service connector space.

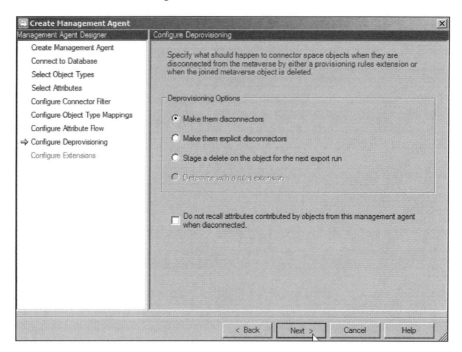

12. By now you might be wondering where the Join and Projection steps you
    had seen in the other MAs went. Well, the FIM Service MA is a little special
    because it has *automatic* join and projection rules. As soon as an object
    appears in FIM Service or FIM Synchronization Service, it will automatically
    be projected to the other, if there is an object type mapping defined. It will
    also automatically join objects using **objectID**.

13. The FIM Service MA does not support any rules extensions; we cannot have any advanced attribute flows or use **Determine with a rules extension** as **Deprovisioning Options**.

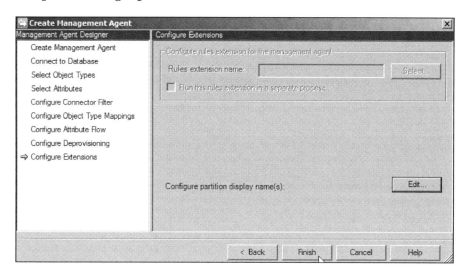

Creating run profiles

Create run profiles for **Full Import, Delta Import, Full Synchronization, Delta Synchronization**, and **Export**:

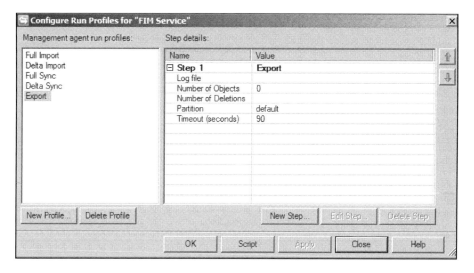

If you click the **Script** button, FIM will create a VB script that can be used to schedule run profiles.

First import

In order to finish the configuration of FIM Service MA, I recommend you run an import before making any changes in FIM Portal. The first import is sometimes called the *Discovery* import. The FIM Service MA and the AD MA both require you to run this first **Full Import** profile before you start to use them.

Select the FIM Service MA, select **Run** in the **Actions** pane, and run the **Full Import** profile. Do **not** run any synchronization profiles.

You will then see the value of **Adds** as 2 in the **Synchronization Statistics** frame:

Profile Name: Full Import User Name: AD\administrator			
Step Type: Full Import (Stage Only)		Partition: default	
Start Time: 1/28/2012 2:04:55 AM		End Time: 1/28/2012 2:04:55 AM	Status: success
Synchronization Statistics		Connection Status	
Staging			
Unchanged	0		
Adds	2	Synchronization Errors	
Updates	0		
Renames	0		
Deletes	0		

If you click the link, you will see two objects with GUIDs as **Distinguished Name**. Every object in the FIM Service database is identified using a GUID.

If you double-click on each of them and view the details, you will see that it is the *Installation* user and the *Built-in Synchronization Account* user. Both of these users are *special* users created during setup.

The Installation user is the account used to install the FIM Service (administrator in my example), and the Built-in Synchronization Account is the account specified during setup as the account used by the FIM Service MA; in our case these are the `Dev-FIMMA` and `svcFIMMA` accounts.

Filtering accounts

In FIM Service, we might have objects that we do not want Synchronization Service to manage. During the first import, described in the previous section, you found two users which were created during setup. We usually do not want to have these users in a Metaverse.

What we need to do is filter out the Installation (administrator) and Built-in Synchronization Account user accounts. We do this by filtering out the GUIDs of these objects.

If you are following this guide, you will have a newly made, first import.

1. Select the FIM Service MA and look in the **Synchronization Statistics** frame.
2. Click **Adds** in the frame.
3. Click the first entry and select the GUID after the Distinguished Name, right-click, and copy. The first entry should be the Installer account, with GUID **7fb2b853-24f0-4498-9534-4e10589723c4**.
4. Click the close button twice.
5. Open properties for FIM **Service Management Agent**.
6. Select the **Configure Connector Filter** step, and select **Person** in the **Data Source Object Type** list.
7. Click **New…**.
8. Paste the GUID into the **Value** field and click **Add Condition**. This will filter the object, where `<dn>` Equals `<guid>`.
9. Click **OK** twice to save the Management Agent configuration.
10. Click **Adds** in the **Synchronization Statistics** frame, and repeat the aforementioned steps to filter out the Built-in Synchronization Account as well.
11. When done, your connector filter should look like the following screenshot:

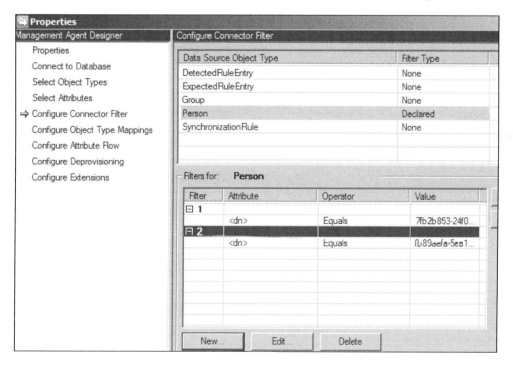

Initial load versus scheduled runs

When we first start to import information into Synchronization Engine it is likely that information already exists in many or all of the connected systems.

We might need to create special synchronization rules just for the initial load, which are not used again unless we need to rebuild the data.

Let me give you an example. At The Company, the basic idea is that users should be imported from the HR system and created in AD. But when we start, there might be existing users in AD and we would need to connect them using a Join rather than provisioning (creating) them in AD. During the initial load we would therefore turn off Provision in FIM, import users from both systems, project them into the MV, and join the users existing in both the systems.

Initial load is usually done manually; that is, we manually start the required run profiles for each MA.

If the environment is large, the initial load might take many hours due to the fact that, when we export our objects into the FIM Service database using the FIM Service MA, there might be many policies configured in the FIM Service that need to be applied for each object. In FIM 2010 R2, major changes have been made to the way the FIM Service MA works, in order to improve performance. Read about it at `http://blog.konab.com/2011/09/performance-improvements-in-fim-2010-r2`.

There are numerous ways of creating scheduled runs. I will show you a way that does not require any coding or third-party add-ons.

If you look at the run profile you would like to schedule, there is a **Script** button to create a script. It will generate a VB-script, which will start the run profile.

The task scheduler in Windows can then be used to create a schedule to run the script by using `cscript runprofilevbscriptname`. Just remember that the account (Network Service, for example) running the scheduled task needs to be a member of the `FIMSyncOperators` group, in order for it to be allowed to run the MA run profiles.

So far, we have the following requirements in our environment:

1. Import from HR.
2. Synchronize the changes.
3. Export to AD.
4. Verify export to AD.

But the logical step 2, *Synchronize the changes*, is actually where we need to export/import/synchronize with the FIM Service MA. So our *run schedule* would be as follows:

1. Import from HR.
2. Synchronize the changes from HR.
3. Export changes from MV to FIM Service.

> If we have very complex rules and workflows in our FIM Service, we might need to give it a little time before importing the result. I usually add a 30-second pause in the schedule.

4. Import changes from FIM Service.
5. Synchronize the changes from FIM Service.
6. Export changes to AD.
7. Import from AD to verify changes.

Moving configuration from development to production

So far, I have done all the changes on the FIM-Dev server, which is my test/pilot/dev environment. We now need to transfer the information from development to production.

The steps to move the configuration vary a little depending on what kind of changes you have made. But basically we have two major areas, FIM Synchronization Service and FIM Service. We move changes to each in different ways.

If I have made any changes to the FIM Synchronization Service schema or any MA, I need to move this configuration as well. Otherwise, I will settle with only moving the FIM Service configuration.

The tool we use to move the FIM Service configuration is PowerShell. When working with FIM, you will realize that PowerShell will be something you will have to learn.

The main steps are as follows:

1. Export the FIM Service schema, FIM Service Policy configuration, and FIM Synchronization Service configuration on both development and production systems.

2. Compare the FIM Service schema and FIM Service Policy, and generate difference files for each.
3. We then import the following to the production environment:
   - FIM Service schema differences
   - FIM Synchronization Service settings (if any changes have been made)
   - FIM Service policy differences

To make it easier to know where files and other scripts and configurations go, I have created a folder structure on the FIM-Dev, FIM Service, and FIM Sync servers to hold the scripts and configuration files. A root folder called `C:\FIMConfig` has been created. In my PowerShell scripts, I set this folder as `$workDir`. I store my scripts in this folder, and this is also where my configuration files exist. I have shared this folder as `FIMConfig` so that I can read the FIM-Dev configuration directly on the production servers without having to copy the files. This is by no means the best practice; this is just the way I do it in this scenario. It is, however, vital that you keep your scripts and files organized, so that you do not risk importing the wrong configuration into production.

In my `FIMConfig` folder, I will create a subfolder called `SyncConfig`, which is where I will create dated folders to store each FIM Synchronization Service export.

Maintenance mode for production

Initially, while the FIM system is still being developed, we do not need to concern ourselves with someone working in the production environment. But later on, we need to make sure that no-one is working in the environment while we import new settings into the production servers.

One way of doing this is to put the servers into *maintenance mode*.

To place FIM Synchronization Service into maintenance mode, ensure that no Management Agents are running; that is, stop all schedules and make sure no MAs are running.

In order to place the FIM Service into maintenance mode, deny it access to port 5725. The steps to deny access to port 5725 are as follows:

1. Open Windows Firewall with Advanced Security. In order to do this:
    i. Click **Start**, and type **Windows Firewall with Advanced Security**.
    ii. Once the search result appears on the Start menu, click **Windows Firewall with Advanced Security**.
2. In the console tree, click **Inbound Rules**.
3. In **Inbound Rules**, right-click on the **Forefront Identity Manager Service (Webservice)** rule, and then click **Disable Rule**.
4. In order to place FIM Portal into maintenance mode, disable FIM Portal with the following steps:
    i. Open **Internet Information Services (IIS) Manager**, click **Start**, type **Internet Information Services (IIS) Manager**, and then click on it when the option appears on the Start menu.
    ii. Expand the objects in the console tree until you see **SharePoint – 80**.
    iii. Right-click **SharePoint – 80**, click **Manage Web Site**, and then click **Stop**.

When you are done importing the new configuration, I recommend that you do some manual testing before putting the system into production again.

Disabling maintenance mode

No change is necessary to bring FIM Synchronization Service out of maintenance mode. If you have scheduled run profiles, you need to start the schedule again.

In order to return the FIM Service to normal operation, allow access to port 5725. The steps to allow access to port 5725 are as follows:

1. Open **Windows Firewall with Advanced Security**.
2. In the console tree, click **Inbound Rules**.
3. On the **Inbound Rules** page, right-click on the **Forefront Identity Manager Service (Webservice)** rule, and then click **Enable Rule**.
4. To return FIM Portal to normal operation, enable FIM Portal using the following steps:
    i. Open **Internet Information Services (IIS) Manager**.
    ii. Navigate to **SharePoint – 80**.
    iii. Right-click on the site, click **Manage Web Site**, and then click **Start**.

Exporting FIM Synchronization Service settings

When exporting the Synchronization Service configuration, the idea is to export from the development environment and import to the production environment. You should, however, always make an export of the configuration in the production environment as well, as this will serve as a backup in case something goes wrong.

The export requires that the target folder be empty, which is why I usually create a new folder for each export with the date (and sometimes time) in it.

In order to carry out the export, follow the ensuing steps on both your FIM-Dev and FIM-Sync servers:

1. Create a new folder with a name reflecting the date and/or time. For example, `C:\FIMConfig\SyncConfig\180312`.
2. Start **Synchronization Service Manager**.
3. In the **File** menu, select **Export Server Configuration...**.
4. Select your newly created folder as the target.

Exporting FIM Service settings

In order to export the FIM Service settings, we run PowerShell scripts. These scripts will generate XML files with the current configuration.

The PowerShell scripts used by The Company are part of the code bundle attached to the book.

> **Note!**
> You cannot use these code bundles as they are, as the paths and names used will need to be changed to work in your environment. But they might serve as a starting point for your own scripts.

> The PowerShell scripts are also available for download from my blog, at the `http://blog.konab.com/fim-2010-r2-book/basic-configuration/` page.

Examples of other PowerShell scripts that can be used to manage the FIM Service configuration, can be found at many places on the Internet.

In some cases, you may have made some *special* changes in the development environment that you do not want to transfer to the production environment. In such cases, you can modify the scripts to exclude these kinds of information.

There are also occasions when migration will have to be made in multiple steps. If we have created dependencies between objects, they need to be in place before we can import the configuration referring to those objects.

Exporting the FIM Service schema

Perform the following steps on the FIM-Dev server:

1. Start the Windows PowerShell command prompt.
2. Run the `FIM-Dev-ExportSchema.ps1` script.

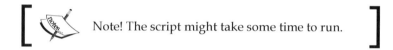
Note! The script might take some time to run.

3. Verify if the resulting XML file is created as expected.

Perform the following steps on the FIM-Service (production) server:

1. Start the Windows PowerShell command prompt.
2. Run the `FIM-Prod-ExportSchema.ps1` script.

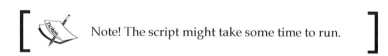
Note! The script might take some time to run.

3. Verify if the resulting XML file is created as expected.

Exporting the FIM Service policy

Perform the following steps on the FIM-Dev server:

1. Start the Windows PowerShell command prompt.
2. Run the `FIM-Dev-ExportPolicy.ps1` script.

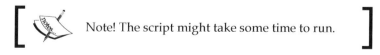
Note! The script might take some time to run.

3. Verify if the resulting XML file is created as expected.

Perform the following steps on the FIM-Service (production) server:

1. Start the Windows PowerShell command prompt.
2. Run the `FIM-Prod-ExportPolicy.ps1` script.

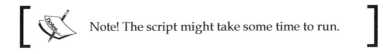

> Note! The script might take some time to run.

3. Verify if the resulting XML file is created as expected.

Generating the difference files

After exporting the configuration from both the development and production environment, we run a PowerShell script that compares the two and generates a difference file.

It is very important that we take a good look at these difference files before we import the difference into production. In some cases, you might manually delete objects in the difference file to prevent them from being imported into the production environment. If you find that this will *always* be required, you might want to take a look at modifying the export script on the Dev environment to exclude those objects.

Generating the schema difference

Perform the following steps on the FIM-Service (production) server:

1. Start the Windows PowerShell command prompt.
2. Run the `SyncSchema.ps1` script.
3. Verify if the resulting XML file is created as expected, and also verify if it contains the changes you expected.

If you get an error "**Changes is null**", it is an indication that there are no differences between the two environments, and that there is actually no error.

Generating the policy difference

Perform the following steps on the FIM-Service (production) server:

1. Start the Windows PowerShell command prompt.
2. Run the `SyncPolicy.ps1` script.
3. Verify if the resulting XML file is created as expected, and also verify if it contains the changes you expected.

If you get an error "**Changes is null**", it is an indication that there are no differences between the two environments, and that there is actually no error.

Importing to production

After validating that the difference files look okay, we can start importing the changes into the production environment.

Importing custom code

If you have installed some third-party add-ons, or prepared some custom code, you will need to import the latest versions of these into production.

How to do this depends on what kind of add-on you are using, and what kind of change is made. So this will vary from just copying a new version of a DLL file to installing a third-party product.

Importing the Service schema difference

Perform the following steps on the FIM-Service (production) server:

1. Start the Windows PowerShell command prompt.
2. Run the `CommitSchemaChanges.ps1` script.

If for some reason the import script is unable to import some objects, it will write them into a `SchemaUndone.xml` file. If this happens, take a close look at the file and check if it has a sign of some misconfiguration, or of what might have caused the import of some objects to fail.

If you think that you have solved the problem, you can then run the `ResumeUndoneSchemaImports.ps1` script to try to import them again.

Importing the Synchronization Service settings

On the FIM-Sync (production) server, we will import the settings from our FIM-Dev Synchronization Service.

While importing the settings, we will import both schema changes and management agent settings. It is typical that we will need to make changes as we import, given that we want production to use other accounts and servers in the MA configuration.

Basic Configuration

In the following guide, I will show you how it looks when I import the settings into my FIM-Sync (production) server for the first time:

1. Start FIM **Synchronization Service Manager** on the FIM-Sync server.
2. In the **File** menu select **Import Server Configuration…**.
3. Browse for the folder that contains the export, which was done on the FIM-Dev server:

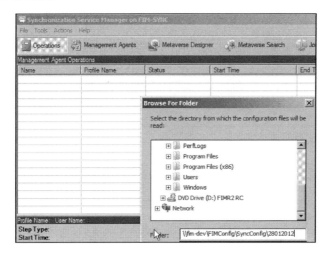

4. While importing new and changed Management Agents, you will need to be aware of the changes done to the account name being used, or the server it connects to. The use of SQL aliases in this case makes it unncecessary to change the **Server** property; we need to change other settings such as the account used in production:

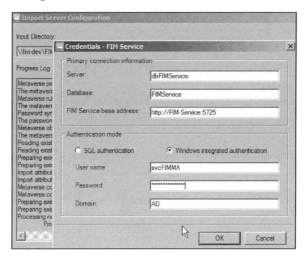

Chapter 4

5. The same goes for the Active Directory MA. This, however, is a special case in our environment. We need to remember to change the container used by the MA before we can start running any synchronizations:

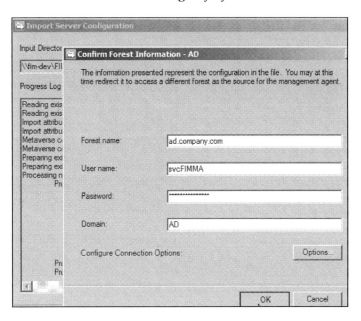

6. The HR MA is also using SQL aliases, so there's no need to change the **Server** property; but, we need to change the account used:

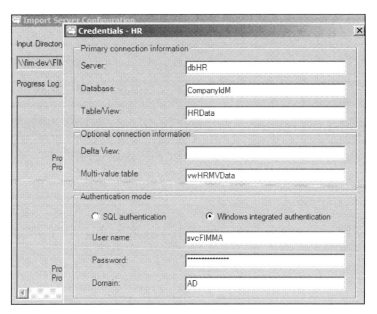

[139]

Basic Configuration

7. As we are using the same AD and just a different OU in this example, we need to remember to change the OU used by the AD MA. If we forget this and start to synchronize data, all sorts of strange things might happen depending on our rules. This is one reason for always doing manual synchronizations after importing new configurations. Doing it manually makes it possible for us to detect errors before we commit them in a CDS, by running an export:

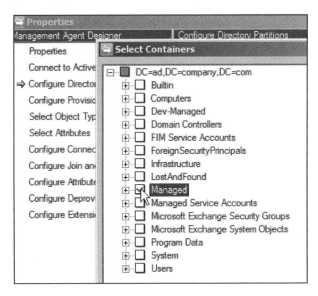

Importing the FIM Service policy

Perform the following steps on the FIM-Service (production) server:

1. Start the Windows PowerShell command prompt.
2. Run the `FIM-Prod-ExportSchema.ps1` script.

If, for any reason, the import script is unable to import some objects, it will write them into a `PolicyUndone.xml` file. If this happens, take a close look at the file and check if it has a sign of some misconfiguration or of what might have caused the import of some objects to fail.

If you think that you have solved the problem, you can run the `ResumeUndonePolicyImports.ps1` script to try and import them again.

PowerShell scripts

The PowerShell scripts used by The Company are a part of the code bundle attached with this book.

> **Note!**
> You cannot use these as they are, since the paths and names used will need to be changed to work in your environment. But they might serve as a starting point for your own scripts.

> The PowerShell scripts are also available for download from my blog at the http://blog.konab.com/fim-2010-r2-book/basic-configuration/ page.

Examples of other PowerShell scripts that can be used to manage the FIM Service configuration, can be found in many places on the Internet.

Summary

In this chapter, we have seen how The Company configured their first Management Agents and prepared the FIM environment for further configuration.

In my experience, the most common source of errors in the FIM environment is the lack of well-documented processes to make sure the development/test and production environments look the same. Learning and documenting how to move your configuration from development/test to production is vital as the configuration gets more complex.

If you take your time to make sure your basic configuration setup is satisfactory, it will save you many hours of troubleshooting later on. If you feel confident that your basic configuration is correct, moving on and making more complex configuration settings will be easier.

We are now ready to actually do something with our FIM environment. In the next chapter, we will start off by looking at how to configure FIM for user management.

5
User Management

User management is the primary goal for most FIM deployments. Synchronizing user information between different Management Agents and managing user provisioning/deprovisioning is often the first thing we focus on, in our FIM deployment.

In this chapter, we will look at:

- How user management is set up in FIM Service and FIM Synchronization Service
- How to manage users in:
    - Active Directory
    - Microsoft Exchange
    - A phone system
- How to enable users to do some self-service

Before we move on, let's make something clear.

In this chapter, and the next on Group Management, all configuration changes are made in the FIM-dev environment and then migrated to the production environment. I will not point out that step.

Modifying MPRs for user management

There are many **Management Policy Rules** (**MPRs**) in FIM Service that control how user objects can be modified by self-service, administrators, or the synchronization engine.

User Management

In many cases, we need to modify the existing MPRs and/or create new ones. Whether we use the existing MPRs or decide to create new ones is something you can decide as you wish. In my examples in this book, I will reuse many of the built-in MPRs and add new ones when needed.

Before we can start our user management, it is a good idea to look at the existing MPRs and try to understand what they will do. If we go into FIM Portal, select **Management Policy Rules**, and search for **user**, we will get around 21 MPRs (many are regarding group management) in our default FIM 2010 R2 setup. Take a quick look at them in the following screenshot and you will notice that many are disabled by default:

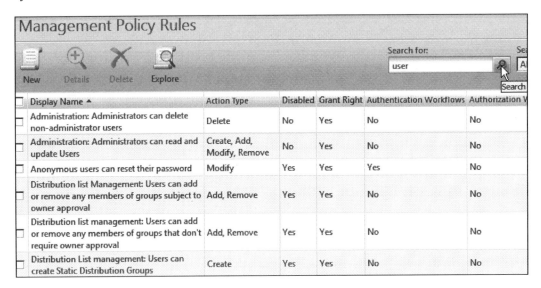

One that is enabled by default is **Synchronization: Synchronization account controls users it synchronizes**. This is the MPR that allows the synchronization account to manage user objects. Let's take a look at this one, so that we will understand later on why synchronization of users might not work as expected.

Click the link to the MPR, **Synchronization: Synchronization account controls users it synchronizes**, to open up its properties.

- In the **General** tab, we can see that this MPR is of type **Request**, since it deals with a request from the synchronization account to modify a user object.

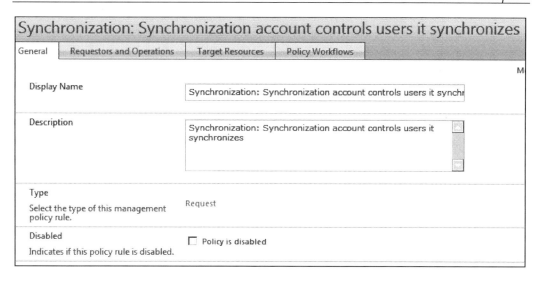

- The **Requestors and Operations** tab shows that this MPR is applied when the **Requestor** is **Synchronization Engine**, and **Operation** is something other than **Read resource**.

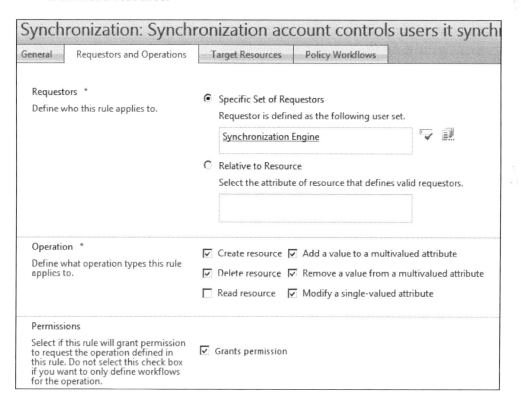

User Management

- In the **Target Resources** tab, we see that the target in this case is the set **All People**. If you look at the definition of that set, you will see that the criterion is that it is a user object.

> If you change the **All People** set, be aware that this and other MPRs might stop working as expected.

Notice that the MPR does not apply to all attributes, only a selection of attributes.

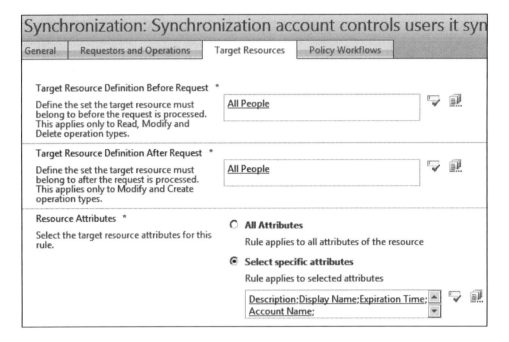

If you click the icon that looks like a stack of papers, you can get a list of all attributes and choose the one you want the MPR to apply to.

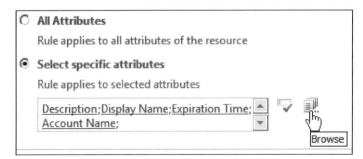

On the **Select Attributes** page, in the **Search within:** drop-down, select **Users**, and then click on the search icon. You will then see all the attributes, bound to user resources, and will be able to select and deselect as you like. Whenever you have added some attribute to the schema, you will have to go back here and select the new attribute, in order for the synchronization engine to be allowed to manage it.

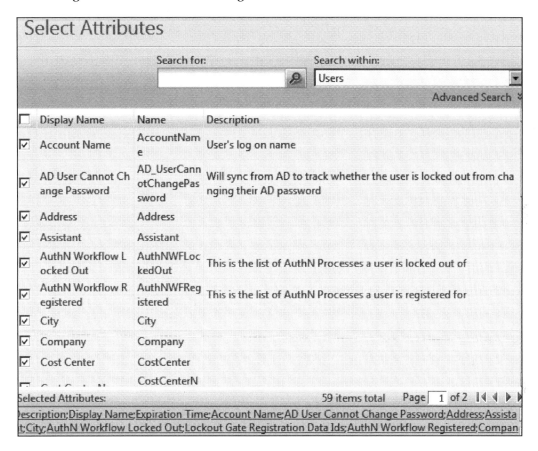

User Management

- There are no policy workflows triggered by this MPR.

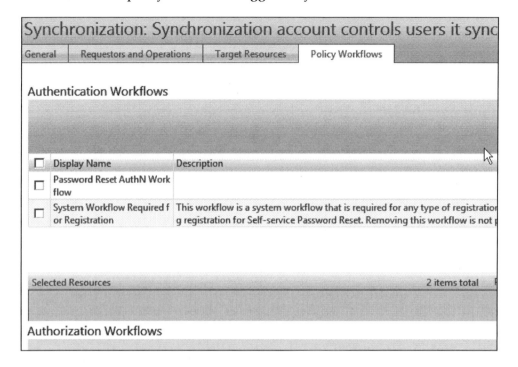

 Please remember that any request made by the synchronization engine will bypass any authentication or authorization workflows. Only action workflows can be triggered when the requestor is the synchronization engine.

Configuring sets for user management

Organizing objects in the FIM Service is done through Set; all MPRs use Set some way or the other. As soon as we start to talk about grouping users rather than managing them individually, we need to create a Set containing those users.

 Sets are *not* groups. Sets are only used within the FIM Service to organize managed objects, while groups are themselves a type of managed object that can be synchronized to other systems.

Chapter 5

It is, for example, very common that different employee types are managed differently. But in order to do that, we need to organize them into different Sets.

If we look at all the Sets that we get out of the box, you will find that many of them have a **Display Name** that you can relate to, and you can choose to reuse them or create your own.

Again, there are some predefined Sets that we can use, such as **All Contractors** or **All Full Time Employees**. However, in our example, **All Full Time Employees** is not correctly configured. In our example, **Employee Type** is not called **Full Time Employee**, it is just **Employee**.

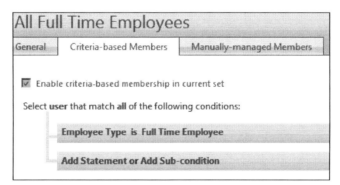

In the **All Full Time Employees** Set, we can see that the criterion is that the **Employee Type** attribute is **Full Time Employee**; we need to change this to **Employee**.

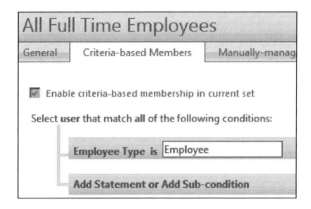

A good idea, in this case, is to also change the display name of the set to **All Employees**.

As we proceed with configuring FIM Service, we will create many new Sets; consider this a short introduction.

Inbound synchronization rules

One of the first things we need to do in order to manage users is to get some users into FIM Synchronization Service and FIM Service. We can create them using FIM Portal or some other interface, but usually there are existing users in some system that we would like to import. In our example, the HR system is our primary source of users.

Importing will require us to create what is called an **inbound synchronization rule**. For one external system, such as the HR system, we might have multiple inbound synchronization rules. One reason for that could be that we have multiple object types in one **CDS (Connected Data Source)** and we can only synchronize one resource type (object) in each rule.

So first of all, we create a synchronization rule to import users from the HR system.

In the **FIM** portal, go to **Administration | Synchronization Rules | New**.

1. When creating synchronization rules, it is a good idea to have some kind of naming standard to make it easier to find the correct rules later on. In my example, I use the syntax *MA ObjectType Direction*, so this one is called **HR Users Inbound**. I tend to create separate synchronization rules for each direction, because it gives me more control. The behavior and settings on inbound and outbound rules are quite different, as you will see once we have created a few synchronization rules. But, as you will see later in this chapter, I do create rules with both the inbound and outbound directions, in some cases.

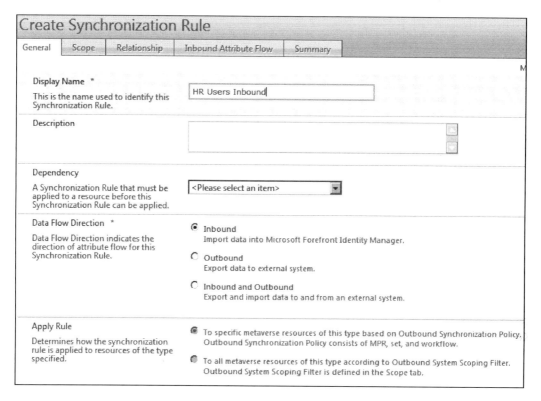

User Management

2. In the **Scope** tab, we define the **Resource Type** involved in FIM and in the Connector Space object for the **External System**. Remember that we are now looking at the FIM Synchronization Service (**Metaverse**) schema not the FIM Service schema.

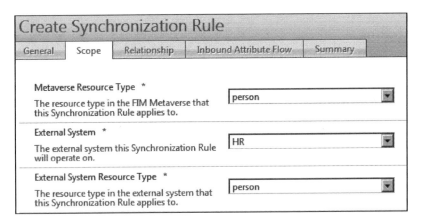

3. In the **Relationship** tab, we define how FIM should try to join the Connector Space object to the Metaverse object. If you add multiple conditions, the objects have to satisfy all conditions. If you need more complex rules to join the objects, you might need to configure the Management Agent join rules instead. If FIM cannot match objects using the Relationship Criteria we would, in this case, like FIM to project a new object into the Metaverse. To project, we then need to check the **Create Resource in FIM** checkbox. So, what FIM will do in this example is first check if it can match **Relationship Criteria**, and if no match is found, it will create a new object in the Metaverse.

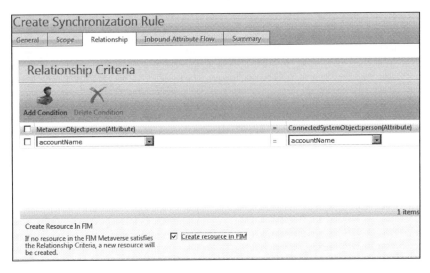

Chapter 5

4. We then define the attribute flows. This tells FIM how to flow data from the Connector Space into the Metaverse. In this example, we have only straight forward, direct flows. Later, we will create some more complex attribute flows. Typically, you just define one or two attributes to begin with, and then go back and add attributes later on, when you know it is all working as expected.

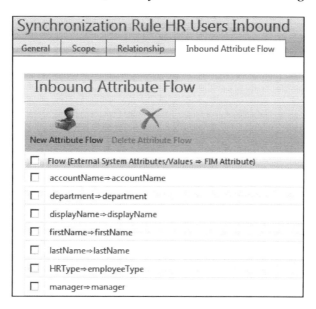

- **Synchronization Rule** cannot be used directly after creation. We first need to import the new **Synchronization Rule** object into the synchronization engine, which is supposed to do the synchronization. An easy way is to run **Delta Import** followed by **Delta Sync** on the FIM Service MA. The synchronization engine will then associate the new rule with the correct MA, HR in our example.

- It is now possible to actually use the new synchronization rule. Test it by running a **Full Sync** on the **HR** MA; I am assuming you have already run the **Full Import** profile.

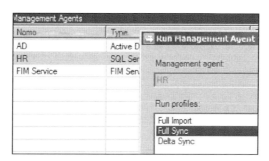

[153]

User Management

- In **Synchronization Statistics**, you will see how many new objects (**Projections**) are projected (created) in the Metaverse.

Step Type:	Full Synchronization	
Start Time:	2/15/2012 8:56:53 AM	
Synchronization Statistics		
Inbound Synchronization		
Projections		2
Joins		0
Filtered Disconnectors		0
Disconnectors		2
Connectors with Flow Updates		2

- Further down in the **Synchronization Statistics**, you will see that for each projection there is also a **Provisioning Adds** option to the **FIM Service** MA. This is caused by the automatic provisioning happening for the FIM Service MA. This is just another example of the special way the FIM Service MA works. As you will see later, for all other MAs, we need to configure the provisioning for it to happen.

Step Type:	Full Synchronization
Start Time:	2/15/2012 8:56:53 AM
Synchronization Statistics	
Disconnectors	2
Connectors with Flow Updates	2
Connectors without Flow Updates	0
Filtered Connectors	0
Deleted Connectors	0
Metaverse Object Deletes	0
Outbound Synchronization	**FIM Service**
Export Attribute Flow	2
Provisioning Adds	2

○ In order for the users to appear in FIM Portal, we need to run an **Export** to the **FIM Service**. Running **Export** to the **FIM Service** MA (and other MAs as well) is a critical step, since we now will start to change data in the connected system. To make sure you are not on your way to doing something stupid, you can check what will happen.

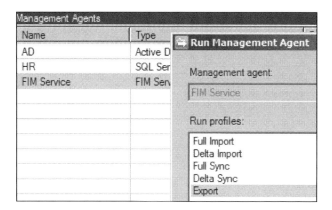

○ It is possible to search the Connector Space for **Pending Export**. By doing this and looking at **Pending Export**, you can verify that the changes that FIM is planning to make in the Connected Data Source are what you expected. If not, you can go back, reconfigure, synchronize again, and check if **Pending Export** is looking better.

User Management

- After running the **Export**, go into the FIM portal and search for **Users**; you will find new users, but they will not have any data. This is because we need to manually configure the FIM Service MA to export the attributes we would like to have in the FIM Service Database and which should be shown in FIM Portal.

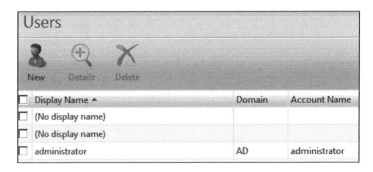

- In the **FIM Service** MA properties, we need to go to **Configure Attribute Flow**.
- Select the correct **Object Type** flow, **Person** <- -> **person** in our example, and find the **Data source attribute** in the FIM Service schema you want the value to be stored in; then find the **Metaverse attribute** you imported the value to.
- For the **Flow Direction** option, select **Export**, and click the **New** button.

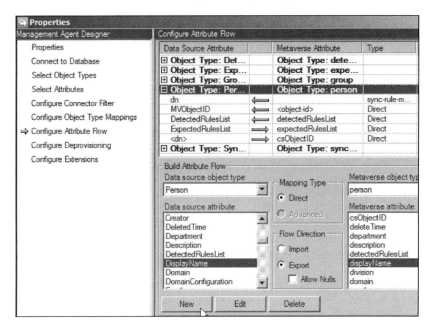

- Repeat this for all relevant attributes.
- After adding the attributes we want to the **Attribute Flow** in the **FIM Service** MA, we need to run **Full Sync** followed by **Export**, for the data to appear in the portal.

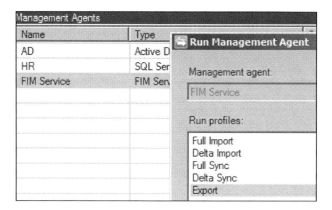

By now, I guess you are starting to understand how the flow of inbound synchronization works. It is very easy to make a mistake that causes strange behavior. The most common one is to mix up the two schemas of the Metaverse and the FIM Service.

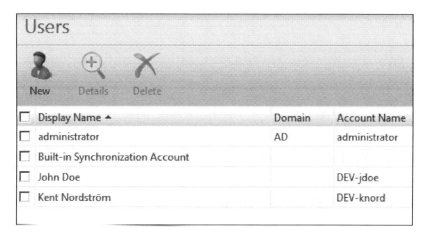

During testing and development of the FIM Synchronization and FIM Service, you will find that you need to make frequent changes and synchronizations to verify your configuration. If your test/development environment contains a large number of objects, it might take hours to run a synchronization cycle, so try keeping the number of objects in your test/dev environment to a minimum.

User Management

> If you are following this example and have one test/development and one production environment, I would recommend that you do frequent migrations of the configuration. It will take some time, but it will also make troubleshooting easier, since you are migrating fewer changes.

Since we are now also starting to configure our environment and might create a situation where we would like to go back, I also suggest that you back up the FIM Service and FIM Synchronization Service databases now and then, and occasionally make some extra configuration exports as well.

Outbound synchronization rules

As you can see, inbound synchronization rules are associated with the Connector Space MA we like to import information from. Outbound synchronization is very different!

This is one reason I tend not to have **Inbound and Outbound Data Flow Direction** in my synchronization rules.

Outbound synchronization rules are associated with each object (user, for example). In FIM 2010 R2, there are two ways of doing this.

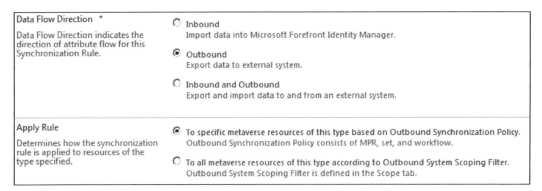

You can either use **Outbound Synchronization Policy** or **Outbound System Scoping Filter**.

> You can only make this choice during the creation of the outbound synchronization rule. You cannot change it once the synchronization rule is created.

[158]

In some scenarios, you will find that it is useful to have multiple outbound synchronization rules for one external system. In those cases, you might mix the two different ways of associating the rule to the object. You will find one example of this later in this chapter, in the *Managing Exchange* section.

You will quickly find out that using Outbound Scoping Filter will be easier. However, there are limitations when you use this approach for outbound synchronizations.

A critical limitation is that you cannot do deprovisioning (trigger a delete), using Outbound Scoping Filter. This I know is a subject for debate and might change in later releases or updates.

Another limitation of Outbound Scoping Filter is that it will not allow you to use workflow attributes (such as generated passwords) in your synchronization rule.

Outbound synchronization policy

The only way, before the FIM 2010 R2 release, is to associate the users with **Expected Rule Entries** (**EREs**). In order for us to do that, we need to create what some people call the **configuration triple**.

We need the following:

- A **Set** containing the objects that should have the ERE
- An action **workflow** that adds the ERE to the object
- An **MPR** that runs the action workflow when the object transitions into the Set

If we want to do deprovisioning as well, we would also need an action workflow to remove the ERE and an MPR that triggers that workflow.

Outbound system scoping filter

If we have a very simple scenario, we can use what is called **Outbound System Scoping Filter** to tell FIM which objects to associate the outbound synchronization rule with.

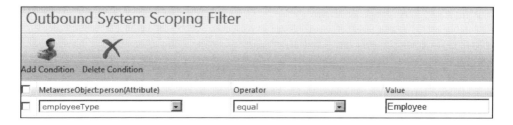

User Management

In the outbound synchronization rule, we define the filter. Something very important to remember here is that, if you add conditions they are ANDed. This means your objects need to match all conditions. At The Company, I will use **Outbound System Scoping Filter** for the phone system.

> **Outbound System Scoping Filter** is a new feature in the FIM 2010 R2 release. You will not find this if you run earlier versions of FIM 2010.

Detected rule entry

If for some reason you would like to know if an object exists in the external system, you can configure FIM to create a **Detected Rule Entry** (**DRE**) and associate it with the object.

One reason for this would be that we need to know if the provisioning is successful and maybe trigger some actions based on that. For **Active Directory** (**AD**), for example, we might use this to trigger the creation of home folders only after a DRE is detected on the user.

We can configure this by adding a small checkbox to our outbound synchronization rule.

If you check **Use as Existence Test** on one of the outbound attribute flows, FIM will create the DRE if it detects a successful export of that value during the next import from the system. The attribute flow you are using should be one that is populated for all objects.

Outbound Attribute Flow

New Attribute Flow   Delete Attribute Flow

	Initial Flow Only	Use as Existence Test	Flow (FIM Value ⇒ Destination Attribute)
☐	☐	☐	department ⇒ department
☐	☐	☐	displayName ⇒ displayName
☐	☐	☐	firstName ⇒ firstName
☐	☐	☐	lastName ⇒ lastName
☐	☐	☐	middleName ⇒ middleName
☐	☑	☑	HRGUID ⇒ objectID

If we synchronize this DRE in to the FIM Service, we can check the **Provisioning** tab on the object, **User** for example.

In **Detected Rules List**, we will see the DREs this particular user is associated with.

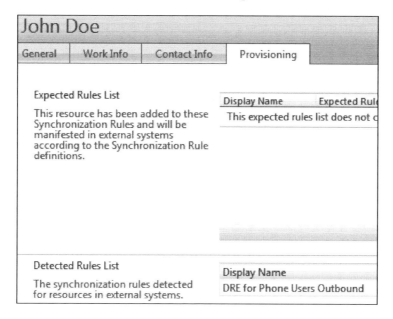

If you plan on using DREs or would like to understand them better, I suggest you begin by reading http://aka.ms/FIMDRE, where the whole concept of DREs is explained in detail. You will also find some nice examples on how to use them.

Provisioning

Provisioning is when we create new objects in a Connector Space using the Metaverse as the source. Before we can start to use provisioning, we need to enable it in **Synchronization Service Manager**.

1. Start **Synchronization Service Manager**, and select **Tools | Options**.

User Management

2. Check the **Enable Synchronization Rule Provisioning** checkbox, to enable provisioning.

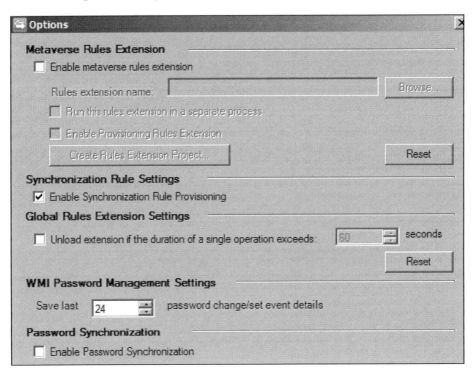

3. In the outbound synchronization rule, we need to place a check in **Create resource in external system**.

Non-declarative provisioning

If you are doing non-declarative classic synchronization using code, you would instead check **Enable metaverse rules extension**, type (or browse for) the name of the DLL files containing your code, and check the **Enable Provisioning Rules Extension** checkbox.

If you are planning on doing non-declarative, classic provisioning, you will find plenty of examples on what the code could look like in the Metaverse Extension DLL. A good starting point can be http://aka.ms/FIMMVExtension. When searching the Internet, make sure to look for the older versions, MIIS and ILM, since most examples are from those older versions. Enabling **Metaverse Rules Extension** also gives you the ability to click the **Create Rules Extension Project...** button; the tool will then create a Visual Studio project for you using either VB.NET or C#, as you choose.

Managing users in a phone system

The phone system at The Company is a simple SQL table in the eyes of FIM. The basic idea is that all employees, but not contractors, should be in the phone system and FIM is responsible for creating them.

Once the users are created in the phone system, this system is responsible for entering phone and office location data, which is then imported back into FIM.

I have earlier stated that I tend not to mix inbound and outbound data flow directions in the same synchronization rule, but the phone system is one where this is possible. Why? Well, because it is very simple and the users are completely managed by FIM.

To manage the users in the phone system, we need to create the MA for the phone system, to begin with. Since we have walked through the steps on how to do this before, I will just point out some basics:

1. Management Agent type is **SQL Server** and I give it the name **Phone**.

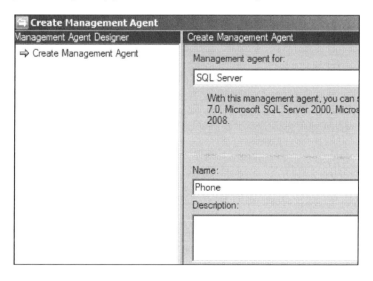

User Management

2. Using a SQL alias of **dbPhone**, I connect to the database—**CompanyIdM**—and table—**PhoneData**—containing the phone data.

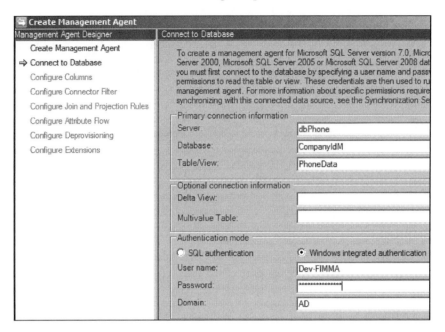

3. I set the **objectID** column as anchor and the **Object Type** is **person**.

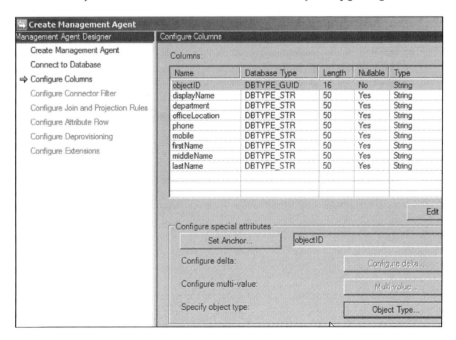

4. FIM will manage the users in the phone system and will also delete them, if they no longer have a connection to FIM. In order for FIM to do that, we select **Stage a delete on the object for the next export run** in **Deprovisioning Options**.

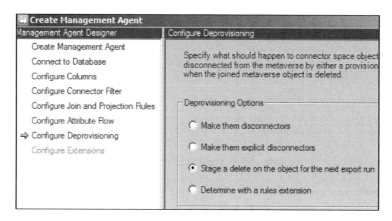

After creating the phone MA, we can go into the FIM portal and create the synchronization rule required for creating users in the phone system and importing the phone related data to FIM.

1. For the phone user's synchronization rule, I choose to do both inbound and outbound in the same rule. To decide which objects to do outbound synchronization for, I use the **Outbound System Scoping Filter** option.

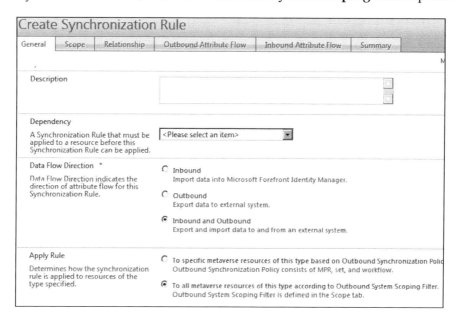

[165]

2. We select the resource types in FIM and the phone system and then define the Outbound Scoping Filter. I use a simple one—**employeeType** equals **Employee**. This will associate all users matching this filter with this synchronization rule.

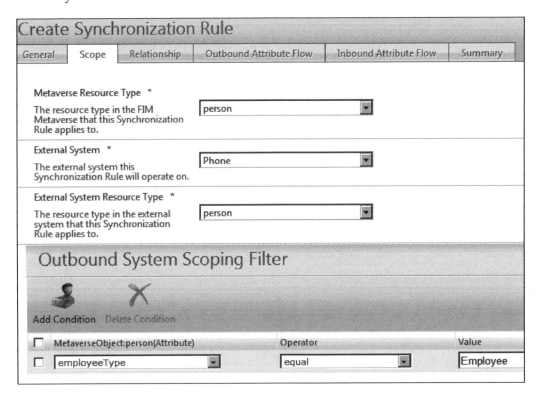

3. To provision the users to the phone system, we place a check in **Create resource in external system**. Configuring **Relationship Criteria** might seem unnecessary, since FIM is creating the users, but we might have a situation where we need to recover from some failures and need to import the existing users in the phone system and join them to existing users in the Metaverse.

Chapter 5

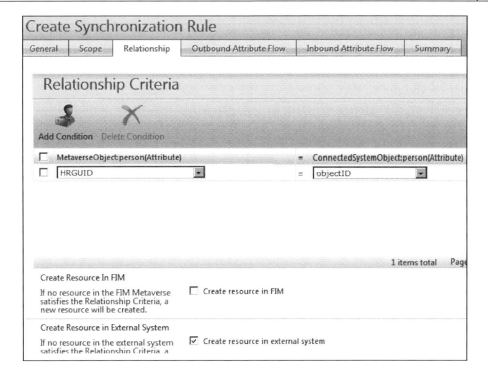

4. Define **Outbound Attribute Flow**. I have, in this case, chosen to define the objectID attribute flow as **Initial Flow Only**. This attribute is not supposed to change.

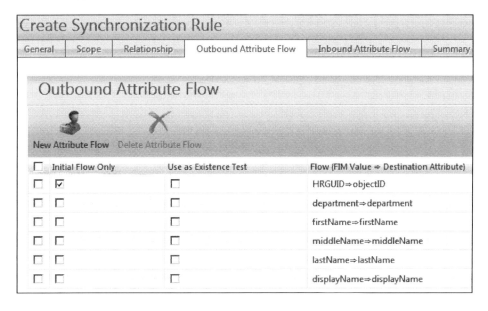

User Management

5. **Inbound Attribute Flow** is just as easy as before. Notice how the mobile attribute flows to the mobile attribute in the Metaverse. This is a classic problem. In the Metaverse, you have both the **mobile** attribute and the **mobilePhone** attribute to choose from. It is quite easy to make the mistake of selecting the wrong attribute in the Metaverse when configuring synchronization rules, when there are multiple attributes to choose from. In my customer projects, I usually delete the attribute we are not using in the Metaverse, to make sure we select the correct mobile phone attribute later on.

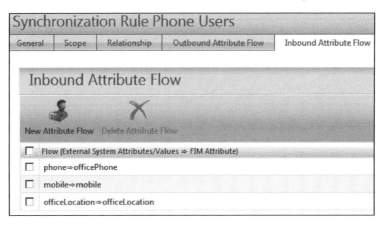

6. As before, we also need to configure the FIM Service MA to **Export** the attributes populated by the phone system, in order for them to show up in the FIM portal. Once again, we need to be careful to choose the correct attributes in each schema.

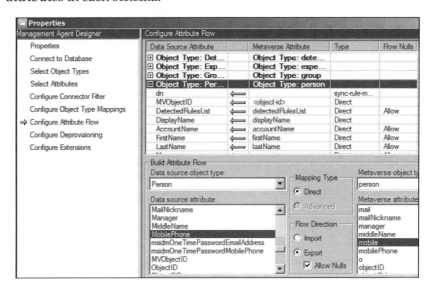

Chapter 5

7. You then need to:
   i. Create the required run profiles on the **Phone** MA.

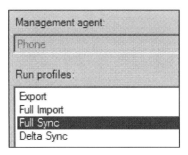

   ii. **Import** and **Sync** the new synchronization rule from FIM Service MA.
   iii. Export the users to the phone system.
   iv. Have the operators of the phone system update the user object with the relevant data.
   v. **Import** and **Sync** the new information from the phone system.
   vi. Export it to the FIM Service.

8. If all works as it should, you will be able to see the information from the phone system on the user in the FIM portal.

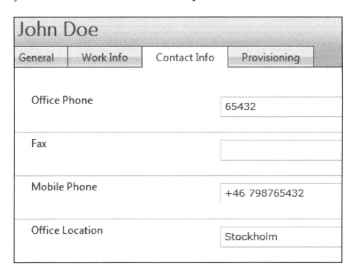

[169]

Managing users in Active Directory

One of the most common external systems we have in FIM is Active Directory. Managing users in Active Directory is very much a question of understanding how Active Directory works. I have seen many FIM designs violating the basic functionality of Active Directory.

There are also quite a few attributes in Active Directory that require special treatment and knowledge. The most common one is the attribute userAccountControl.

At The Company, the idea is that management of normal users in Active Directory is to be made using FIM. A few things, however, are not managed by FIM; one is the initial password.

At The Company, the initial password is set by the users themselves when they visit the security officer's desk to identify themselves and sign a form about account usage. At the desk, there is a small web application where the user can fill in his initial password.

The initial password, as well as account name and e-mail addresses, are common attributes in Active Directory where FIM is missing some components out-of-the-box. If we would like to manage the creation of a complex initial password or the creation of a unique account name, we need to add some additional workflow capabilities to FIM. We can either write our own add-ons or buy from third-party vendors.

What I have found in many cases is that the processes and functionality are already in place to manage these problems. Many companies already have a system in place for generating unique account names and procedures to set and distribute the initial password. Moving the responsibility for this function to FIM is often a separate project.

userAccountControl

The userAccountControl attribute is most commonly used to enable or disable a user account. But, if you look at http://support.microsoft.com/kb/305144, for example, you will find that this attribute is actually a bunch of bit flags. To control it, we need to understand the meaning of each bit, and we need to modify just the bits we are interested in.

Look at the following table:

Property flag	Value in hexadecimal	Value in decimal
SCRIPT	0x0001	1
ACCOUNTDISABLE	0x0002	2
HOMEDIR_REQUIRED	0x0008	8
LOCKOUT	0x0010	16
PASSWD_NOTREQD	0x0020	32
PASSWD_CANT_CHANGE	0x0040	64
Note that you cannot assign this permission by directly modifying the UserAccountControl attribute. For information about how to set the permission programmatically, see the *Property flag descriptions* section in KB305144.		
ENCRYPTED_TEXT_PWD_ALLOWED	0x0080	128
TEMP_DUPLICATE_ACCOUNT	0x0100	256
NORMAL_ACCOUNT	0x0200	512
INTERDOMAIN_TRUST_ACCOUNT	0x0800	2048
WORKSTATION_TRUST_ACCOUNT	0x1000	4096
SERVER_TRUST_ACCOUNT	0x2000	8192
DONT_EXPIRE_PASSWORD	0x10000	65536
MNS_LOGON_ACCOUNT	0x20000	131072
SMARTCARD_REQUIRED	0x40000	262144
TRUSTED_FOR_DELEGATION	0x80000	524288
NOT_DELEGATED	0x100000	1048576
USE_DES_KEY_ONLY	0x200000	2097152
DONT_REQ_PREAUTH	0x400000	4194304
PASSWORD_EXPIRED	0x800000	8388608
TRUSTED_TO_AUTH_FOR_DELEGATION	0x1000000	16777216
PARTIAL_SECRETS_ACCOUNT	0x04000000	67108864

So, if we would like to create a normal, enabled account we set the userAccountControl attribute to 512, and if we would like create a normal, disabled account we add the ACCOUNTDISABLE flag (2) and set it to 514. But, disabling an account by just setting this value to 514 is *not* the way to do it because then we might change other flags as well. What we need is to do bit operations to just modify the flag in question.

User Management

ACCOUNTDISABLE is the flag we need to modify in order to enable or disable a user account. To do this, we have to use the **BitAnd** and **BitOr** functions in our synchronization rules.

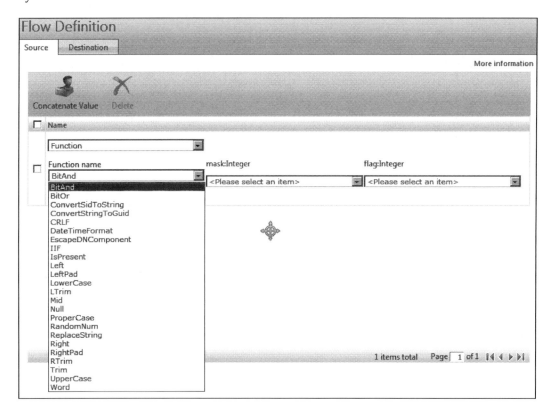

BitAnd and **BitOr** are just two of the built-in functions we can use in our synchronization rules. I will not give you a complete description of each function in this book, as they are well described on the Microsoft TechNet site (http://aka.ms/FIMFunctions), if you need the information.

What I have found in my deployment is that I usually end up doing a CustomExpression instead of using the function builder.

This could then end up with an expression such as the following:

```
IIF(active,IIF(IsPresent(userAccountControl),BitAnd(9223372036854775808
5,userAccountControl),512),IIF(IsPresent(userAccountControl),BitOr(2,u
serAccountControl),514))
```

In this example, I have added a Boolean attribute active to the schema, and the value of that attribute controls whether the Active Directory account should be enabled or disabled. In this example, I also check if userAccountControl has a value or not. If it has an existing value, I just modify the bit flags; otherwise I set it to the standard 512 or 514 values. If you wonder where I got the "9223372036854775805" to do my **BitAnd** operation to enable the user, I suggest you search the Internet. But basically, this value 9223372036854775805 is the maximum value of the 64-bit signed integer, 9223372036854775807, minus 2.

A deeper explanation and more information on this can be found at http://social.technet.microsoft.com/wiki/contents/articles/how-to-enable-or-disable-accounts-in-active-directory-domain-service-using-fim.aspx.

userAccountControl is just one of many Active Directory attributes with strange behaviors that we need to understand before we use.

Provision users to Active Directory

Creating users in Active Directory requires two attributes to be present.

- sAMAccountName
- dn

The dn (distinguished name) tells FIM where in Active Directory to put the user, and the sAMAccountName is the login name we use for Active Directory.

One special attribute in Active Directory is unicodePwd; this can be used to set the initial password of a user, and this attribute can only be used with **Initial Flow Only**. You cannot use a synchronization rule to set unicodePwd to change the password on the user after it has been created.

Let's walk through the very basic way of provisioning users to AD using EREs (Outbound Synchronization Policy). This involves creating the following:

- A synchronization rule
- A Set
- A workflow
- An MPR

User Management

Synchronization rule

We start by creating the outbound synchronization rule.

1. When working with Active Directory, I almost always separate outbound and inbound synchronization. So, we create a synchronization rule with **Outbound** as **Data Flow Direction** and select the resources based on Outbound Synchronization Policy for the **Apply Rule** option.

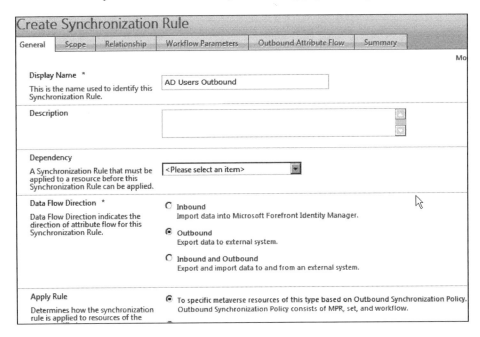

2. The resource types are **person** in the Metaverse and **user** in the **External System Resource Type**.

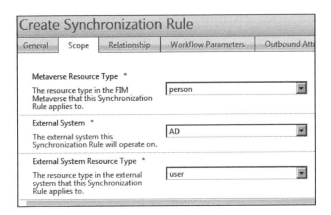

3. We check **Create resource in External System**, to enable provisioning. Since you are doing an outbound-only rule and the plan is that FIM should create all users in AD, it is easy to forget the **Relationship Criteria**.

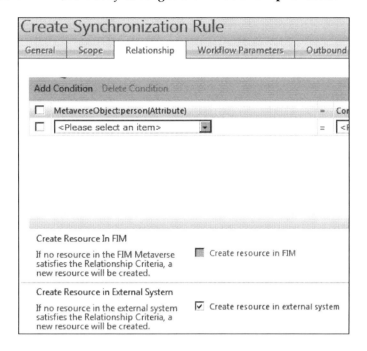

4. If you forget the **Relationship Criteria**, you will get an error reminding you to configure it. You are correct in wondering why, since this is not used in this type of rule. In future releases or updates, this requirement might disappear for outbound only rules.

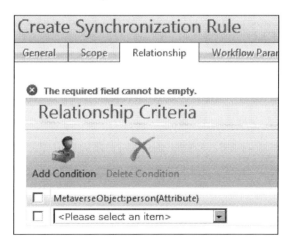

User Management

5. In this example, we have no **Workflow Parameters**. But, in many cases, an FIM deployment has some custom workflows that will give parameters to use in your synchronization rule. A typical example in this case, when doing AD provisioning, would be a custom workflow creating the initial password.

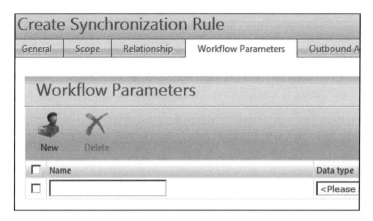

6. When defining the attribute flow for AD, there are many times when the built-in functions are useful. This example shows how the **Distinguished Name (DN)** is built. The DN is often also dependent on things such as department, since many companies store user objects from different departments in different OUs in Active Directory. At The Company, all users are in **OU=Managed**.

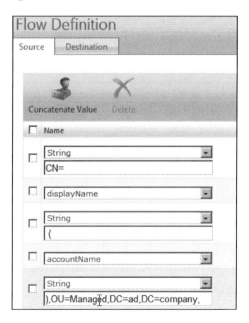

7. To provision users to AD, the dn attribute flow should be marked **Initial Flow Only**. However, if you also want to support moving or changing the dn of the user, you also need to add the same flow without the **Initial Flow Only** checkbox.

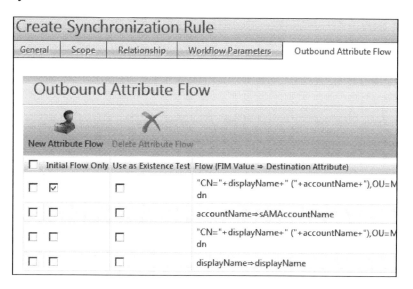

Set

We then need to create the Set that contains the users we would like to provision to AD.

1. Before we start to create a Set, we need to decide its purpose and content. That way, we can give it a descriptive name. Since FIM contains a large number of Sets out-of-the-box, I usually recommend that my customers prefix their own sets with something to make them easier to find and distinct from the built-in ones.

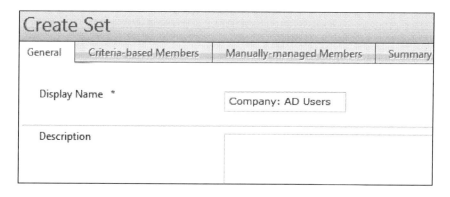

2. The Set used to determine who should have an account in Active Directory, is usually based on some criteria. At The Company, the criterion is that **Employee Type** is either **Employee** or **Contractor**. Try keeping your criterion as simple as possible, otherwise troubleshooting Set membership can become quite problematic. Use the **View Members** button to verify you got the correct content in your Set.

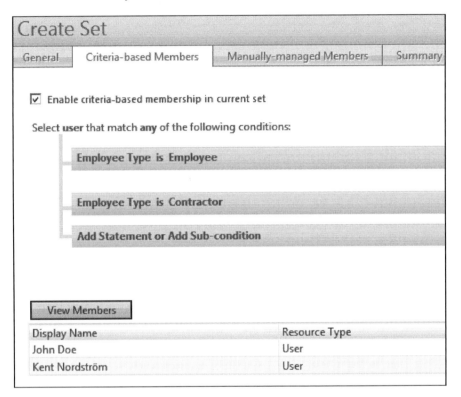

Workflow

We need a workflow to add the synchronization rule as an ERE on the user.

1. We need a workflow of type **Action** that is used to add the Outbound Synchronization Rule to the user objects.

Chapter 5

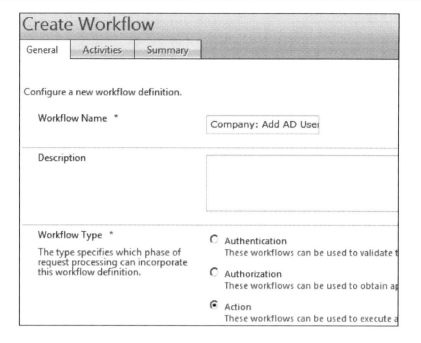

2. There is a vital checkbox on the **General** tab called **Run on Policy Update**. This is required if you have users that are already members in a Set that you would like to apply the workflow on. This will be clear when we do the MPR, but basically what we will say is that FIM should run this workflow when users become part of the Set. For existing members, that event has already occurred, so FIM will not apply the workflow. Checking this box will make FIM apply the workflow to existing members.

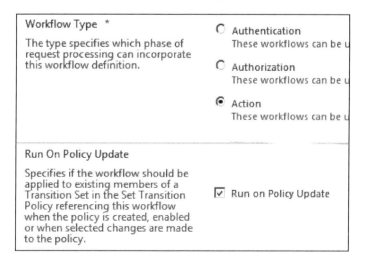

[179]

User Management

3. In the **Activities** tab, in this case, select the **Synchronization Rule Activity** option. In rare cases, you might also want this workflow to do more than one activity, such as sending a notification.

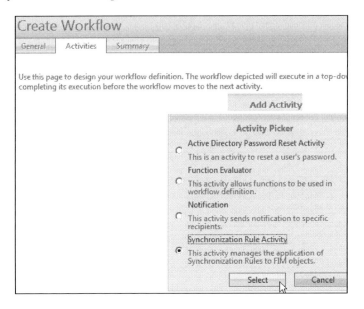

4. Select the synchronization rule and the action to perform. In this case, it is **AD Users Outbound Synchronization Rule**, and select **Add** for the **Action Selection** option.

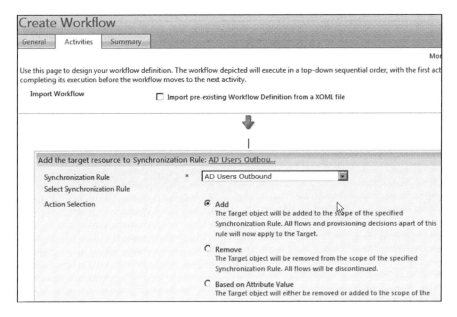

MPR

Finally, we need to create the MPR that will trigger the workflow.

1. Once again, since there are many built-in MPRs, I recommend using some kind of prefix to distinguish your own. The **Type** for this MPR is **Set Transition**. This means it will trigger due to some object entering or leaving a Set.

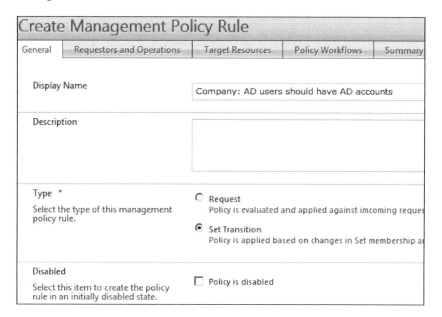

2. The Set we are interested in is our newly created one containing the users we would like to have in AD. This MPR should get triggered when there is a **Transition In** event, that is, when someone becomes a member of this Set.

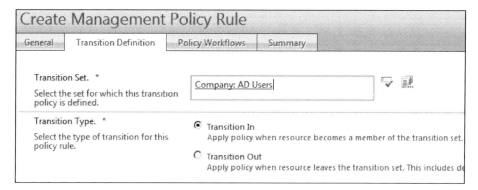

3. When the **Transition In** event occurs, the MPR should run the workflow that adds the synchronization rule to the user object. You might have additional workflows defined that you would like triggered in this case, such as sending a notification.

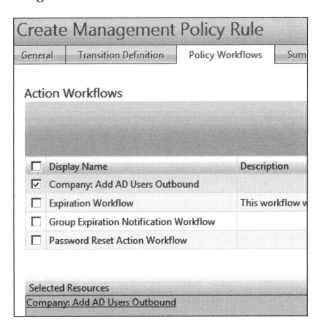

4. After creating the MPR, you can look at a user in FIM Portal. On the **Provisioning** tab, you will see that you have a new ERE in the **ERL** (**Expected Rules List**) with a status of **Pending**, since we have not run any synchronization yet. If you run a cycle of synchronizations, you will be able to verify that the users are created in Active Directory, and the status of the ERE on the user in the FIM portal will then change to **Applied**.

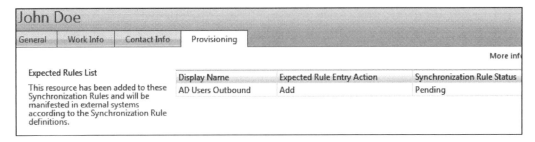

5. When running the synchronization and actually trying to create the user in Active Directory Connector Space, you might get an error—as shown in the following screenshot—stating that the user does not have a parent object in the management agent AD. This is because in order for you to create users in the Connector Space, you need to run at least one **Import** from AD, so that the OU structure is imported. This is usually called the **discovery import**. Without the discovery import, FIM is unable to know if the OU that you try to create the user object in is present.

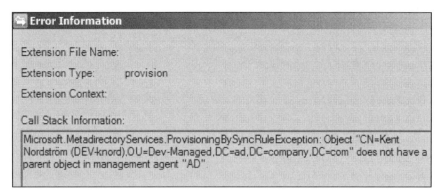

Inbound synchronization from AD

Depending on what we would like to do, there are some attributes required in FIM that AD can provide. In order for a user to be able to log in to the FIM portal or authenticate against the FIM Service using some other client, the FIM Service DB requires three attributes:

- `AccountName`
- `Domain`
- `ObjectSID`

In FIM Service, the combination of `Domain` and `AccountName` has to be unique. In this context, `Domain` is the NetBIOS name of the Active Directory.

If you, like The Company, have a single-domain forest, you can import `Domain` as a constant. If you have a multi-domain forest, you need to add some logic to get the correct `Domain` value.

User Management

Inbound Attribute Flow might look somewhat as shown in the following screenshot:

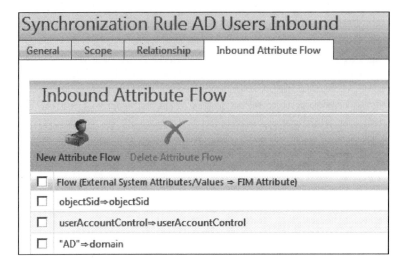

In order to import `userAccountControl`, I have in this example extended the Metaverse schema with a new attribute named `userAccountControl`.

The **Attribute type** for **userAccountControl** is **Number**, and we will store the decimal value of the attribute.

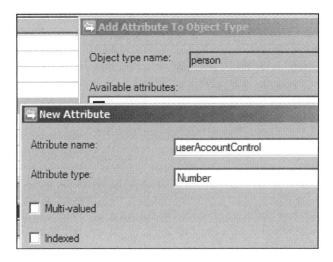

And, as always, we need to modify the FIM Service MA to export the required attributes, `AccountName`, `Domain`, and `ObjectSID`, to the FIM Service in order for the user to be able to log in to the portal.

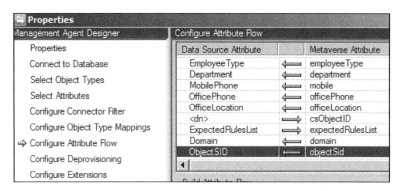

Temporal Sets

In many situations when we manage users, we are working with time-dependent actions.

For example, we might state that a user should be disabled in Active Directory the day employment ends but should be deleted from AD 30 days after employment has ended. How do we do that in FIM?

First of all, we need to get the employment dates into FIM. Usually, we get them from the HR system. It is a bit tricky to work with date/time attributes since localization and formatting can require us to do some troubleshooting before we get it right. You will very likely end up using the built-in `DateTimeFormat` function when importing the date/time data from HR or some other source and converting it to the format *yyyy-MM-ddTHH:mm:ss.000* used in FIM.

We then create what is called a **Temporal Set**. This is just a normal Set, but we use a criterion that is time dependent.

User Management

We can then use this Set to trigger an MPR that modifies an attribute, such as the active attribute I used in my previous example, or an MPR that triggers some workflows.

In FIM Service DB, there is a SQL job that evaluates these temporal Sets once a day; the default time is 1 AM. If that is the time at which you also have some backups or run profiles scheduled, you should consider changing the schedules to avoid conflicts.

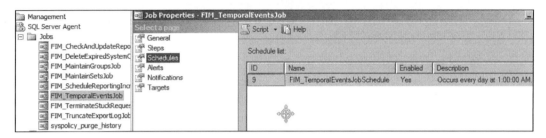

Self-service using the FIM portal

For users to be able to log in to the FIM portal and authenticate to the FIM Service, we need, as I said before, three attributes populated for the user—`AccountName`, `Domain`, and `ObjectSID`.

But even if we have populated these attributes in FIM Service and a standard user tries to log in to the portal (`https://FIMPortal/IdentityManagement`) he will get the message shown in the following screenshot:

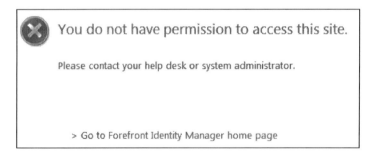

Why? Well because there is no MPR enabled, by default, to allow users to access the FIM portal and/or FIM Service. The MPRs required allowing access to users is disabled by default. We just need to enable them in order for users to have access.

The MPRs we need to enable are as follows:

- **General**: Users can read non-administrative configuration resources
- **User management**: Users can read attributes of their own

[186]

Also if you look back, you might recall that we had some options during installation talking about user access as well. It was a checkbox with **Grant Authenticated Users access to the FIM Portal Site**. If you forgot to allow that during setup, don't panic. This setting is only to allow SharePoint access, and we can fix this now if we had forgotten earlier.

If you start the FIM portal as administrator, you will find **Site Actions** in the upper-right corner, and from there you can access **Site Settings**. In **Site Settings**, below **Users and Permissions**, you have **Site permissions**. Follow that link into **Permissions**, and add **Authenticated Users** with **Read** permissions.

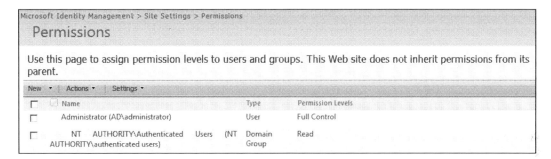

After fixing the MPRs and verifying that users have SharePoint permissions, the user can access the portal.

User Management

Compared to the view the administrator has, it's quite limited. If the user tries to do something, he will find that he is unable to do anything except look at some of his own attributes. He cannot modify anything or see any other users. For that to be possible, we need to enable yet some other MPRs and maybe configure new ones in order for the user to be able to work in the portal.

Managers can see direct reports

Just to exemplify, I will walk you through the creation of a new MPR allowing managers to read information about their direct reports.

1. This MPR is of type **Request**. If you are to use FIM for self-service, you will likely end up with quite a few MPRs. Make sure you give them good descriptive names and also a good description, so that it will be easy to understand the purpose even when looking at them 6-12 months from now.

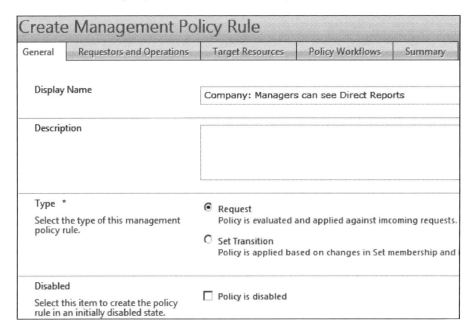

2. We will now start to see the beauty of using FIM to manage users. We can define the **Requestor** as **Relative to Resource**. Hopefully, you also see how using reference attributes plays a role in this. What we say is that the **Requestor** should be the user referenced in the **Manager** attribute of the user we try to look at or modify. The **Operation** in this case is just **Read resource**, but you can easily see how a similar MPR might allow a **Manager** to modify some attributes as well. Finally, we need to check **Grants permission**.

Chapter 5

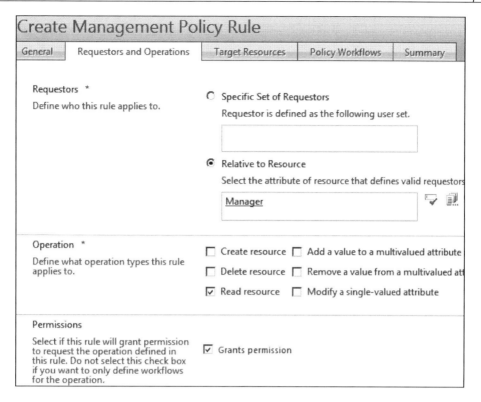

3. The target resource in this case could be **All People** or some other Set containing the users we want managers to see. In this case, I simply allow the managers to see all attributes of their direct reports.

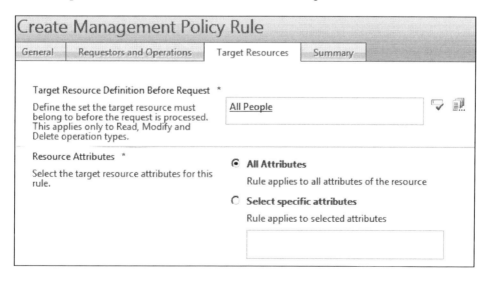

4. If you want to limit the attributes read by managers in this example, just select **Select specific attributes** and type (separated by semicolons)—or search and select—attributes in the list of available attributes. Just remember that you will have to update this MPR as soon as there is a new attribute you would like managers to see.

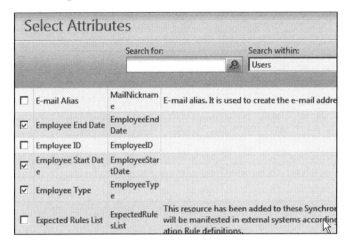

5. The result of this MPR will be that when John (a manager) searches for users in FIM Portal, he will not only find himself but also his direct report, Kent (the consultant that had John as his manager).

Users can manage their own attributes

Another typical scenario is that we want users to manage some attributes of their own. This could, for example, be information such as mobile phone number.

In order for this to work, we need to create a new MPR that gives the users permission to change selected attributes.

1. This MPR is of type **Request**. If you are to use FIM for self-service, you will likely end up with quite a few MPRs.

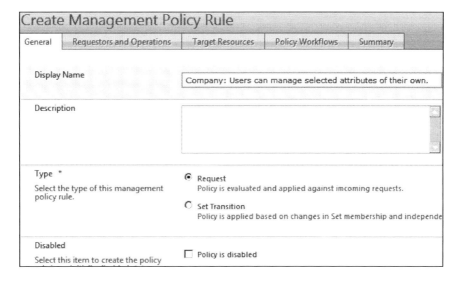

2. This time we set the **Requestor** as **Relative to Resource**, based on **Resource ID**. This is the same as saying self. We want to allow **Modify a single-valued attribute**. If you are to allow the users in this scenario to manage a multi-value attribute, you will need to also allow both adding and removing a value in multi-valued attributes.

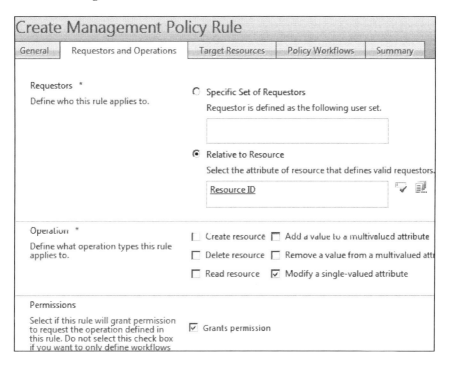

User Management

3. If you would like, say, only contractors to have this ability, you could set the target to **All Contractors**, rather than **All Users**. And in this case, when we talk about modifying, we always define the attributes. You shouldn't even allow administrators to modify **All Attributes**.

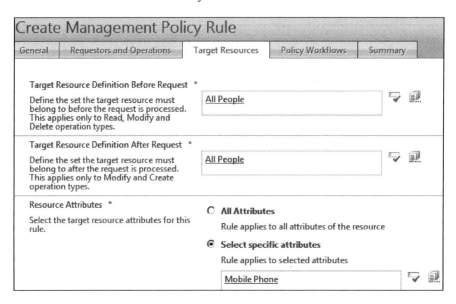

4. For some scenarios, you might want to also kick off some workflows as the request is made. It could, for example, be an authorization workflow requesting that the change be approved by a manager before being applied, or maybe an action workflow sending a notification to the user himself about the change.

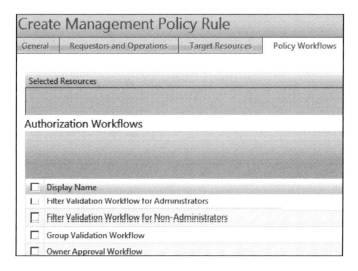

5. It is likely that we would also want this change exported to some other system. We then need to modify **Attribute Flow**, in the FIM Service MA, to import the attributes into the Metaverse.

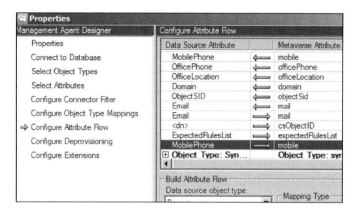

6. Importing the attribute from the FIM Service MA (allowing an attribute to be changed using the FIM portal or the FIM Service) might cause a problem with **Attribute Flow Precedence** in the Metaverse. We need to decide how we are to handle this. In our example, we now have both the FIM Service and the phone system trying to populate the `mobile` attribute in the Metaverse. If a conflict occurs, we need to decide who will be the winner. Or maybe we can just decide that the `mobile` attribute is no longer managed by the phone system and remove the attribute from the inbound flow and add it to the outbound flow in the phone system synchronization rule.

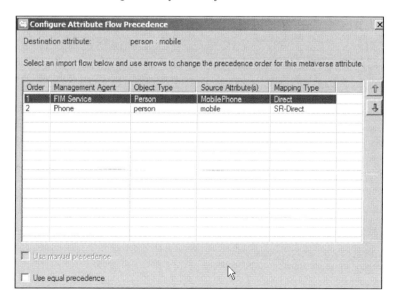

User Management

I always avoid using the **Use equal precedence** setting, when configuring **Attribute Flow Precedence**, since this means that the last writer wins. Usually, this causes a situation where attribute data is not set to the expected value.

Managing Exchange

When managing users, we usually also find that we need to manage e-mail settings or even e-mail systems. Microsoft Exchange is the most common e-mail system but I also have quite a few customers running other e-mail systems, such as IBM Lotus Notes.

In order for FIM to also manage Exchange, there are some configuration settings and permissions required.

Basically, what happens is that FIM adds attributes to the object in Active Directory and makes a call to Exchange to update the recipient.

In order to do this, the AD MA account needs to be a member of the **Exchange Recipient Management** group.

If there is a need for more complex Exchange management, such as moving mailboxes, the built-in functionality will not be enough. I would then suggest that you take a look at some third party PowerShell MA.

In order for us to manage the attributes used and required by Exchange, we will need some knowledge about Exchange. There are, for example, multiple types of recipients to deal with.

At The Company, they have decided that all employees should have a mailbox (Recipient Type: `UserMailbox`) but contractors should be mail enabled users (Recipient Type: `MailUser`). Each recipient type requires a different set of attributes configured for them to work.

Exchange 2007

If you are still using Exchange 2007, it is required that you install the management tools for Exchange 2007 on the FIM Synchronization Service server. FIM will use the Exchange PowerShell tools to tell Exchange to update the recipient information.

On the Active Directory MA, on the **Configure Extensions** page, you select **Exchange 2007** for the **Provision for** option. Optionally, you can also configure which **RUS** (**Recipient Update Service**) Server FIM should use.

Exchange 2010

Managing Exchange 2010 does not require any extra installation of tools on FIM, unless you consider PowerShell 2.0 extra.

On the Active Directory MA, on the **Configure Extensions** page, select **Exchange 2010** for the **Provision for** option.

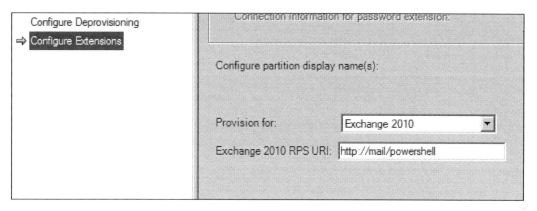

You also need to configure which **CAS (Client Access Server)** FIM should use to make the remote PowerShell call to update the recipient.

Synchronization rule for Exchange

Since we are creating different types of recipients for different employee types, The Company decided to manage this by adding separate synchronization rules to manage each type. These rules will work in addition to the general Active Directory synchronization rule responsible for creating the users in Active Directory.

First of all, we need to add some attributes to the AD MA. The attributes listed next are a sample. In reality, you might manage more attributes or like to import more Exchange-related attributes.

The Company added the following:

- homeMDB
- mail
- mailNickname
- mDBUseDefaults
- msExchHomeServerName
- targetAddress

User Management

In this example, we create two separate outbound synchronization rules, one for employees that should get mailboxes and one for contractors that should be mail-enabled users.

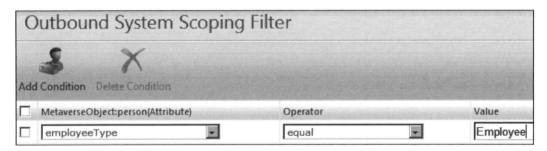

Mailbox users

The rule for mailbox users use **Outbound System Scoping Filter**, where **employeeType** equal **Employee**.

The attributes required to create a mailbox user are as follows:

- `homeMDB`
- `mailNickname`
- `msExchHomeServerName`

As you can see, I do not set `ProxyAddresses`. This is because, at The Company, the generation of e-mail addresses for mailboxes is the responsibility of Exchange.

The tricky part is to find the `homeMDB` and `msExchHomeServerName` values we need to use. Your Exchange admin should be able to provide them to you.

Outbound Attribute Flow will look as shown in the following screenshot:

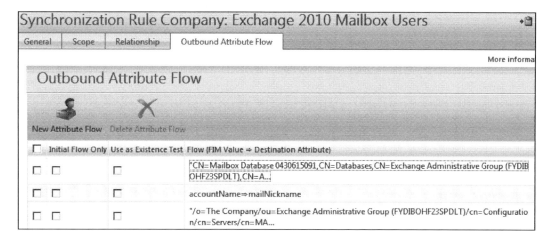

In FIM, it is required to have the `Email` attribute in the FIM Service database populated, if we are to use any workflows relying on e-mails.

To get this information into FIM, we can add a flow of the `mail` attribute in AD; this usually contains the primary e-mail address of the user when you are using Microsoft Exchange as the e-mail system, and add mail to `Email export` attribute flow in the FIM Service MA.

Mail-enabled users

The rule for mail-enabled users use **Outbound System Scoping Filter**, where **employeeType** equal **Contractor**.

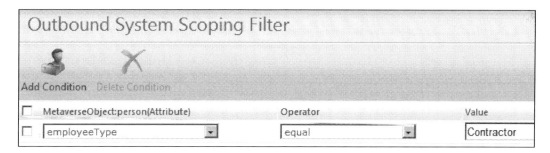

The **Outbound Attribute Flow** option required to create a mail-enabled user in Exchange 2010 is shown in the following screenshot:

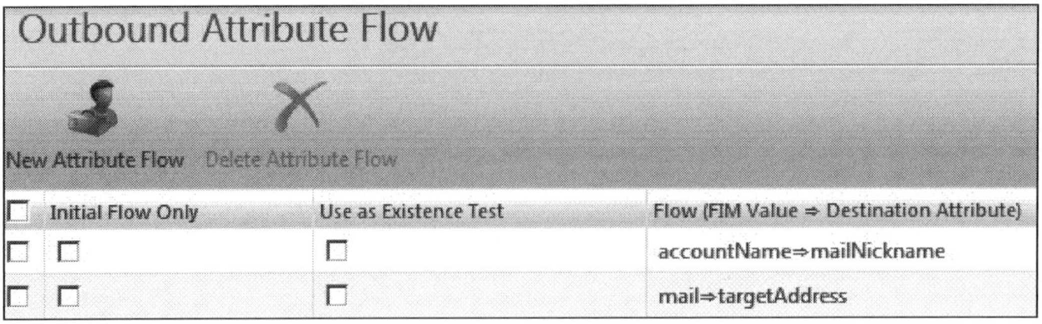

Initial Flow Only	Use as Existence Test	Flow (FIM Value ⇒ Destination Attribute)
☐	☐	accountName⇒mailNickname
☐	☐	mail⇒targetAddress

Summary

In this chapter, we have seen how the power of the FIM engines allows you to manage users out-of-the-box. But as you might soon discover, some things require you to add some customization.

The important thing is to start off easy and not try to make the implementation too complex at once.

When managing users, you will need to decide early on where required unique attributes are to be created. I mean attributes such as `AccountName`, first-time password, and e-mail address.

In this chapter, we have also seen how easy it is to implement basic self-service using the FIM portal, allowing you to delegate some administration to the users themselves.

In the next chapter, we will extend this to groups and look at how FIM 2010 R2 can be used to enhance your group management.

6
Group Management

Once you have user management in place, it is usually time to start looking at group management. In many FIM implementations I have done, the group management capability has been the key reason for choosing FIM. But still, in order to manage groups, we need to also have the users that are supposed to be members, managed by FIM.

In this chapter we will look at:

- Different group scope and types in AD and FIM
- How to manage groups using the Outlook add-in
- How to synchronize groups between HR, AD, and FIM

Group scope and types

We need to understand how groups in FIM work, and since AD (Active Directory) is so common, I will use that as a comparison.

Active Directory

If you go into AD and create a group, you are asked about **Group scope** and **Group type**.

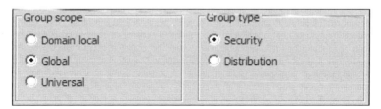

Group Management

This selection will end up in the attribute in AD called `groupType`. This is a bitmask value, as described in the following table (as well as described at http://msdn.microsoft.com/en-us/library/cc223142):

Value	Description
1 (0x00000001)	Specifies a group that is created by the system. If you look in AD in the `CN=Builtin` container you will find groups with this flag set.
2 (0x00000002)	Specifies a group with global scope.
4 (0x00000004)	Specifies a group with domain local scope.
8 (0x00000008)	Specifies a group with universal scope.
16 (0x00000010)	Specifies an `APP_BASIC` group for Windows Server Authorization Manager.
32 (0x00000020)	Specifies an `APP_QUERY` group for Windows Server Authorization Manager.
2147483648 (0x80000000)	Specifies a security group. If this flag is not set, then the group is a distribution group.

As with the `userAccountControl` attribute on user objects, we need to make sure we manage this attribute using bit handling.

However, the bit for the Security group is 2^31 and the rule is that if the value of a 32-bit integer is larger than 2^31 - 1, subtract 2^32 (which is 4,294,967,296). The value of the `groupType` attribute for a universal security group becomes:

2,147,483,656 - 4,294,967,296 = - 2,147,483,640, where 2,147,483,656 is 2,147,483,648 (Security) + 8 (Universal).

So what we then end up with is the following table describing the values we need to set in AD on the `groupType` value for each group scope and type:

Group Scope/Type	groupType Value
Universal Distribution Group	8
Global Distribution Group	2
Domain Local Distribution Group	4
Universal Security Group	-2,147,483,640
Global Security Group	-2,147,483,646
Domain Local Security Group	-2,147,483,644

If you are changing these values using FIM, you might need to consider if you are required to do a bit operation or if you can just change the values. Today, there is a tendency towards creating only universal groups, and therefore changes of the scope are rare. In AD, we also need to remember that there are rules controlling the group types, a given type of group can have as member. This is also one reason for creating universal groups.

FIM

In FIM however, the schema for groups looks quite different.

In FIM, we not only have the scope and type, but also need to look at other attributes.

Type

If you look at the schema in FIM, you will find that the group type can be **Distribution**, **Security**, or **MailEnabledSecurity**.

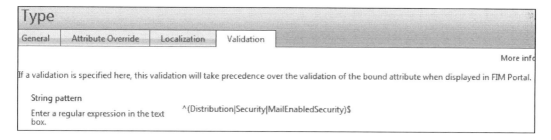

This means that if I import a group from AD into FIM, I need to check the bits of the `groupType` attribute and set the type in FIM, accordingly.

It might look similar to the following statement in our inbound synchronization rule:

```
IIF(Eq(BitOr(63,groupType),63),"Distribution","Security")
```

The preceding statement does not however take care of groups that might be mail-enabled security groups. If I am using FIM portal to create a **MailEnabledSecurity** group, it will require me to also fill in the **E-mail Alias**.

Group Management

In AD, this is represented by `mailNickname`, if you are running Microsoft Exchange as the e-mail system.

Scope

The scope is very similar to the corresponding setting in AD. If you look in the FIM schema, you will find that scope can be **DomainLocal**, **Global**, or **Universal**.

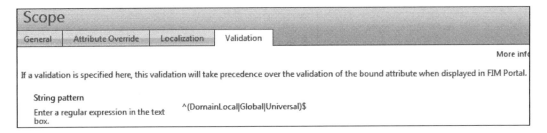

So if I am to import groups from AD, I need to check the bits for scope in the AD `groupType` attribute, when importing groups.

So the inbound synchronization rule that we use to import groups from AD, might contain something similar to the following:

```
IIF(Eq(BitAnd(2,groupType),2),"Global",IIF(Eq(BitAnd(4,groupType),4),"DomainLocal","Universal"))
```

As you can see, we need to use the bit operating functions to check the bits, rather than checking the value of the `groupType` attribute.

Member Selection

When you try to create a group using FIM Portal you will be asked about **Member Selection**.

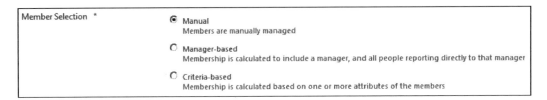

Depending on what we choose here, there are a few attributes involved. **Member Selection** does not correspond to just one attribute but will affect several.

In FIM, we have two types of groups when it comes to membership selection. They can be **Manual** (Static) or **Criteria-based** (Dynamic); **Manager-based** is just a special case of **Criteria-based**.

Manual

If you choose **Manual**, the Boolean attribute `MembershipLocked` will be `false`. This also means that, if I want to import groups with memberships from AD or some other source, I need to set this to `false`.

When creating a manual group, we also get the opportunity to set **Join Restriction**.

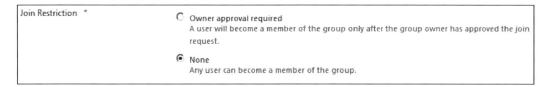

The **Join Restriction** selection corresponds to an attribute called `MembershipAddWorkflow`. If we look in the FIM schema, we will see that this attribute can have three values—**None**, **Custom**, and **Owner Approval**.

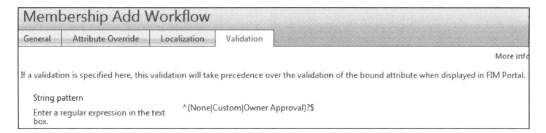

If we import a group from an external system, such as AD, the `MemebershipAddWorkflow` should be set to `None`.

> Keep in mind that when a request is made from Synchronization Service, using the Built-in Synchronization account, the authorization workflow step is skipped.

Hence, since authorization workflows are skipped when requests come from Synchronization Service, we cannot have `Owner Approval` on a group managed by an external system through Synchronization Service.

In order for us to use `Owner Approval`, we also need to configure the owner.

In FIM, there are two owner attributes, **Owner** and **Displayed Owner**.

Group Management

The **Owner** attribute is used for Owner Approval workflows. This is a multi-value attribute in order for us to define multiple owners that can approve the request.

The **Displayed Owner** attribute is a single-value attribute that corresponds, for example, to the single-value `managedBy` attribute in AD.

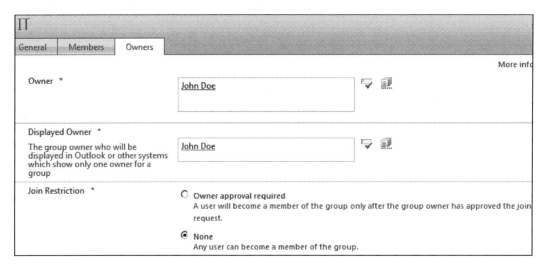

Typically, **Owner** and **Displayed Owner** have the same value in FIM.

Manager-based

Manager-based is essentially a **Criteria-based** (Dynamic) group. The difference is that when creating manager-based groups, the wizard in FIM will only ask you for the **Manager**. This type of group is very useful, since it gives us a way to allow a Manager to have a group with the direct reports.

The result is that `MembershipAddWorkflow` is set to `None` and `MembershipLocked` is set to `true`.

The criteria used in **Criteria-based** groups are stored in the **Filter** attribute. But when creating a **Manager-based** group, you will not be asked to fill in the criteria, since the filter will be generated automatically.

Filter	
A predicate defining a subset of the resources.	xmlns="http://schemas.xmlsoap.org/ws/2004/09/enumeration">/Person[(Manager = 'c66e3869-6662-42fc-91a7-c292e47d6c44') or (ObjectID = 'c66e3869-6662-42fc-91a7-c292e47d6c44')]</Filter>

In the previous example, **Filter** defines that members should all be **Person** objects, where **Manager** is the selected manager or the **Person** object itself is the selected manager.

Criteria-based

A **Criteria-based** group is the most flexible version. Here, you have the power to decide what the criteria for membership should look like.

As with **Manager-based** groups, `MembershipAddWorkflow` is set to `None` and `MembershipLocked` is set to `true`. But here, you will have to define the **Filter** yourself.

Group Management

In complex scenarios, you might not even be able to define the criteria using the wizard but will instead open up the advanced properties of the group and manually edit the **Filter** attribute.

Your criteria could contain some time references, like the ones in the following screenshot:

The **Temporal** attribute of the group object is set to `true`.

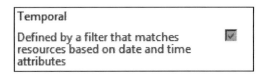

Please remember that **Temporal** groups are only recalculated every 24 hours (by default), depending on the SQL job, as covered in *Chapter 5, User Management*, around Temporal Sets.

Installing client add-ins

It is now time for the client add-ins to be installed. If you are using some approval workflows in your user management, you might have a need for the add-ins, earlier in your implementation.

There are two pieces of client software packaged with FIM—*Add-ins and extensions* and *CM Client*. In this chapter, I will only use *Add-ins and extensions* and will leave the *CM Client* for *Chapter 12, Issuing Smart Cards*, where FIM CM and Smart Card management are discussed.

Add-ins and extensions

The following steps show what the manual installation of the add-ins looks like, but in practice, you will deploy the MSI package using your favorite deployment tool and manage all the settings using group policies. Read more about your options, at http://aka.ms/FIMAddIn.

Chapter 6

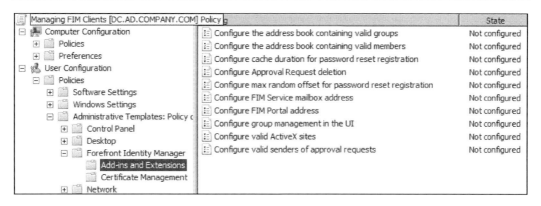

To install manually, locate your FIM 2010 R2 media and follow the ensuing steps:

1. The add-ins and extensions are available in multiple languages. Be aware that there are both x64 and x86 versions. Run **setup.exe** as administrator, on the client.

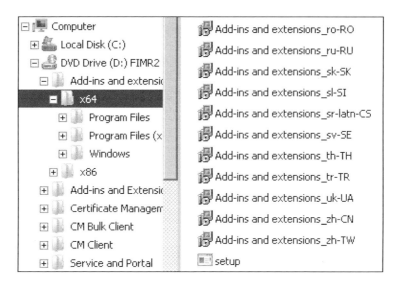

2. After some default steps about licensing agreements and some other stuff you will need to decide what to install. The only actual choice is if you are using Outlook and would like to install **FIM Add-in for Outlook** or not.

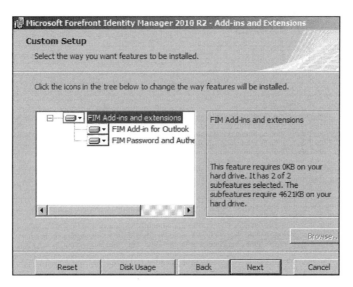

3. The FIM Portal Server address is the hostname, not the URL, that the client should use. The FIM Service service account e-mail address is the address used by FIM Service when sending e-mails to clients. If you look carefully at the following screenshot, you will notice I misspelled the e-mail address, causing the client to not accept the e-mails from the service. This little typo caused me about one hour of troubleshooting before I realized my error.

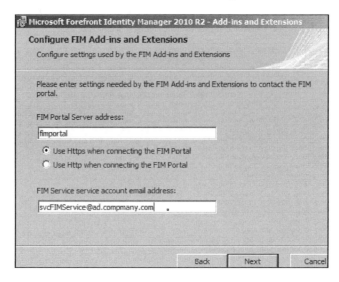

4. Enter the hostname used by the client to talk to FIM Service. Do not add protocol such as `http` or `https`. If you are using the standard port 5725 for FIM Service, you do not need to add it.

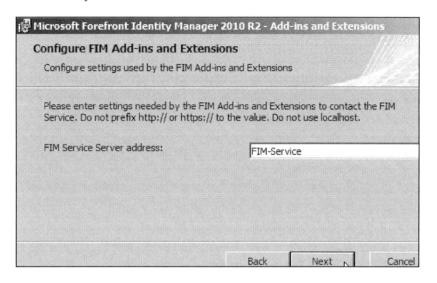

5. When asked about the URL for the Intranet Password Registration portal, you are requested to actually enter the complete URL with both protocol and hostname. Yes, I know this setup UI is not 100 percent consistent in its behavior.

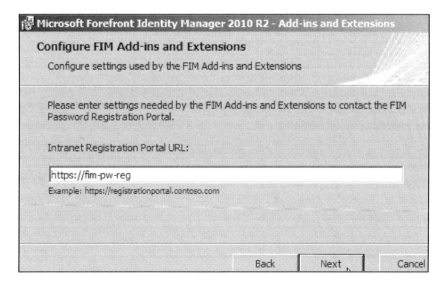

6. After finishing the installation, you are required to reboot before you can start using the client.

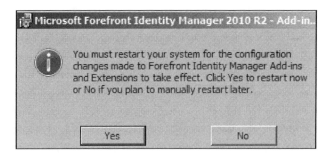

In this chapter, we will only discuss the Outlook add-in. In *Chapter 7, Self-service Password Reset*, we will take a look at how to use the self-service password reset support which we also installed at this point.

Modifying MPRs for group management

There are many MPRs that control how group objects can be modified by self-service, administrators, or synchronization engine. But when it comes to group management, almost every MPR is disabled by default.

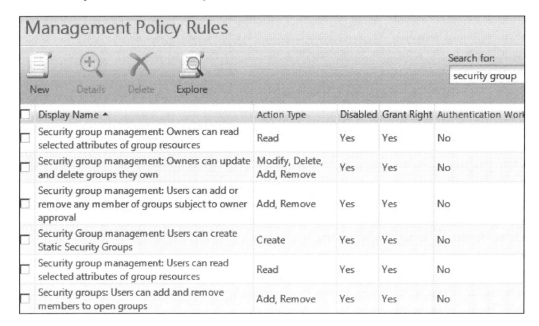

Let's look at distribution groups, to start with.

The Company only wants *Employees* to be able to create *static* distribution groups. The following steps will be required, to allow that:

1. Enable and change the MPR **Distribution list management: Users can create Static Distribution Groups**. The MPR allowing the creation of this type of group is **Distribution list management: Users can create Static Distribution Groups**.

2. The set called **All Active People** is the default value of **Requestor**. We need to change that to the **All Employees** set that we modified in *Chapter 5, User Management*.

3. In order for users to be able to add themselves and the owners to approve the requests, we need to also enable the following MPRs:

    ◦ **Distribution list management: Owners can read attributes of group resources**
    ◦ **Distribution list management: Owners can update and delete groups they own**
    ◦ **Distribution list management: Users can add or remove any members of groups subject to owner approval**

Group Management

- ◦ **Distribution list management:** Users can add or remove any members of groups that don't require owner approval
- ◦ **Distribution list management:** Users can create Static Distribution Groups
- ◦ **Distribution list management:** Users can read selected attributes of group resources

Creating and managing distribution groups

After allowing employees to create distribution groups, we can now see what they would look like from a user perspective.

There are different parts and steps involved in managing distribution groups. Let's start with how John creates a new distribution list.

1. John (who is an employee) logs on to FIM Portal and selects **My DGs**. So far, it is empty. He would like to create one, so he clicks on **New**.

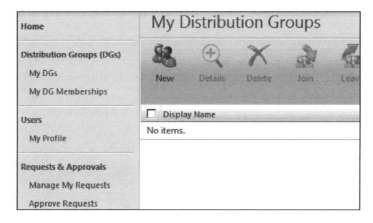

2. He gives his new group a display name, **Golfers**, and an e-mail alias, **golfers**. A good description is always useful so others can decide whether this is a group they would like to join.

3. John will automatically be added as the first member, and he is given the chance to add others as well, at this point.

4. John, as the creator, will automatically be set as **Owner** and **Displayed Owner** of this group. John has also chosen that he wants to approve join requests.

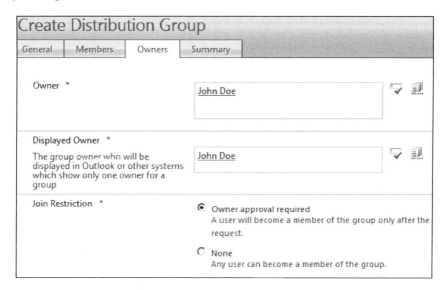

5. In the **Summary**, John can verify his settings before submitting the request.

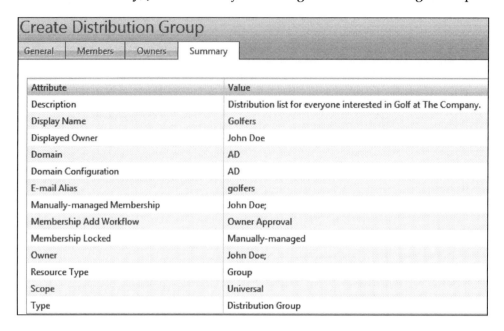

6. When John looks in the FIM Portal, he will now find his new group in **My DGs**.

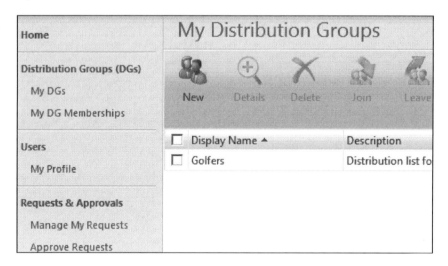

Chapter 6

After creating the group, there might be users that would like to join the group. At The Company, they have a consultant, Kent, who likes golf and would like to be part of this distribution group. Let's see how Kent can use FIM Portal to join the group.

1. Kent logs on to FIM Portal and searches for distribution groups, using the keyword `Golf`. He finds John's **Golfers** group, selects it, and clicks on **Join**.

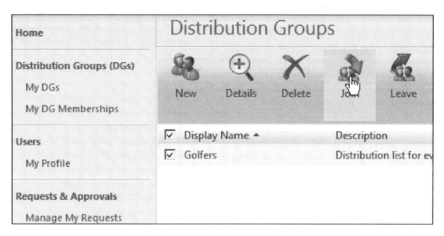

2. When he submits the request, he will see in the **Status** that his request is **Pending approval**. Remember, John had decided to choose **Owner Approval** for this group.

Join Group		
Summary The following summarizes the operation or operations that you are requesting.	Join to groups ▪ Joining group Golfers	
Status		
Description	Date	Status
Joining group Golfers	3/10/2012 2:20:02 AM	Pending approval. [Details]

[215]

Group Management

What happens now is that FIM will wait for John to approve the request. The MPR triggered by Kent's request to join the group is also configured to send John this request as an e-mail, making it possible for John to use the Outlook add-in installed on his computer to **Approve** or **Reject** this request.

With the Outlook add-in installed, he can **Approve** or **Reject** the request directly from the **Preview** pane in his Outlook window.

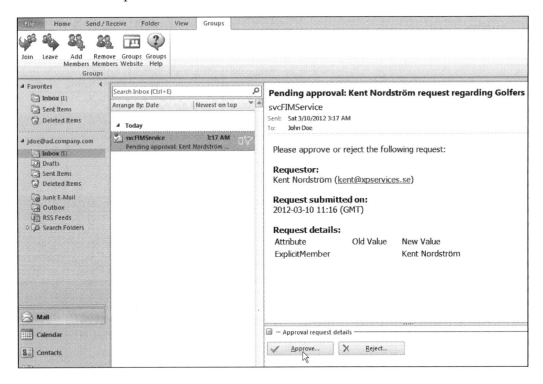

In the e-mail sent back to FIM Service, John can give a reason (not required) for his approval (or rejection) and the text entered in the **Reason** field will in that case be part of this request.

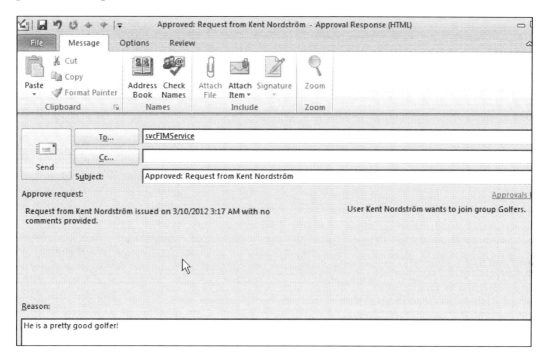

If he had not had the Outlook add-in available, he could have gone to FIM Portal to **Approve** or **Reject** the request there instead.

Having Exchange and using Outlook are by no means required to work with self-service group management like this. The difference is that you would have to use FIM Portal for approval. In those cases, it would be a good idea to change how the e-mail templates used by FIM look, so that they include a link to FIM Portal.

Group Management

The e-mail template used is the one configured in the MPR triggered by this event.

The MPR **Group management workflow: Owner approval on add member** triggers the authorization workflow **Owner Approval Workflow**.

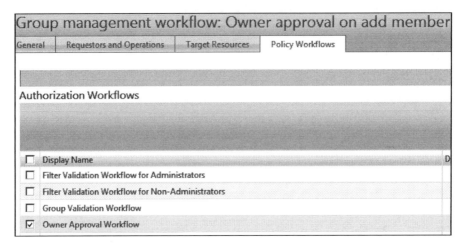

If you look into that workflow, you will find some settings you might want to change, but you will also find the e-mail templates used by FIM for the different steps in this workflow.

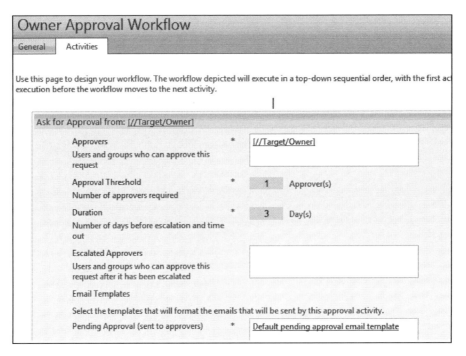

You can change these templates or create a new one and use that in your workflow. If you are changing the built-in, default e-mail templates, be aware that they might be used in other workflows as well.

 I recommend that you create your own e-mail templates and use them instead of modifying the built-in ones.

Another risk of modifying the built-in e-mail templates is that future updates and service packs might reset your changes.

 We have *not* yet synchronized this group into Active Directory (Exchange), so it will not yet show up in any address book or even have an email address.

Importing groups from HR

It might not be the case that groups are created and managed in FIM. There might be an external system with information about groups and their members.

At The Company, all groups related to the Organization are managed in the HR system. The membership—the `member` attribute—is made available through the multi-value setting in the HR MA.

Group Management

First of all, we need to import the group data from HR, using an Inbound synchronization rule.

We are getting the hang of this by now, so let's look at it quickly.

1. Select the **Inbound** button for **Data Flow Direction**.

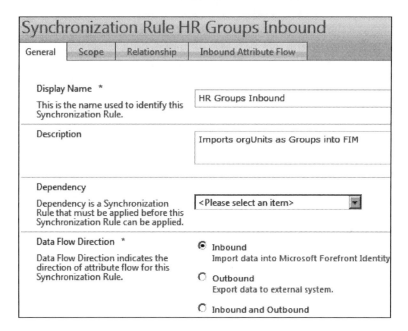

2. In the HR system, at The Company the object type **Resource Type** is **orgUnit**, but in our FIM we want these set as **group**.

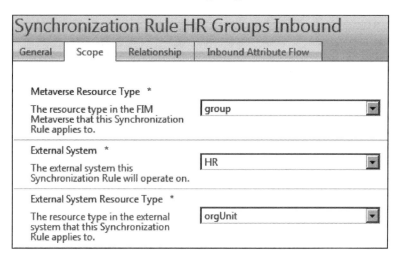

3. In this example, I use **accountName** to check if the group already exists, in order to make a join. **Create Resource in FIM** (projection) should likely be enabled in this scenario. At The Company, it is:

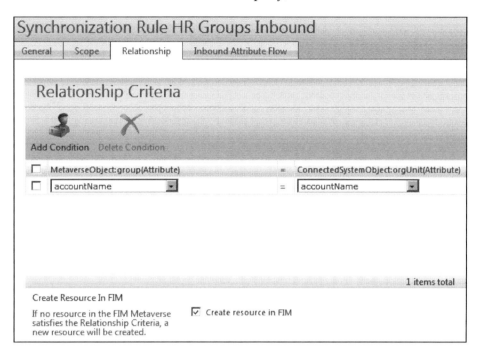

4. The Company has decided that all groups based on **orgUnit** and coming from HR should be **Universal** (scope), **Security** (type) groups and that the manager should be defined as the owner of the group. Note the required flows for the attributes:
    - **domain**
    - **membershipLocked**
    - **membershipAddWorkflow**

Group Management

> If you forget these, you will be able to import the groups into the Metaverse, but you will not be able to export them to FIM Service, since you will be violating the FIM Service schema.

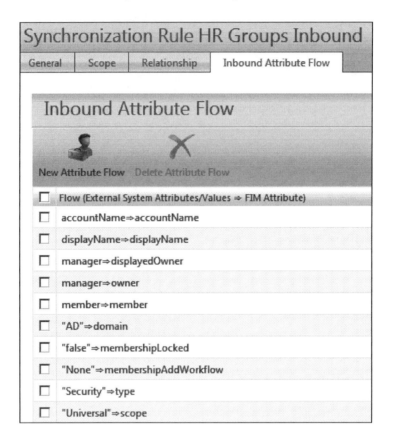

After synchronizing this new synchronization rule into FIM Synchronization Service, we can import the groups from HR into the Metaverse. But, in order for the information about the groups to also be able to synchronize into FIM Service and be viewed in FIM Portal, we need to add some attribute flows to the FIM Service MA.

FIM Service and Metaverse

We now have a scenario where we create distribution groups in FIM and import security groups from HR. So, how do we configure this in respect to the FIM Synchronization Service and the Metaverse?

Well, first of all, we need to configure the attribute flows on the FIM Service MA.

As you can see, we will need to both import and export many attributes regarding **group** objects between FIM Service and the Metaverse.

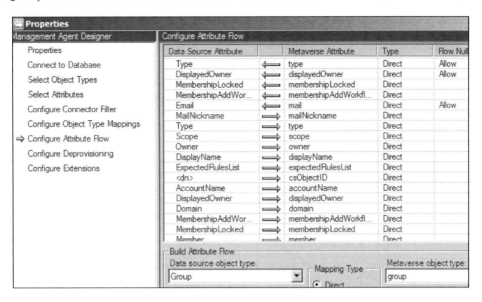

We are using the same Metaverse object type, **group**, in our inbound synchronization rule for **orgUnit**, from the HR system. This will cause a precedence problem in the Metaverse.

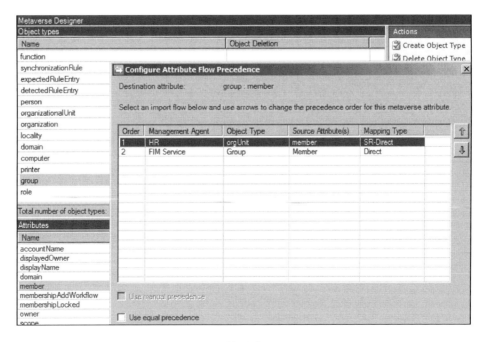

We need to go through all attributes with multiple import flows and make sure the precedence is correctly configured. In this case, we want the HR system to have higher precedence in order for FIM Service to accept values from it. There is no conflict in the other direction, since no groups managed in FIM should also be managed in HR.

 If you change and import new configurations of FIM Synchronization Service, you need to recheck all **Attribute Flow Precedence** settings again.

If you have a scenario where groups are managed in multiple systems and both imported and exported to the same systems, we might run into an unsolvable situation. If for example, members are to be added in two systems, say HR and FIM, you might be tempted to check **Use equal precedence**. But be aware that this might cause deletions in one system.

Let me give you an example.

Let's say you have a group in both FIM and HR. You update the group in FIM but do not export the change to HR before someone changes the same group in HR. The result will be that, depending on how we synchronize, we will end up losing one of the changes. Equal precedence basically is *last writer wins*. So, please don't use it unless you are really sure of what you are doing.

Ok, we have configured the precedence and are able to synchronize the group information entered in FIM and HR. The result will be that all groups will show in both FIM Service (viewed in FIM Portal) and in the Metaverse.

Managing groups in AD

We now have some groups in FIM. Both the ones created in FIM and those that come from the HR system.

We now need to configure FIM to export these groups to AD.

As discussed earlier, we now need to consider the `groupType` attribute in AD.

We also need to consider if we have different needs depending on group type.

At The Company, they have decided that FIM should not delete security groups once created in AD. This is a common approach, since deleting a security group—and thereby its SID (Security ID)—might cause dramatic events, if the group is used for some kind of permission. Recreating a group with the same name will not recreate the SID and will not fix the permissions.

On the other hand, when talking about distribution groups, we want FIM to be able to delete them. The owner might want to delete it and will use the FIM Portal interface to do so. Or, it could be that we have a policy stating that distribution groups where the owner has left the company and no new owner has been assigned should be deleted.

We end up with two ways of managing groups in AD.

Security groups

Since we do not need support for deletions, we can use a synchronization rule based on **Outbound System Scoping Filter**. The following steps show what this synchronization rule might look like:

1. I use, in this case, the **Inbound and Outbound** direction. The key is that it is configured for **Outbound System Scoping Filter**.

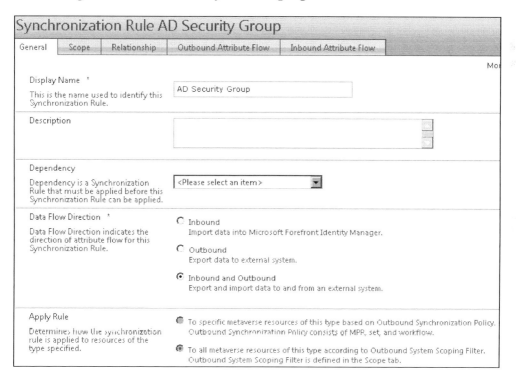

Group Management

2. The definition of the scoping filter is **MetaverseObject:group(Attribute) (domain)**, **Operator (equal)**, **Value (AD)** and **type, equal, Security**. Note that this will *not* cover a `MailEnabledSecurity` group type. If we are to support that as well, we would need to create a similar rule with **type, equal, MailEnabledSecurity**, in the filter.

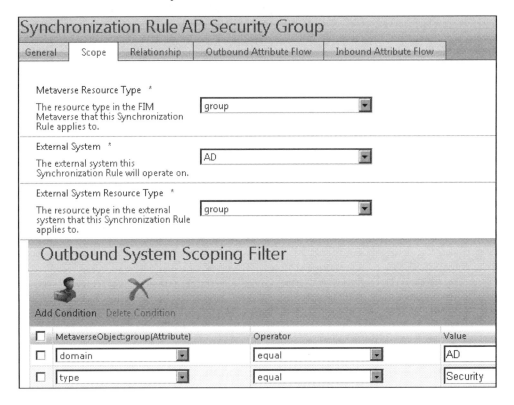

Chapter 6

3. To be able to rejoin, in case we lose the connector to AD, we set up a **Relationship Criteria**. Since these are only security groups, the **objectSid** attribute can be used. To create the group in AD, we check the **Create resource in external system** box.

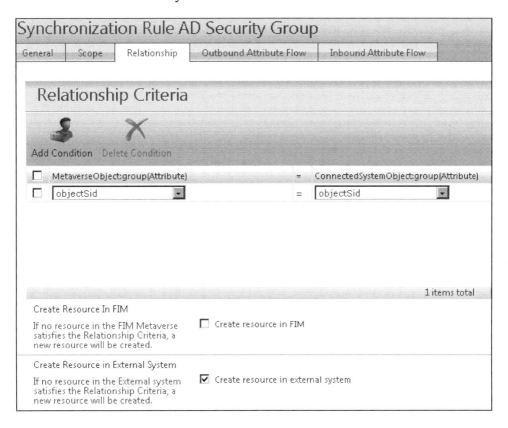

4. As we saw when managing users in *Chapter 5, User Management*, it is required to select the **Initial Flow Only** setting for the **dn** attribute flow. We then need the same attribute flow without the **Initial Flow Only** setting in case we want to support renames. The flow for **groupType** is not that complex, since we *know* these are only security groups. In this example I use `CustomExpression IIF(Eq(scope,"Universal"),-2147483640,IIF(Eq(scope,"Glob al"),-2147483646,-2147483644))`.

5. In **Inbound Attribute Flow**, I only import the **objectSid** attribute. It's not that I need it in FIM, but it is a good identifier of the object in AD. The GUID would have been another option.

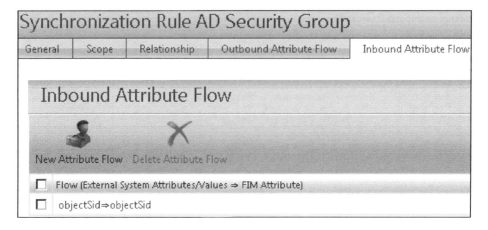

If we synchronize after creating this rule, we will get **Pending Export** to AD, for the security groups we got from HR.

Distribution groups

Since we would like to support *deprovisioning*, this synchronization rule needs to be based on Outbound Synchronization Policy. As discussed earlier, this means creating the configuration triple with Set, Workflow, and MPR, to control when to add or remove the synchronization rule.

Synchronization rule

The synchronization rules for the distribution groups could be created using the following steps:

1. I use, in this case, the **Inbound and Outbound** direction. The key is that it is configured for Outbound Synchronization Policy.

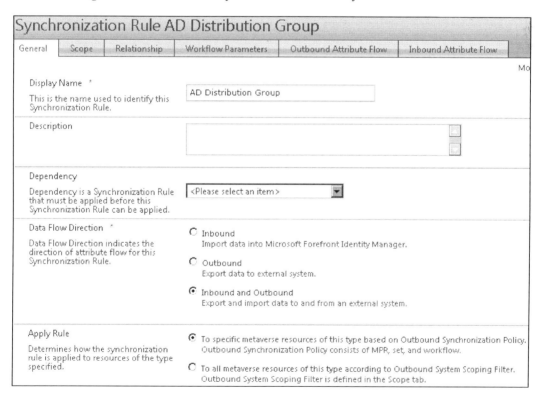

Group Management

2. Scope is **group** in both systems.

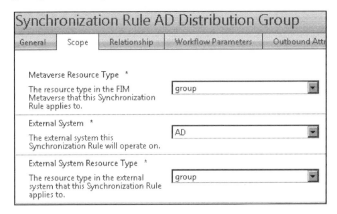

3. These objects are fully managed by FIM. We manage provisioning by checking **Create resource in external system**. We also manage deprovisioning by checking **Disconnect FIM resource from external system resource when this $**. The **Disconnect FIM resource from external system resource when this $** checkbox will not automatically delete the objects in AD; it will just disconnect the connector space object from the Metaverse if this rule is not applied to the object anymore.

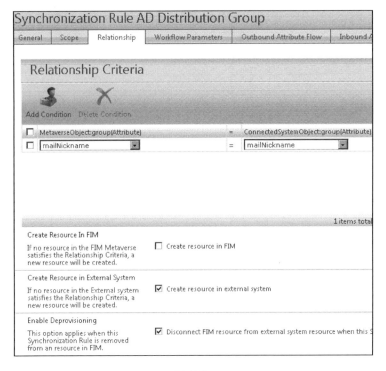

4. Once again, we need double **dn** flows to support renames. The **groupType** is again quite simple since we *know* this is only distribution groups. In this example I use `CustomExpression IIF(Eq(scope,"Universal"),8,IIF(Eq(scope,"Global"),2,4))`.

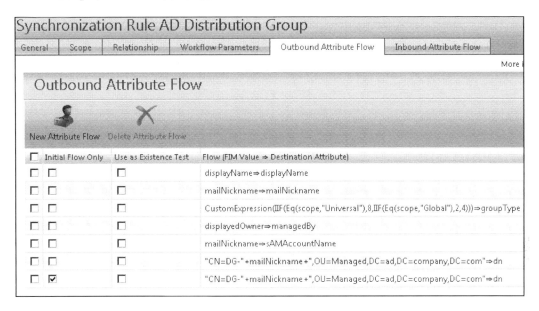

5. On **Inbound Attribute Flow**, we import the **mail** address generated by the e-mail system, Exchange.

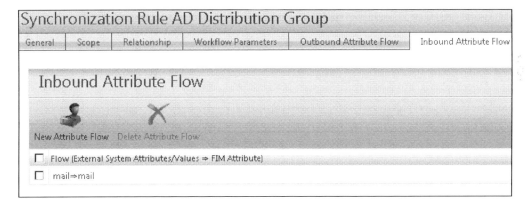

In the synchronization rule, we checked the **Disconnect FIM resource from external system resource when this Synchronization Rule is removed** box. This will, as it says, disconnect the object in the AD Connector Space from the object in the Metaverse.

Group Management

The next step, then, is to look at the settings of the AD MA.

If we set **Deprovisioning Options** to **Stage a delete on the object for the next export run**, the objects disconnected from the Metaverse will be deleted in AD, on the next export run.

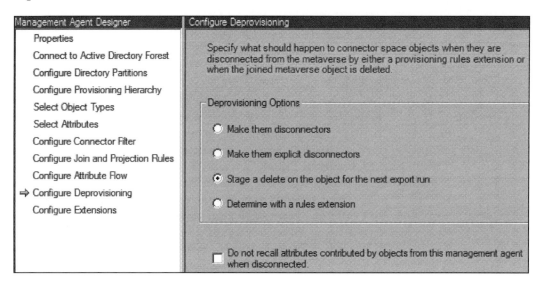

As you can see, this is a setting on the MA and will apply to all object types, not just the distribution groups. If you are concerned about FIM accidently deleting other object types, you can solve this in three ways, as follows:

- Use the **Determine with a rules extension** setting. This would require you to create a rules extension project and write a few lines of code. Read more about this option and more on deprovisioning at http://aka.ms/FIMDeprovisioning. This is the option I would recommend in the example we are looking at. It would require about five lines of code to *delete* distribution groups but to only *disconnect* security groups.

- Use the **Make them disconnectors** option and configure FIM to send a notification about the group being *ready for deletion* to, for example, the Exchange admins, and they will carry out the actual deletion of the group.

- By narrowing the permission used by the account that is used by FIM to access AD.

Set

The set we can use for the provisioning, in this case, is the built-in set called **All Distribution Groups**.

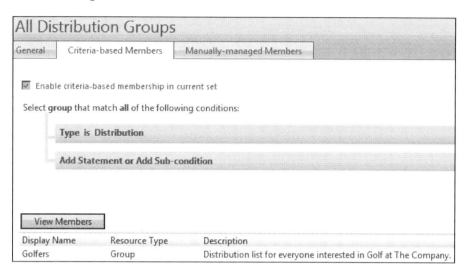

If we need to have a difference in synchronization rules or deprovisioning behavior for different distribution groups, we would have to create our own sets.

To support deprovisioning based on some criteria, we need to use a set using that criteria. The **All Distribution Group** set might otherwise trigger FIM to provision the group again.

Our custom set could look something like the following screenshot.

This set will contain all **Distribution** groups where **Displayed Owner** is in the set **Company: Active Employees**.

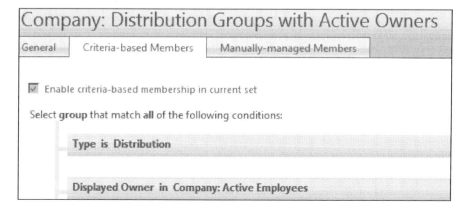

Group Management

The set **Company: Active Employees** in turn might look something like the following screenshot:

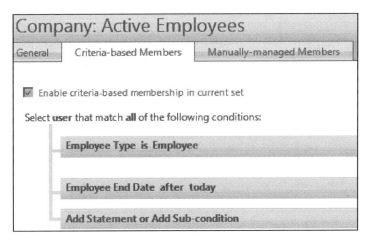

We can now satisfy a policy saying that distribution groups in AD must have an Active Employee as owner; otherwise they should be deleted from AD.

Workflow

We need a workflow that adds our synchronization rule to the resource (the distribution group).

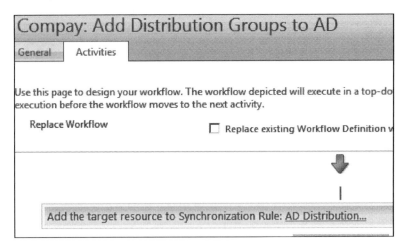

If we want to support deprovisioning as well (based on some criteria), we also need a workflow that removes the synchronization rule.

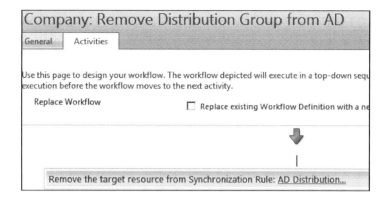

It is quite common to also have some kind of notification workflow activity. If we were to use an approach where the Exchange admins must manually delete the groups, we would certainly have some kind of notification activity.

If we added some custom workflow activity, we might have FIM create a case in our service management system.

If we delete the object in FIM, the workflow to delete the synchronization rule will not work, since it is of type *action* and happens *after* the delete. To support actual deletes in FIM, we need to configure **Object Deletion Rule** to delete the Metaverse object when it is deleted in FIM Service (using FIM Portal, for example).

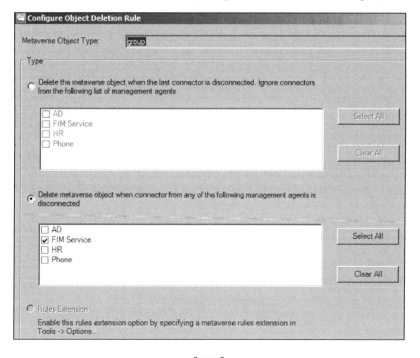

Group Management

We have to remember that FIM, by default, is not configured to delete objects, such as users and groups, once they are created in the Metaverse.

MPR

The MPR to trigger the correct workflow to add the synchronization rule is a simple set transition MPR acting on the **Transition In** event, when the object becomes a member of the set.

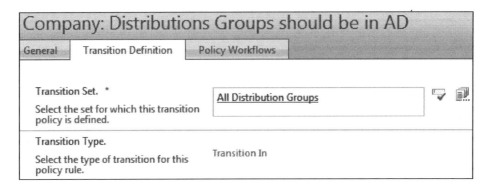

The MPR will then trigger the Action Workflow to add the synchronization rule.

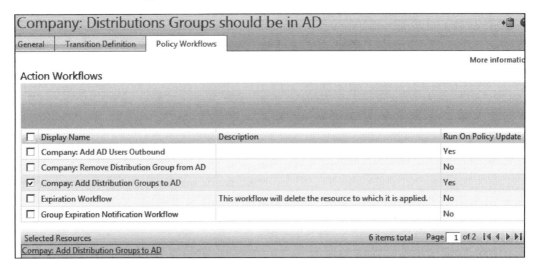

Once again, to deprovision, we need to figure out some criteria FIM can use to decide when to remove the synchronization rule from the resource.

We could use the example of the distribution groups having active owners described previously to provision and deprovision the groups in AD. In that case, it would also be likely that we want to trigger some kind of action to check if this group should be deleted altogether or whether a new owner should be assigned.

Summary

The group management features we have in FIM allow us to work with both static and dynamic groups and also allow users to manage groups by themselves. Deletions are by design difficult to implement since the objects by default remain in the Metaverse as long as a connector exists.

In this chapter, we have seen how the Outlook add-in makes self-service easier when it comes to groups.

In the next chapter, we will look at another self-service feature in FIM 2010 R2, the **Self-Service Password Reset (SSPR)**.

7
Self-service Password Reset

By now, we have a functional FIM 2010 R2 able to manage our users and groups, and maybe also some self service. It is now time to look at one of the features of FIM that many customers believe is the most cost saving one.

The feature is **Self-service Password Reset (SSPR)**, which will allow users to reset their own passwords if they have forgotten them, so they will not have to contact a help desk. Through that, we not only save ourselves a help desk call, but also allow the user to be productive again, quicker. This saves money!

In this chapter we will cover:

- Enabling password management in AD
- Allowing FIM Service to set passwords
- Configuring FIM Service
- The user experience

Anonymous request

What we need to keep in mind when looking at this feature is that the user, as he has forgotten his password, is unable to authenticate properly to FIM. So, the key problem with SSPR is how to authenticate the user.

Let's take an example.

Kent, our contractor, has forgotten his password. He then makes a request anonymously to FIM to reset the password of the user account Kent. Well, FIM won't just do that! So, we tell FIM to try to figure out who the *requestor* is. We add an Authentication (AuthN) workflow, which gives Kent a chance to prove his identity. If the AuthN workflow proves to FIM that the requestor is indeed the user Kent, it will allow Kent to reset his password.

Self-service Password Reset

In FIM 2010 R2, there are two built-in ways for FIM to find out who the user is—we can use either a **Question and Answer (QA)** gate or a **One Time Password (OTP)** gate.

QA versus OTP

There are two different ways of doing SSPR in the R2 release—QA (Question and Answer) and OTP (One Time Password).

QA basically means that a user can reset his password by giving the correct (the same) answers to a couple of questions the user was presented with during registration of this service.

OTP is a solution where we distribute a one-time code to the users by SMS or e-mail. The user then uses that code to reset his password.

Enabling password management in AD

The goal for SSPR is, usually, to reset the password of users' account in Active Directory, but the SSPR feature in FIM is not limited to that. It can be used to reset passwords in other CDSs as well.

In order for FIM to change the password of a user in AD (or any other CDS), the account used by FIM needs to have the **Reset password** permission in AD, or a similar permission in another CDS:

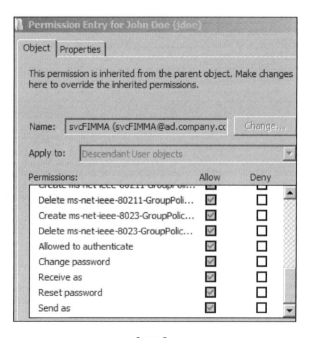

Chapter 7

In **Management Agents** for the target CDS, in this case the AD, we need to check the **Enable password management** checkbox:

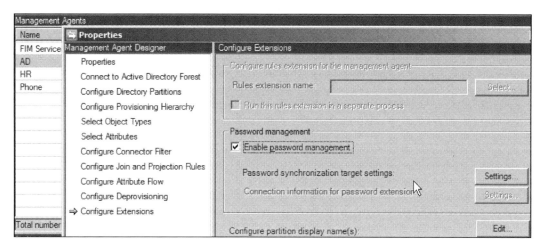

If we then look at the settings, we can make some adjustments, as shown in the following screenshot:

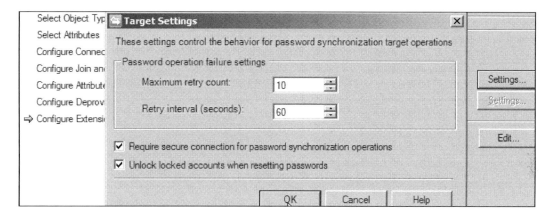

> The **Unlock locked accounts when resetting passwords** option is not enabled by default, but I would think that most implementations of SSPR will use that setting. It might be that the user actually locked his own account before realizing he forgot his password.

The Management Agent for AD is now ready for SSPR.

Allowing FIM Service to set passwords

The FIM Service account will be the account that calls FIM Synchronization Service, and tells it to reset the password in AD. But in order for the FIM Service account to be able to do that, we need to assign it some permissions with the following steps:

1. We need to add the account to a couple of groups created during installation (see *Chapter 3, Installation*) of FIM Synchronization Service.

2. Add the FIM Service account to the **FIMSyncBrowse** group:

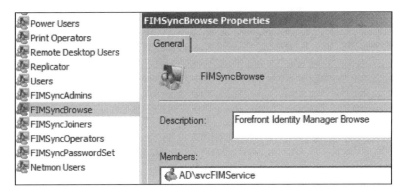

By default, this is a local group on the FIM Synchronization server; but you might have chosen to use groups in Active Directory instead. This will give FIM Service the ability to read information in FIM Synchronization Service.

3. To actually be allowed to initiate a password reset, we also need to add the FIM Service account to **FIMSyncPasswordSet**:

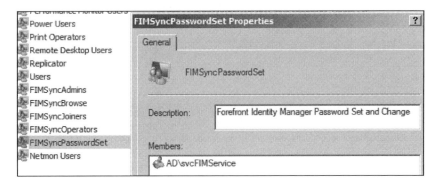

The call from FIM Service to FIM Synchronization Service to do a password reset is made using **Windows Management Instrumentation (WMI)**. This in turn means we need to give FIM Service the WMI permissions as well. This is not something we do on a daily basis and is somewhat tricky.

Chapter 7

Because we have, in our example, separated FIM Service and the FIM Synchronization server, it will be remote WMI calls that demand a few extra steps. A few of these steps can be ignored if the services are running on the same server. You would then need to remember to make the changes when/if you separate the services:

1. Open up the properties of **WMI Control** in **Server Manager (FIM-SYNC)**:

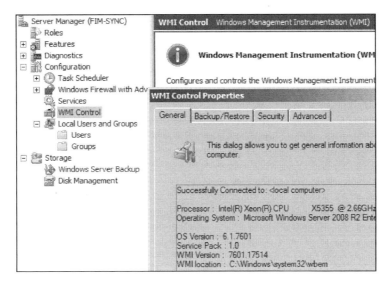

2. In the **Security** tab, expand the **Root** namespace and select the **CIMV2** namespace. Then click the **Security** button at the bottom:

Self-service Password Reset

3. Add the FIM Service account and assign the **Enable Account** and **Remote Enable** permissions. This will allow the FIM Service account to connect to this namespace:

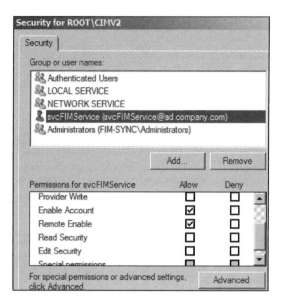

4. But we need to give access to sub namespaces as well. Click the **Advanced** button.
5. In the advanced security settings for CIMV2, select the entry with the FIM Service account and edit it. Change the **Apply to:** from **This namespace only** to **This namespace and subnamespaces**. Click **OK** a few times, to save your settings:

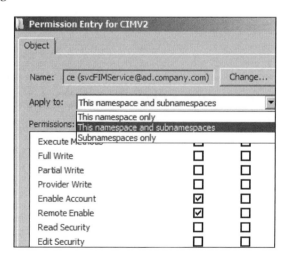

Chapter 7

As we have separated the servers, we also need to allow WMI calls through the firewall in FIM Synchronization Server, with the following steps:

1. In the **Control Panel | System and Security** section, click the **Allow a program through Windows Firewall** link:

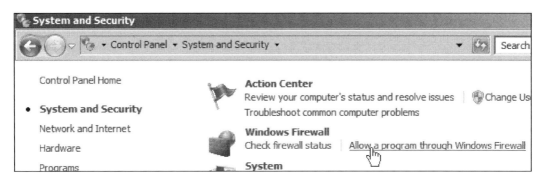

2. In the **Allowed Programs** setting, check the **Windows Management Instrumentation (WMI)** program:

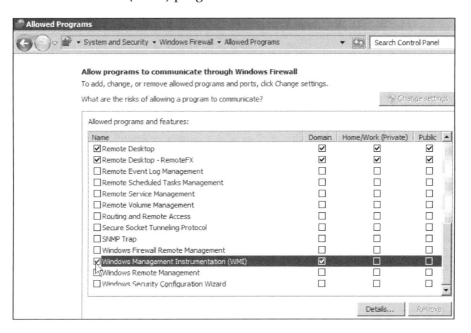

This can be done using GPOs, if that is your preferred way of managing the local firewall on your servers. When allowing WMI to communicate through the firewall, it will create a firewall rule. If you would like to narrow down the IP addresses allowed to use the remote WMI, you can do so by modifying that rule.

Self-service Password Reset

The FIM Synchronization groups are assigned some DCOM permissions during setup, but we need to make some adjustments in order for SSPR to work. The following are steps for the same:

1. Under **Component Services** (in the FIM Synchronization server), in the **COM Security** tab of the properties of **My Computer**, click **Edit Limits...**.
2. Assign the **Local Launch** and **Remote Launch** permissions to the **FIMSyncPasswordSet** group:

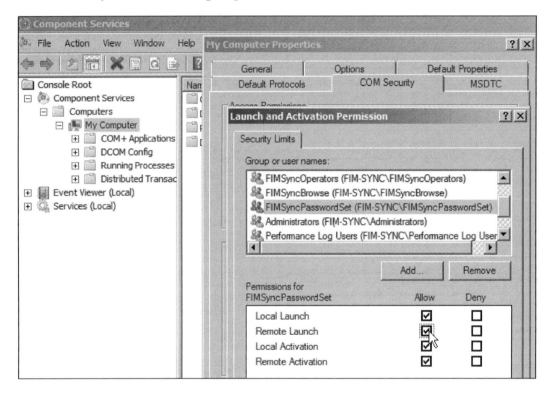

Now the FIM Service account has the permissions required to make the calls to FIM Synchronization Service, to tell FIM Synchronization Service to reset the password in the target CDS (AD).

Configuring FIM Service

SSPR is not enabled by default in FIM Service, so we need to enable some MPRs and configure some *sets* and *workflows*.

Security context

I am not sure if you remember the steps when we installed the FIM password registration and reset portals back in *Chapter 3*. But let me remind you of one critical part in that setup:

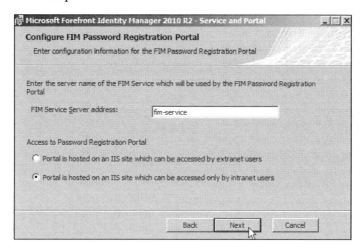

During the setup, we decided that the portal should be used for Intranet users. While configuring SSPR, we can configure some settings to only apply to Extranet users. At The Company, we only have one set of password registration and reset portals. But the idea is that you might also want to have a special set for Extranet users. Later, we will refer to this as *security context*. Security context can either be *All* or *Extranet*, where All means it applies to both Intranet and Extranet users.

Password Reset Users Set

The default MPRs around SSPR use a predefined set called **Password Reset Users Set**. If you look at the criterion for that set, you will find it applies to all users:

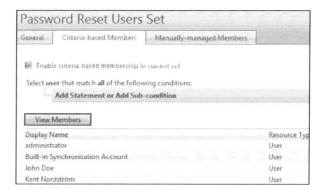

Self-service Password Reset

Allowing SSPR for all users is likely not the case in reality. So, we need to modify the criterion in this set. We could also create a new one, but then we would also need to modify all MPRs to reflect the new set. Initially at The Company, this feature will be used by Employees:

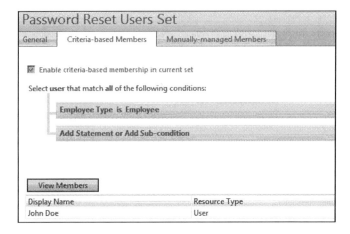

We have now defined users for whom we would like to use the SSPR feature.

Password Reset AuthN workflow

As we discussed earlier, we need to have at least one Authentication workflow in our SSPR implementation. The default one is called the **Password Reset AuthN** workflow. The default activity used in this workflow to authenticate the users is the QA gate:

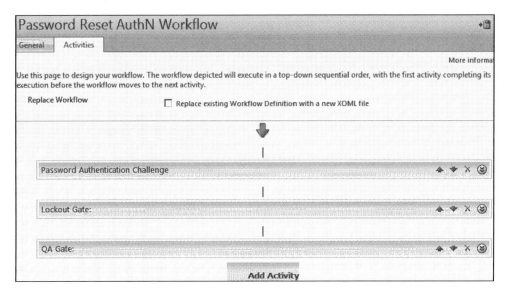

There are also some activities to support the SSPR feature; we will look at those now.

The **Password Authentication Challenge** activity is used during registration and will force the user to reenter their current password during the registration process:

The **Lockout Gate** activity decides how many tries a user will get, and how we should handle lockout if users fail to authenticate correctly:

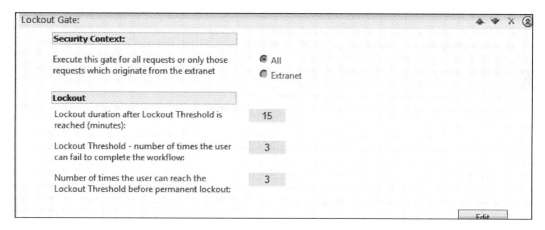

In the previous screenshot, note that the **Security Context:** in this activity is, by default, set to **All**.

Configuring the QA gate

Finally, the QA gate activity needs to be configured with the following steps:

1. As with **Lockout Gate**, the **Security Context:** section is, by default, set to **All**:

   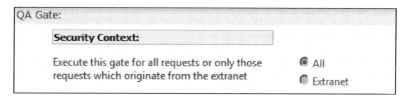

Self-service Password Reset

2. We need to decide how many questions to ask and how many questions users are required to answer:

Step 1 - Question Settings	
Enter the total number of questions for this gate:	3
Number of questions displayed during registration:	3
Number of questions required for registration:	3
Number of questions randomly presented to the user:	3
Number of questions that must be answered correctly:	3
Allow duplicate answers:	☐
Answer constraint:	^.{4,}$
Message to user that describes uniqueness and answer text constraints:	Each answer must contain at least four characters, and no two answers may be the same.
Terse inline error message to user for answers that violate uniqueness or text constraints:	Answer is duplicated or has less than four characters.

Note that the default value of **Answer constraint** requires the answer to contain at least four characters. This you might need to change if you, for example, ask a question such as favorite car, as the answer *BMW* will not work. In the R2 release, the duplicate check and answer constraints were added to prevent users from answering, for example, *123* on all questions.

3. Then, we need to define the question pool to be used by the QA gate. This can be a very time consuming task, as there are many thoughts on what a good question is. You need to ask questions such that they prove a person's identity, but are not likely to be easily guessed by other people.

In many cases, the questions also need to be reviewed by the legal department to make sure that we do not violate any rules or laws. I mean, asking a person about sexual preferences, for example, might not be such a good idea.

There are no best practices in this case. But in my opinion, it is better to have a few good questions than many bad ones. One way is to have the users generate new information with a question, such as asking to "enter a personal PIN (4 digits)". But this kind of information is easier to forget, even though it is a good identifier. In the following example, I ask about Social Security number. This might seem like a good question, but we need to remember that it might be illegal to store this information in our database:

Step 2 - Enter Questions	
1.	Mothers maiden name?
2.	Favorite car?
3.	Social security number?

4. Finally, we need to set the compatibility level. If you have an existing pre-R2 implementation of FIM, and have installed the earlier (pre-R2) add-ins and extensions for Windows, you might need to allow them to use the SSPR feature without the duplicate and regular expression check. If you are upgrading from an earlier version of FIM 2010, please read http://aka.ms/FIMR2Upgrade.

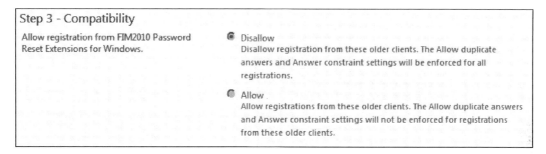

The OTP gate

If we do not want the QA gate, or we need to support more ways (two-factor authentication) of resetting passwords, we can use the OTP gate included in FIM 2010 R2.

If you click **Add Activity** in the workflow, you will get the following page:

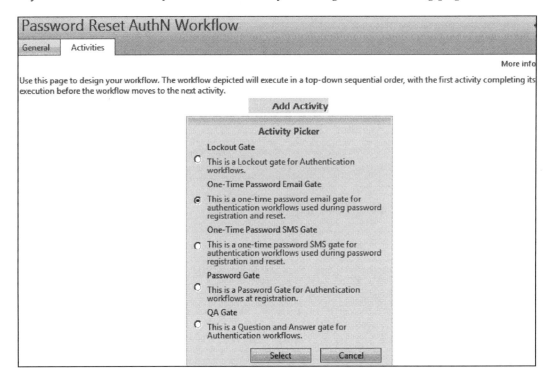

As you can see, there are two OTP gates—one is **One-Time Password Email Gate** and the other is **One-Time Password SMS Gate**.

The e-mail gate can be used pretty much out of the box, as long as FIM Service is allowed to send e-mails to external e-mail addresses. Just remember that it might not be useful for internal users, whose only e-mail address is the internal one. For external users, such as consultants or partners, this might be an easy way of implementing SSPR. During the registration, the users will provide the email address they want to use for SSPR. As you can see, there is an option to have the e-mail address as read-only. This is used when FIM will get the e-mail address to be used, from some other source:

Chapter 7

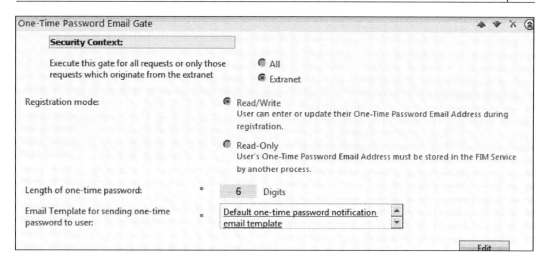

If you look in the schema of FIM Service, you will find that there is a special set of attributes that are used by the OTP gates. If you are providing the e-mail address used for the e-mail gate, or the mobile phone number used by the SMS gate, you need to make sure the values are stored in the attributes **One-Time Password Email Address** and **One-Time Password Mobile Phone**, respectively:

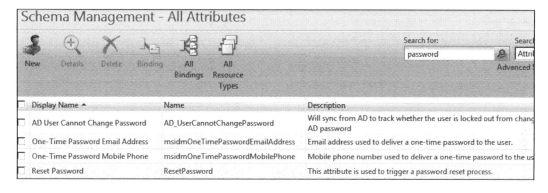

The OTP attributes are **not**, by default, allowed to be managed by the synchronization engine or by users, if that is what you want. Changes in the MPRs are required for this to be possible.

Self-service Password Reset

The SMS gate has almost the same settings as the e-mail gate, but requires some additional coding to take place, as we need to compile the DLL files that FIM should use to send the SMS. If you go to `http://aka.ms/SSPRconfigureSMSOTP`, you will find an example of how to create the `SmsServiceProvider.dll` file. You would, of course, also need a provider to send the SMS:

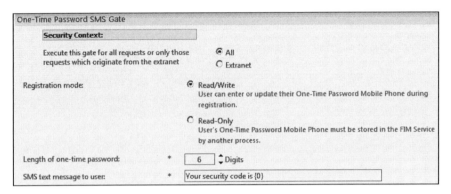

The reason I do not have an example of this in my book is that the solution varies a lot, depending on how you are calling your SMS provider. I would guess your SMS provider will be a good source of information on how to programmatically call their endpoint using .NET code.

Require re-registration

If for some reason, you would like users to re-register to the SSPR—the reason could, for example, be that you have redesigned all your questions in the QA gate—you need to check the little **Require Re-Registration** box in the **Password Reset AuthN Workflow** page. This will prompt the users to register again:

SSPR MPRs

Now that we have decided the set and the gate we want to use, we need to enable and configure the relevant MPRs to get the SSPR started.

There are three MPRs that we need to enable; they are as follows:

- **Anonymous users can reset their password**
- **Password reset users can read password reset objects**
- **Password Reset Users can update the lockout attributes of themselves**

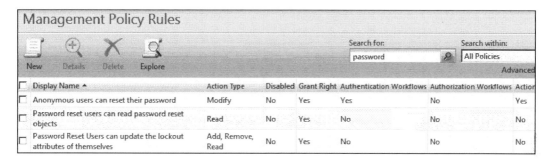

The first one, **Anonymous users can reset their password,** is the one that does the trick. It will fire off the Password Reset AuthN workflow we talked about earlier and the Password Reset Action workflow that will do the actual reset.

If we haven't done it before, we also need to enable the following MPRs:

- **User management**: Users can read attributes of their own
- **General**: Users can read non-administrative configuration resources

The user experience

So what does this look like for the user? In my little example, the employees are the ones that will be using the SSPR to begin with.

In order to get the best user experience, requirement number one is that the client computer has the FIM client add-ins and extensions installed, as we talked about in *Chapter 6, Group Management*.

As soon as we enable the MPRs and John (a member of the Password Reset Users set) logs on to his computer, which has the FIM add-ins and extensions installed, it will start up a browser window connecting to the Password Registration portal, which we defined during the installation of the add-ins in *Chapter 6*.

Self-service Password Reset

He could also access the Password Registration portal manually; the experience is similar, but using the add-ins and extensions will likely increase the number of users actually taking time to register, as they will be automatically prompted to do so.

If we used FQDN for the Password Registration portal URL, we should make sure that the URL is in the local Intranet zone of the client, so that IE can use Integrated Authentication. To get a good experience with FIM, I recommend adding `*.ad.company.com` to the local Intranet zone:

1. First the user has to prove he knows the current password. This is the Password Authentication Challenge activity we have in our workflow kicking in:

Chapter 7

2. The user is then asked to answer the questions we configured in the **QA Gate** activity. If the QA gate is configured with five questions, but is only supposed to ask three, the three questions asked are randomly picked among the five:

3. If we also used the OTP e-mail gate, the user might be asked to also register the e-mail address to be used for the OTP:

[257]

4. When the user has completed the guide, he is informed that he might use the Password Reset portal to reset the password. This is, however, not the only way for the user to reset his password. If he has the add-ins and extensions installed, he can also use the Windows logon screen:

5. If a user who is not a part of the Password Reset Users set tries to manually access the Password Reset Registration portal, he will be duly notified that he is not authorized to register:

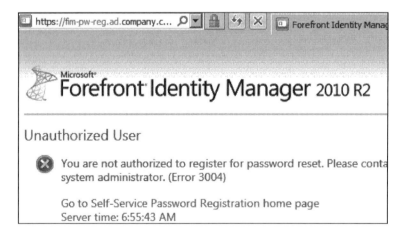

Chapter 7

So, what happens when the user finds himself forgetting his password?

Well, there are two options here—he can either access the Password Reset portal from some internal kiosk computer, or maybe we could have the Password Reset portal published to the Internet, using, for example, Microsoft Forefront UAG. But, as we have also installed the add-ins and extensions on his computer, he can use that as well:

1. At the Windows logon screen, the user can just click the **Forgot your password?** link:

2. To authenticate himself, he answers the QA gate questions:

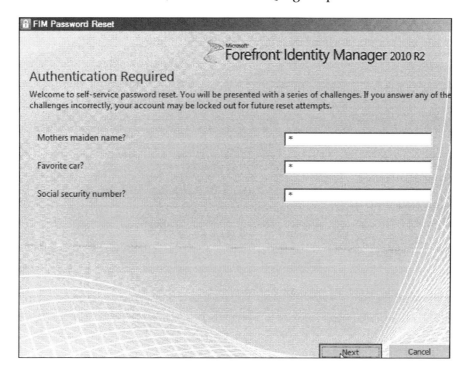

[259]

3. If he answers the gate correctly, he is given the chance to enter a new password. He then clicks **Reset**. Normally, the user can then log on using the new password immediately:

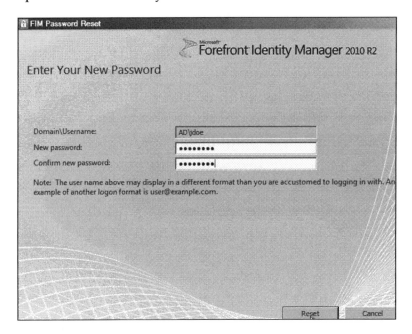

4. As an option, the user can also go to the Password Reset portal and do the following:

   a. Enter his username:

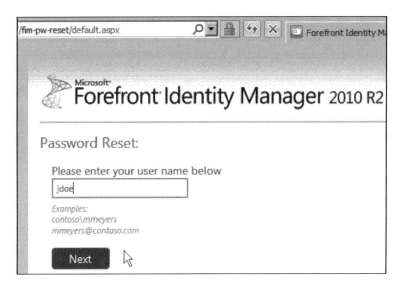

b. Answer the questions:

c. Enter a new password:

d. Finally, start using his new password:

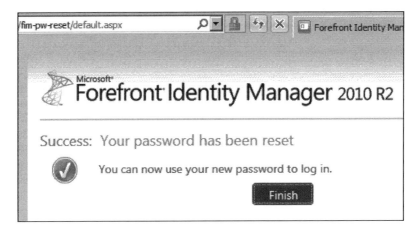

As you can see, the user experience is quite friendly; especially the fact that it integrates with the Windows logon screen, if we install the add-ins and extensions.

Summary

The SSPR feature is a very nice one, which can save companies that are using passwords a lot of money. In this chapter, we have seen how easy it is to enable and configure the Self-Service Password Reset feature. If you look at http://aka.ms/FIMR2QuickStart, you will see that there is a **QuickStart** tool to get started with SSPR even quicker.

We need to decide early on whether we want the same solution for both internal and external access to the SSPR feature. If we would like to separate them, we need to install a separate set of SSPR registration and reset portals and modify the FIM Service MPRs and workflows, accordingly.

Talking about external, *what if the identities we manage are in the cloud?* The next chapter will discuss how FIM can be used when managing *cloud* identities.

8
Using FIM to Manage Office 365 and Other Cloud Identities

When I started writing this book, there was a rumor that Microsoft would ship a new Management Agent for Office 365 in FIM 2010 R2. It is now clear that this will not be the case. In this chapter, I will show how FIM 2010 R2 might fit into the puzzle of managing Office 365 identities, and also how FIM might play a role in Identity Federation scenarios.

In this chapter I will:

- Give an overview of Office 365
- Show some tips for setting up DirSync
- Discuss the role of FIM in Federation and OTP scenarios

Overview of Office 365

Office 365 is Microsoft's cloud-based service offered to companies for end-user services such as Exchange, SharePoint, and Lync. It is constantly evolving, so the information I give in this chapter might get outdated quite soon.

Let's take a quick look at Office 365 as it looks today:

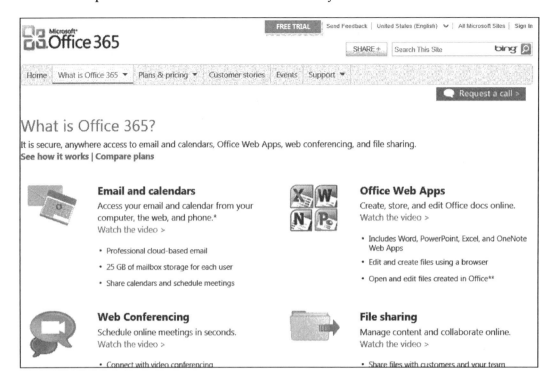

There are three main services being offered to customers at the moment, namely:

- E-mail services using Exchange Online
- Collaboration services using SharePoint Online
- Online chat and conferencing using Lync Online

It is very easy to start using these services, so long as you do not have an existing environment that you want to interoperate with.

If some of your users are using Office 365, but are still also using an on-premises solution, it gets a bit trickier.

> From the end-user perspective, the best solution, in my opinion, is to configure Federation as soon as users are to exist in both Office 365 and on-premises.

If you have an existing environment and would like to start using Office 365, FIM can help you manage identities in both locations, whether you are using federation or not.

Chapter 8

An administrator can use the administrative website to manage users and applications:

There is also a PowerShell-based interface, which can be used to manage most of the day-to-day tasks of Office 365. You just need to download and install the Microsoft Online Services Module for PowerShell, use your Office 365 administrative credentials, and connect:

```
Administrator: Microsoft Online Services Module for Windows PowerShell
PS C:\> $cred = Get-Credential

cmdlet Get-Credential at command pipeline position 1
Supply values for the following parameters:
Credential
PS C:\> Connect-MsolService -Credential $cred
```

There are actually some tasks that can only be done using the PowerShell interface; one example is the New-MsolFederatedDomain cmdlet.

The New-MsolFederatedDomain cmdlet adds a new, single sign-on domain (also known as an identity-federated domain) to Office 365, and configures the relying party's trust settings between the on-premises Active Directory Federation Services 2.0 server and Office 365. Due to domain verification requirements, you may need to run this cmdlet several times, in order to complete the process of adding the new, single sign-on domain.

If you are looking at starting to manage your Office 365 Identities using FIM, it is essential in this case (as in any other case) that you learn how this new Connected Data Source (CDS) works.

We have discussed CDSs such as AD and HR systems, so far. If you look at the properties of a user in Office 365, you realize this is quite different:

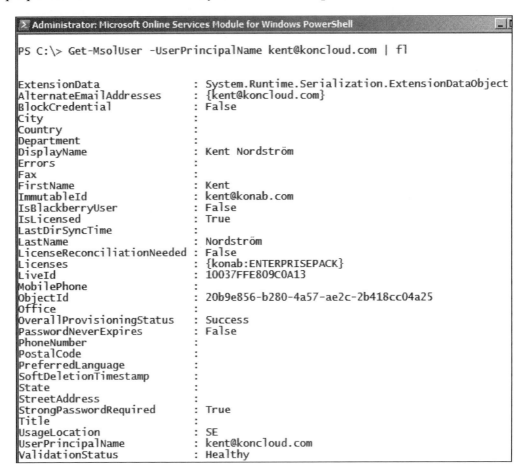

Although many attributes look familiar, there are some odd ones. There are also some restrictions, which we need to understand, such as the fact that the **UserPrincipalName** attribute has to be the same as the e-mail address of the user. This is the username used by the user, when they log in to Office 365 using the web interface.

Now that we understand a little bit more about how Office 365 looks and works, we can start to think about how to manage it using FIM.

But wait… there is no Management Agent for Office 365, so how do we do that?

Well Microsoft does have a Management Agent for Office 365 available, it is just not available for you to install in FIM; instead they offer you **DirSync**.

DirSync

DirSync is a tool that synchronizes users and groups between Active Directory and Office 365.

To download it, go to your Office 365 administration portal, and go to **User Management | Active Directory synchronization**, and click **Setup** (step 4 in the following screenshot):

Set up and manage Active Directory synchronization

Synchronize your local Active Directory® and see your global address list in Microsoft Office 365 for enterprises.

If you haven't done so already, we strongly recommend that you set up single sign-on to allow users to sign in to Microsoft Office 365 with their corporate credentials.

1. **Prepare for directory synchronization**
   Check prerequisites, including computer requirements and user permissions.
   Read: Prepare for directory synchronization

2. **Verify domains**
   For a better user experience, go to the domains page to add and verify your company's domains before you continue with the steps on this page.

3. **Activate Active Directory synchronization**
   Activate directory synchronization to use your local Active Directory to add or remove users and security groups and sync to Microsoft Office 365. After you activate directory synchronization, you cannot deactivate it. Learn more

   Active Directory synchronization is activated.

4. **Install and configure the Directory Synchronization tool**
   Download the Directory Synchronization tool and then configure it to set up synchronization from Active Directory to Microsoft Office 365.
   Read: Install the Directory Synchronization tool

   ● Windows 32-bit version
   ○ Windows 64-bit version

   [Download]

5. **Verify directory synchronization**
   Make changes to your local Active Directory and verify those changes in Microsoft Office 365.
   Read: Verify directory synchronization

6. **Activate synchronized users**
   Go to the users page, select the "Unlicensed users" view, select all of those users, and then click "Activate synced users".

DirSync should be installed on a dedicated machine.

If you download the 32-bit version, you will essentially get the ILM version of the synchronization service, and if you download the 64-bit version, you will get the FIM 2010 version of the synchronization service.

Even though you will get your version of the synchronization service in the end, it cannot be used for anything but its dedicated purposes.

During the setup and configuration of the DirSync tool, I would like to point out some steps that might confuse you:

1. When the setup is finished, it will start the configuration wizard:

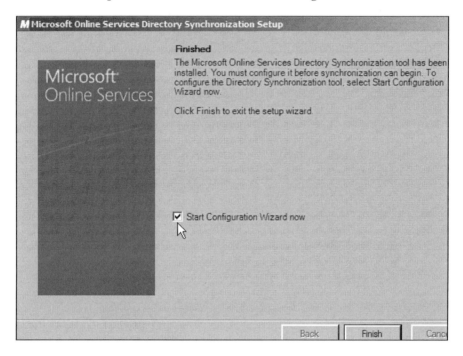

2. The configuration wizard will not ask many questions. First, you need to give it the administrative account that you want it to use, to connect to your Office 365. I would suggest that you create a separate account in your Office 365 environment, with administrative privileges:

Chapter 8

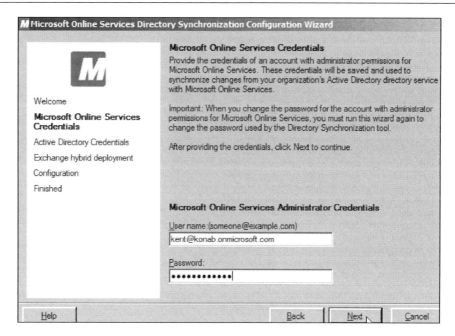

3. When asked for Active Directory credentials, it is easy to make the mistake of using something like our `svcFIMMA` account, which we used in our FIM deployment. Well it will not work, and if you read the text on the following page carefully, you will understand why:

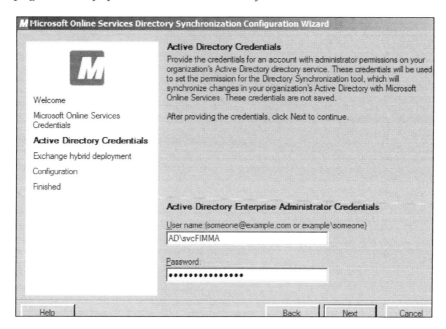

4. If you make the aforementioned mistake, you will get an error about the account not being a member of the Enterprise Admins group:

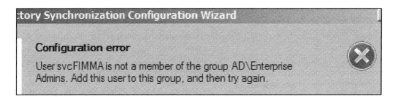

5. The account you specify is **not** the account DirSync will use to synchronize your users; that account will only be used during the configuration step. One step will be to create the account (MSOL_AD_SYNC) actually used by DirSync when synchronizing with AD:

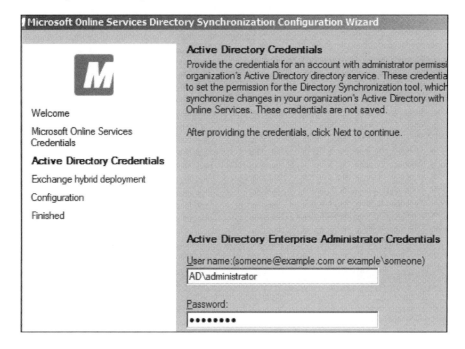

Chapter 8

6. When the configuration wizard is finished, it will, by default, synchronize directories now. I would suggest that you uncheck that for now, and verify your configuration before starting to synchronize your users. Otherwise, every user and group in your AD will be synchronized to your Office 365 environment:

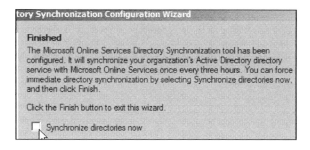

As you can see, you do not get many options while installing and configuring the DirSync tool. So, how can we use FIM to control this?

Well, the DirSync tool is not supposed to be configured, and if you do so, you might end up in an unsupported state. With a few of my customers, I have implemented some customizations to the DirSync tool, which are as follows:

If you start the user interface, `C:\Program Files\Microsoft Online Directory Sync\SYNCBUS\Synchronization Service\UIShell\miisclient.exe`, you will get a familiar interface:

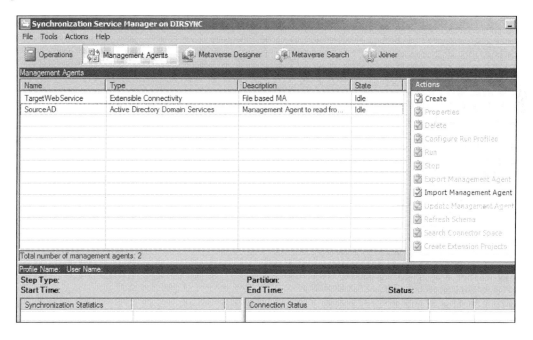

[271]

Using FIM to Manage Office 365 and Other Cloud Identities

 I would suggest that you take your time to look around in this interface and get a feel for the MAs. Also, get to know how they operate before starting the synchronization of your AD objects into your Office 365 environment.

One option you have for limiting the users that are synchronized, is to configure the connector filter on the SourceAD MA. If you look at it, you will find that there are quite a few filters in place, by default:

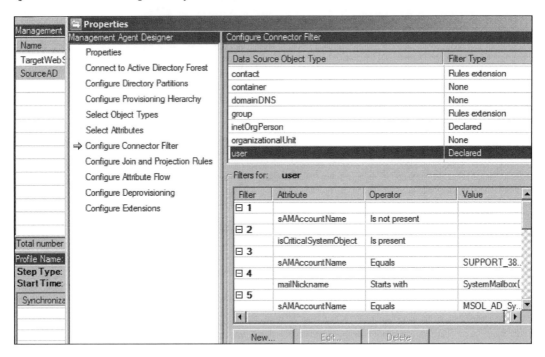

If you have users that you do **not** want DirSync to synchronize from your AD to Office 365, you can add a connector filter. For example, adding `title` (**Attribute**) `Equals` (**Operator**) `student` (**Value**) will filter out all users that have the title of student. This way, FIM can be used to manage the attribute you use in your connector filter, in AD, and thereby control which users get synchronized to Office 365.

If you are using a custom filter, be aware that DirSync is configured to delete objects in Office 365, if they are not present or filtered from your AD.

 Remember that you might end up in an unsupported state, as soon as you make changes to the DirSync tool in this way.

Another option is to look at **Deprovisioning Options** on the **TargetWebService** MA:

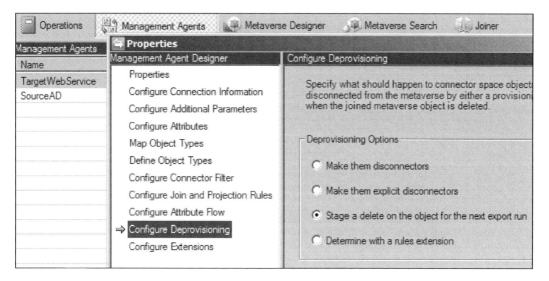

During testing and development, I usually change this setting to **Make them disconnectors**, until I am confident about the behavior of the design.

As you can see, the DirSync tool is a very specialized version of the synchronization service. Although we might feel tempted to use it for other purposes, or make changes to it, we are not allowed to. But I do use the UI of the DirSync tool to troubleshoot synchronization issues the same way I do in my real FIM deployment.

The DirSync tool is highly dependent on good data quality in the Active Directory, and this is where FIM comes in. Using FIM, you can make sure the data in your AD is correct, and feel confident that DirSync will synchronize correct data to Office 365.

Federation

When users get an account in your Office 365, they are by default, given a username, UserPrincipalName, and a password to use during login.

Many companies, however, would like users to use their local Active Directory credentials instead, to authenticate against the Office 365 services.

The solution is to configure your Office 365 environment for **Federation**. This will, if configured correctly, give your internal users the **Single Sign-On (SSO)** login when accessing the Office 365 services.

What you need now is **Active Directory Federation Services (ADFS)**. I will not dive deep into how ADFS or Federation (claims-based authentication) works, but will give a quick overview and try to point out how FIM might play a part in this configuration.

The steps outlined in the following diagram are a very simplified model on how this works:

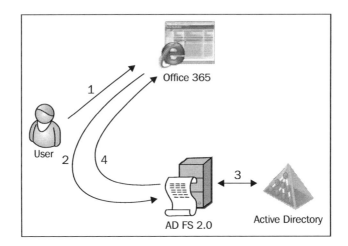

 For more details on this, I refer to ADFS and Office 365 documentation on Microsoft TechNet.

The following are the details of the steps outlined in the diagram:

1. A user tries to access Office 365.
2. Office 365 redirects the user to ADFS.
3. ADFS authenticates the user against AD and gets information about the user to put in the *claim*.
4. The user takes the claim and authenticates it against Office 365.

So where does FIM fit into this?

Well, in step 3, where ADFS authenticates the user against AD, the user needs to be in AD and the authentication method needs to work. FIM can be used to make sure the user is provisioned, updated, and deprovisioned correctly in AD. If passwords are used, then SSPR discussed in *Chapter 7, Self-Service Password Reset*, might come in handy.

Chapter 8

ADFS also needs some storage, where it can pick up the information to generate the claim. This is usually AD, but can also be other sources, such as SQL Server. Whenever claims are used, whether we are talking about ADFS or some other claims provider, the quality of the storage used to generate the claim is vital. By now you know that FIM is the perfect solution to make sure that storage is kept up to date.

In the previous scenario, Office 365 is what's called the *relying party*. When you run the PowerShell commands to configure your Office 365 for federation, it will automatically configure your ADFS server.

If you open up your ADFS 2.0 management console and look at **Relying Party Trusts**, you will find your Office 365. If you go to properties and take a look at the rules used to generate the claim, you will find that it gets `UserPrincipalName` from Active Directory, and puts it into something called `ImmutableID`:

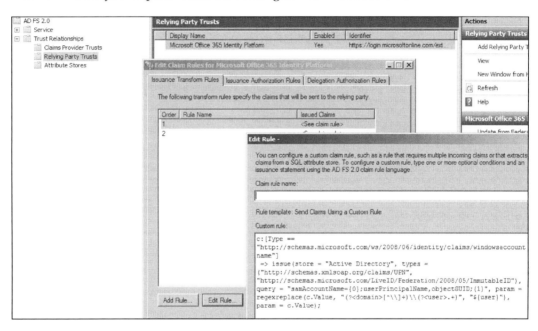

If you look back a few pages, you might recall this `ImmutableID` property being one of the attributes we have in our Office 365 user objects.

You can imagine what might happen if the `UserPrincipalName` attribute in Active Directory becomes incorrect—the authentication might fail, or worse, a user might get access to some other user's information. This is just one example to show how data quality in the storage used by a claims provider needs to be very high. Using FIM, we can make sure that is indeed the case!

If you are using cloud services other than Office 365, the process is almost the same even though the claims provider might be something other than ADFS. FIM can in any case be used to make sure that the claims issued are correct.

FIM can make sure that the *attribute store* used by ADFS has the correct data. But ADFS only supports a few attribute stores out of the box:

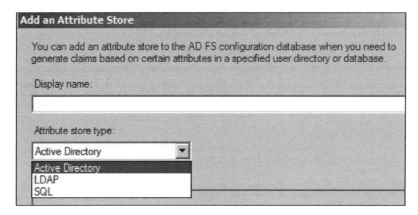

In FIM, there are built-in Management Agents for all three data stores, which are available, by default, in ADFS. This makes them easy to manage using FIM.

ADFS also supports adding custom attribute stores. One example out there that integrates ADFS and FIM is the *ADFS 2.0 Attribute Store for Forefront Identity Manager* that can be found at http://fimattributestore.codeplex.com.

This will give you an ADFS 2.0 Attribute Store that will allow you to fetch attribute values directly from the Forefront Identity Manager Service Database, and issue them as claims.

For example:

- Attributes in the *person* resource can be fetched and issued as claims
- Groups, sets, and roles in FIM can be issued as group or role claims

Using this you might skip the step of configuring FIM to export information to some external source such as AD or SQL that can in turn be used by ADFS to build the claims.

PowerShell or Custom MA

Once you have created your users in Office 365 either manually or using DirSync, they need to be licensed in order to start using Office 365. There is nothing out of the box in FIM 2010 R2 that can help you do this. Usually, administrators use PowerShell to do this, and that is how you typically implement it in FIM as well.

What you need is either a PowerShell Workflow Activity that can run the required PowerShell commands, or you need a Management Agent capable of calling PowerShell scripts. Both might work, but I prefer to use the Management Agent approach, as it is easier to troubleshoot and get feedback from the system verifying if it worked or not. If not, then retrying is easier.

So where do you get your PowerShell Activity or PowerShell capable MA?

There are a number of third-party PowerShell MAs, or you can build your own if you like. Buying a Management Agent from a third-party vendor will possibly give you support that you would like, rather than starting an in-house development project.

For testing and proof-of-concept solutions, you might start off by using the open source versions you can find at http://fim.codeplex.com. I will talk a little bit more about this in *Chapter 11, Customizing Data Transformations*.

However when working with Office 365, some kind of PowerShell capability is more or less required in FIM, if you want to automate the process and/or use FIM Service and Portal for some self-service steps. Office 365 is not the only system that requires PowerShell capabilities in FIM; another example is Microsoft Lync.

At present, there is a version of the Management Agent used by DirSync available for use in FIM, if you engage Microsoft Consulting Services. This would give you much more control on who, what, and how objects are synchronized to Office 365.

If there will be a Management Agent for Office 365 available from Microsoft or not in the future, no one can tell at the moment.

Working with a PowerShell MA is a bit different. You will, for example, have to write the scripts that will generate import data, as well as performing exports.

Let's look at an example—the Søren Granfeldt PowerShell MA. While I was writing this book, information about this MA could be found at http://aka.ms/PowerShellMA.

The Management Agent runs as an import/export Management Agent, which allows for PowerShell scripts to be run to collect objects for an import (only full import is supported in the current version) and export script for the Connector Space (CS) object of the Management Agent.

The names of the PowerShell scripts are defined in the global parameter section of the configuration of the MA, as shown in the following screenshot:

Name	Value	Encrypted
BeginExportScriptname	BeginExport.ps1	No
EndExportScriptname	EndExport.ps1	No
ExportScriptname	Export.ps1	No
ImportScriptname	FullImport.ps1	No

In the documentation for this MA, we can read the following information about the scripts:

BeginExportScriptname: This script is run once at the start of Run Profile, with an Export step. A sample for this script is provided in the kit as `BeginExport.ps1`. The connection information of the configuration of the MA is passed as parameters to this script (parameters are `ConnectTo`, `User`, and `Password`).

EndExportScriptname: This script is run once at the end of Run Profile, with an Export step. A sample for this script is provided in the kit as `EndExport.ps1`. The information from the connection information of the configuration of the MA is passed as parameters to this script (parameters are `ConnectTo`, `User`, and `Password`).

ExportScriptname: This script is run once for each object exported by Run Profile, with an Export step. A sample for this script is provided in the kit as `Export.ps1`. All attribute values present from the defined MA schema are passed as parameters to the script. Also, the information from the connection information of the configuration of the MA is passed as parameters to this script (parameters are `ConnectTo`, `User`, and `Password`).

ImportScriptname: This script is run once for each Run Profile that includes a full import step. A sample for this script is provided in the kit as `FullImport.ps1`. This script **must** send a hash table matching the schema of the MA with all objects to the pipeline. The objects passed from this script will be handed over to FIM. The information from the connection information of the configuration of the MA is passed as parameters to this script (parameters are `ConnectTo`, `User`, and `Password`).

One nice thing, in my opinion, when using a PowerShell MA is that the administrators of the system you are talking to can be the ones writing the scripts. It does not matter if you are using it for Home Folder management or Office 365 License management. This makes it relatively easy to get a clear line of where responsibility shifts.

Using UAG and FIM to get OTP for Office 365

One small side note is that customers might want users on the Internet to use some custom authentication method, such as SMS OTP for example, when accessing Office 365. This is not supported by either Office 365, or ADFS, or AD. So how do we solve this problem?

Well, first of all, we need some product that can translate the SMS OTP into Kerberos, which ADFS and AD understand. One such product is Microsoft Forefront **UAG (Unified Access Gateway)**.

If we look at the steps in our aforementioned Federation model, we need to add some steps to it. What we do is put UAG in front of the ADFS server. UAG is then configured to authenticate the user using SMS OTP, but continues to use Kerberos Constrained Delegation to ADFS.

In this case (typically), the UAG uses Radius authentication against some SMS OTP provider. The SMS OTP provider in turn uses some storage to look up and verify the user. Being a reseller, I use PointSharp ID, `http://www.pointsharp.com`, in much of my deployment, as an OTP provider service. I then use **Active Directory Lightweight Directory Services (AD LDS)** as storage for PointSharp ID.

FIM is then used to manage that storage, giving you the ability to get the same control of this service as you get for any other Identity stores managed by FIM.

Summary

It does not matter how you are managing your Office 365 identities, if you are Federating or not. FIM is a key component in all scenarios, as identity information's data quality is essential in all these scenarios.

In this chapter, we have seen how FIM is used to make sure that Office 365 users are managed correctly. We have seen how DirSync and Federation benefit from the increased identity information's data quality, which we can get from using FIM.

So, FIM increases our data quality. But how do I check the status of the data historically?

In the next chapter, we will look at FIM Reporting and see how we can track changes and create reports to, for example, show how a user has changed his role within the company over time.

9
Reporting

One of the new features in FIM 2010 R2 is built-in Reporting support. During the installation, we discussed the need for System Center Service Manager 2010 in order for Reporting to work.

Once you have managed to install and configure the SCSM environment, using the built-in Reporting feature is quite easy.

In this chapter, we will discuss the following:

- Verifying the SCSM setup
- Default reports
- The SCSM ETL process
- Looking at reports
- Modifying the reports

Verifying the SCSM setup

I usually start by looking at the SCSM Management Console and verify that the FIM settings are there. In *Chapter 3*, *Installation*, I showed you how to install the SCSM infrastructure. If you have an existing SCSM 2010 deployment that you are using, don't forget the post-installation step to run the FIM Post Install scripts for data warehouse.

Reporting

On the FIM Service server, where you have installed the FIM Reporting feature, start the System Center Service Manager console. It will ask you to connect to your SCSM Management Server:

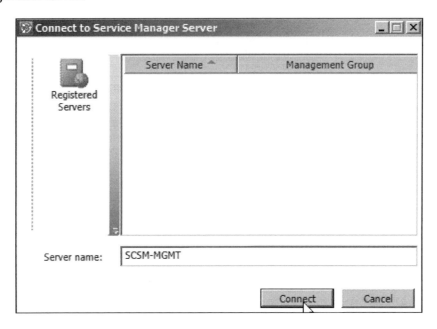

What usually happens (but not all the time) is that you will find that the **Reporting** node is missing in the navigation pane, as shown in the following screenshot:

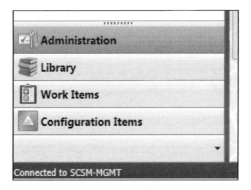

Don't worry! It just takes some time. On occasion, you might also need to restart the SCSM Management console for it to appear. I have not yet figured out what causes this issue. A few forums on the Internet are debating the cause, but so far no clear answer can be found.

But finally, you will see the **Reporting** tool and the default, **Forefront Identity Manager Reporting** reports.

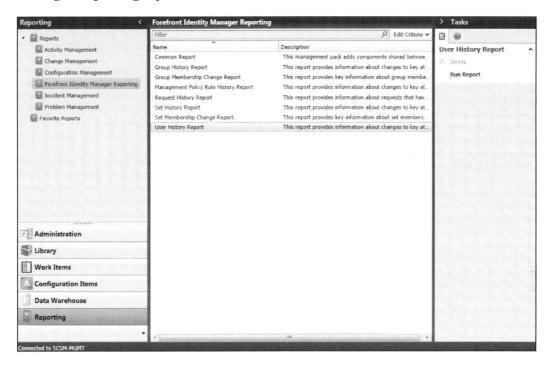

This at least shows us that FIM Reports are imported into SCSM; however, don't try them just yet! We have a few more things to do before we will have useful data in the reports.

Synchronizing data from FIM to SCSM

Before we can start generating any reports, we need to make sure that information is synchronized from the FIM Service database to the SCSM Data Warehouse. We can do this with the following steps:

1. Open up a PowerShell command window and navigate to `C:\Program Files\Microsoft Forefront Identity Manager\2010\Reporting\PowerShell`.

    This is the location of some PowerShell scripts you use to manage the Reporting feature.

2. On the SQL server used by FIM Service, you will find a SQL server Agent Job that is scheduled to run every 8 hours:

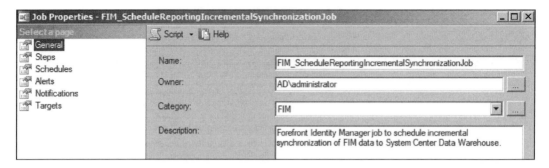

This, however, is running an incremental synchronization between the FIM and SCSM data warehouses.

3. Once we have decided that it is time to start using the Reporting feature, we need to run an initial synchronization. We do that by running the Start-FIMReportingInitialSync.ps1 PowerShell script from the Reporting folder of our FIM Service machine.

The feedback from this PowerShell script is nothing; it just kicks off a job, and you will have to check the status of that job manually.

4. In FIM Portal navigate to the **All Resources** section in the **Administration** panel, and search for **Reporting** resources:

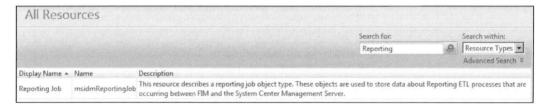

5. The **Reporting Job** resource will contain information about the manual and scheduled jobs transferring information from FIM to SCSM.
6. If you click **Reporting Job**, you will see all the reporting jobs in the order of old to new, so the newest one will be on the last page.

7. If you click on the **Created Time** column, you can reorder them so that the last one comes first. You can then open up the newest reporting job to verify the status:

If you look at the initial job you just started, you will see if it has been completed without errors. If the **Reporting Job Status** still shows as **Running**, just wait a few minutes and check the status again.

8. Once you have completed the initial sync job, you should also run an incremental job by firing the Start-FIMReportingIncrementalSync.ps1 script. Once that is completed successfully, you will soon have some reports to look at.

Default reports

The FIM Reporting service automatically installs management packs to create a number of reports. At http://technet.microsoft.com/en-us/library/jj133843, the default reports are described, but I have the information copied here for your convenience:

- **Group Membership Change report**: This report provides key information about group membership modifications in FIM, including the user account that approved the group change, the type of change, and any related requests or policy rules related to this change.

- **Set Membership Change report**: This report provides key information about set membership modifications in FIM, including account information about the user who joined or left a set, approvers (if any), and any related requests or policy rules related to this change.
- **Group History report**: This report provides information about changes to key attributes on group resources in FIM, including group filter, owner, type, domain, and membership.
- **Management Policy Rule History report**: This report provides information about changes to key attributes on management policy rule resources in FIM, including MPR type, principal set, and change type.
- **Request History report**: This report provides information about requests that have been committed to the database in FIM, including request originator, request target, approver account name, and any modified attributes.
- **Set History report**: This report provides information about the changes to key attributes on set resources in FIM, including set filter, change type, membership, and creator.
- **User History report**: This report provides information about changes to key attributes on user resources in FIM, including account name, e-mail, job title, and employee start/end date.

When looking at the default reports, many of my customers start to talk about how nice it would be to track user and group changes. In my opinion, however, the real power is within the **set** reports. If you look at how we configure FIM, the sets are the ones governing all our processes; therefore, tracking changes by looking at the Set Membership report is often very useful.

The SCSM ETL process

The **Extract, Transform and Load (ETL)** process refreshes the data in the warehouse. This is logically a sequential flow of data:

- The Extract job acquires data from registered management servers
- The Transform job optimizes the data for reporting needs and shapes the data according to the defined business rules
- The Load job populates the data mart for long-term retention and access

Our problem is that there will be no data in our reports until the ETL process has done its job. If you would like to speed up that process, you can save and run the following PowerShell script on your FIM Service server:

 Remember to change the $dwMachine value to the actual name of your SCSM DW server.

```
if (@(get-pssnapin | where-object {$_.Name -eq "SMCmdletSnapIn"}
).count -eq 0)
{
    Add-PSSnapin SMCmdletSnapIn
}

$dwMachine = "SCSM-DW"

Function WaitForId($id)
{
Write-Host ("Waiting on the job " + $id)
    do
    {
        $job = Get-SCDWJob -ComputerName $dwMachine
            -JobBatchId $id
        Start-Sleep -milliseconds 5000
        Write-Host (".") -nonewline
    }
    while ($job.EndTime -eq $null)
    Write-Host ("Job " + $id + " is done")
}

Function FindId($jobName)
{
    $job = Get-SCDWJob -ComputerName $dwMachine
        -JobName $jobName
    if($job.Status -eq "Running")
    {
        return $job.BatchId
    }
    else
    {
        return $null
    }
}

Function GetExtractJobNames
```

```
{
    $results = New-Object System.Collections.ArrayList
    $jobs = Get-SCDWJob -ComputerName $dwMachine
    foreach ($job in $jobs)
    {
        if($job.CategoryName -eq "Extract")
        {
            [void]$results.Add($job.Name)
        }
    }
    return $results;
}

Function RunJob($jobName)
{
    $currentId = FindId($jobName)
    if($currentId -ne $null)
    {
        Write-Host ("Waiting for the previous job " + $jobName)
        WaitForId($currentId)
    }
    Write-Host ("Starting the new job " + $jobName)

    Start-SCDWJob -ComputerName $dwMachine -JobName $jobName

    $currentId = FindId($jobName)
    if($currentId -ne $null)
    {
        Write-Host ("Waiting for the new job " + $jobName)
        WaitForId($currentId)
    }
}

Function RunETL()
{
    $extractJobs = GetExtractJobNames
    foreach($jobName in $extractJobs)
    {
        RunJob $jobName
    }
    RunJob "Transform.Common"
    RunJob "Load.Common"
}
```

```
if ( $dwMachine -eq $null)
{
Write-Error ( "IMT.DataWarehouse was not set ")
}
else
{
$start = Get-Date
RunETL
$end = Get-Date
$ts = New-TimeSpan -Start $start -End $end
Write-Host ("Took " + $ts.TotalMinutes + " total minutes for ETL")
}
```

 The script can also be found at http://technet.microsoft.com/en-us/library/jj133844.

Looking at reports

There are several ways of looking at the FIM reports. You can use the SCSM Management console, but you can also use the web interface of SQL Reporting Services.

Using the SCSM Management console (from the FIM Service server, for example) is a means for you, as an administrator, to verify if everything looks okay.

Reporting

It is not uncommon for the reports to be empty, with the message, **There is no data available for this report.**. This is due to the fact that, by default, the reports show data of the last three days.

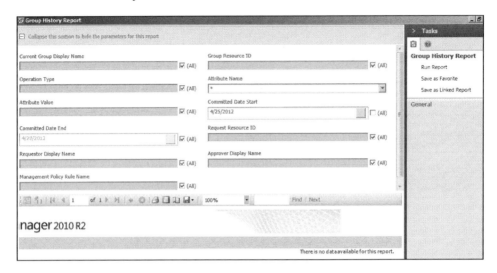

What you need to do is expand the **Parameter** section at the top of the console, and modify it to match your needs. Once you have done that, you can click **Run Report** in the **Tasks** pane to regenerate the report:

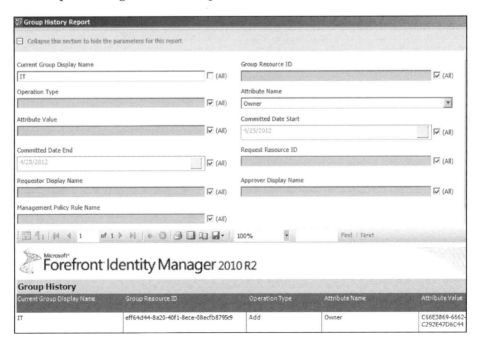

[290]

The aforementioned example shows a report filtered to show all events regarding the **Owner** attribute of the group, with the display name **IT**.

Another way to do this is to use the web interface of Reporting Services. This would typically be the way normal users would access the reports. However, if John (our manager) would like to look at the reports, and does not have sufficient permissions to do so, he will receive the error page shown in the following screenshot:

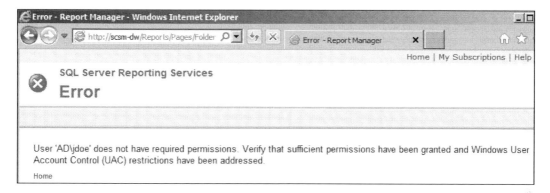

Allowing users to read reports

In order for selected users to read reports, we need to give them some permission on the Reporting server side.

Service Manager supports a delegation model for different user roles. However, if you want non-administrators to see and use specific reports, this is not possible using one of the default roles. To make that happen, we need to use the permission model of SQL Reporting Services.

Let's take a look at how we can give John (our manager) exclusive permission to only look at the **FIMUserHistory** report, and nothing else:

1. As an administrator, access the web interface of the Reporting Services server. In our example, that is `http://SCSM-DW/Reports`.
2. Navigate down the tree to **Forefront.IdentityManager.Reporting**.

3. Drop down the little menu to the right of the **FIMUserHistory** report, and select **Security**:

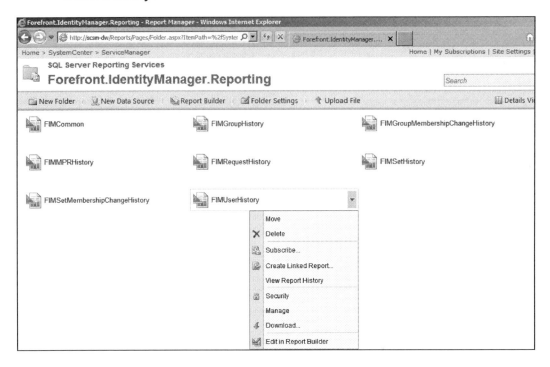

4. Click the **Edit Item Security** option to change the security setting for this particular report:

5. A warning appears, asking if you really want to have special permissions and to stop using the inherited security settings:

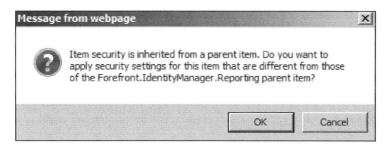

If we had wanted John to run all FIM Reports, we could have done this at the folder level instead.

6. After clicking **OK**, the user interface changes and allows you to assign new roles:

7. We can now click the **New Role Assignment** option, and give John the **Browser** role, which will give him permission to run this report:

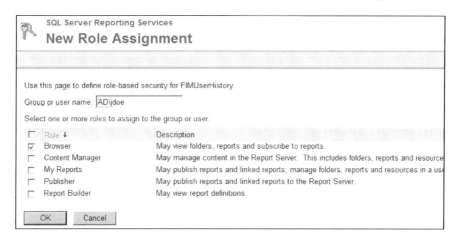

Reporting

As you can see, we have the opportunity to allow John to get additional roles as well. In most real cases, I would be using Active Directory Groups managed by FIM to assign these permissions, rather than assigning them to individuals.

One problem remains though. This does not allow John to access the default Report site and navigate himself down to the **FIMUserHistory** report. One way of solving that problem is to give him a direct URL to this report. Once he has that, he can access the **FIMUserHistory** report using his browser:

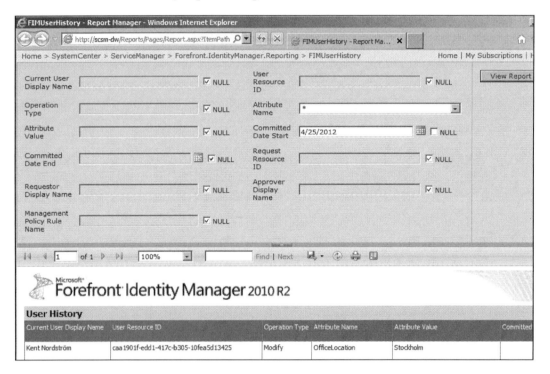

Modifying the reports

While FIM 2010 R2 provides reports based on the default FIM schema, you can also extend FIM Reporting to accommodate custom resources and attributes that you have created in the FIM schema, or customize the way the reports are displayed.

 For detailed guidance on extending FIM Reporting, see http://aka.ms/FIMReporting.

As mentioned earlier, the FIM Reporting service automatically installs several SCSM management packs to define the default FIM schema and reports. Once you have modified the FIM schema with new resources or attributes, you will need to create another management pack, so that SCSM is aware of the new resources.

The following is a summary of this process from the TechNet article at `http://technet.microsoft.com/en-us/library/jj133861`. It outlines the general process of extending FIM Reporting:

1. Create a new Schema management pack for SCSM, which contains definitions for the new schema elements.
2. Create a new FIM Reporting Binding file. A FIM Reporting Binding file is an XML file that is used to define the resource mapping between the data warehouse and FIM. A default binding file `DefaultBinding.xml` is installed with FIM and can be used as a template for your customized reports.
3. Using a PowerShell script, import the Schema management pack to the SCSM server.
4. Using a PowerShell script, import the FIM Reporting Binding file to the FIM server.
5. Using SQL Server Management Studio, create a new, stored procedure to return the data that you require for your report.
6. Create a new **Report Definition Language (RDL)** file using the stored procedure from the previous step. The RDL file defines how the report is structured and displayed to the end user.
7. Create a new Report management pack that uses the stored procedure and RDL file from the previous steps. This management pack will define a new report in the SCSM Service Manager console.

At this point, all the required customization work has been done. Next, you will run a PowerShell process that will:

1. Verify that the FIM and data warehouse schemas referenced in the FIM Reporting Binding file are valid and free of collisions.
2. Create management pack files (.MP) from the Schema and Reporting management packs that you created.
3. Bundle the .MP files and RDL files into a new management pack bundle.
4. Import the bundle into SCSM.
5. Import the FIM binding into FIM.

The last step is to synchronize the new management packs on the data warehouse.

This process instructs the data warehouse to look for any new management packs that have been added, create any new schema elements that have been defined, and deploy any new reports that have been defined.

Once the management packs have been synchronized, you must take the following steps to see if the new data appears in the data warehouse:

1. Run the FIM Reporting Initial-Partial ETL process. This will move the new schema elements, which you have just defined, over to the data warehouse.
2. Once that is complete, you may optionally start a FIM Reporting Incremental ETL process to pick up any changes that have occurred since Incremental ETL was last run.
3. Either start the SCSM ETL processes manually, or wait for a scheduled run to occur. Once a full cycle completes (Extract, Transform, and Load), you will see the data appear in the SCSM console or SSRS web view.

Summary

The FIM Reporting feature is a great way of tracking historical events relating to your FIM objects. But the setup dependency using the SCSM functionality for Data Warehousing and Reporting makes it hard to troubleshoot and get set up correctly the first time.

The use of standard SQL Server Reporting Services does, however, make it very easy to make your own custom reports and also to granularly define permissions around your reports.

We mentioned that we need to give John a way of finding his reports easily. One way would be to give him a link to the FIM Portal page. This and other FIM Portal modifications, I will show you in the next chapter.

10
FIM Portal Customization

Using the FIM Portal as an administrator to manage users or as a self-service portal for end-users will likely mean you would like to make some changes to UI. These can be easy things such as changing the logo or more complex things such as changing how the forms look and behave.

In every FIM project I have been involved with, at least some changes have been made. So learning how to make adjustments, is in my opinion, a must.

I will not cover all the possible ways you have for making changes to the FIM Portal in this chapter, but rather give some examples of things I usually run into in my customer projects, and some tips and tricks around them. Check out `http://aka.ms/CustomizeFIMPortal` to get a more complete guide on how to change everything.

In this chapter, we will take a quick look at how to:

- Modify the basic FIM Portal UI
- Customize search scopes
- Customize forms

Components of the UI

The Portal UI is composed of several different blocks, as described in the following screenshot:

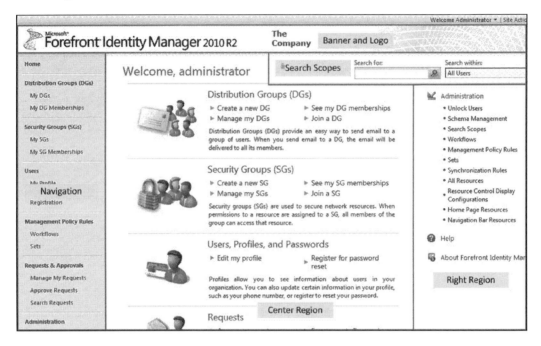

If you have ever worked with SharePoint, you will see some familiar stuff. One thing to remember though is that the FIM Portal is not *just another* SharePoint site; you will realize this as soon as you start to look at, for example, the forms we use in FIM.

But many of the graphical changes we can make are the same as in SharePoint.

In the upper-right corner, we will find some familiar menus if we have worked with SharePoint.

If we go into **Site Settings** and click on the **Site Theme** option, we will see that FIM installed its own SharePoint theme called **FIM**, which is used by the FIM Portal site.

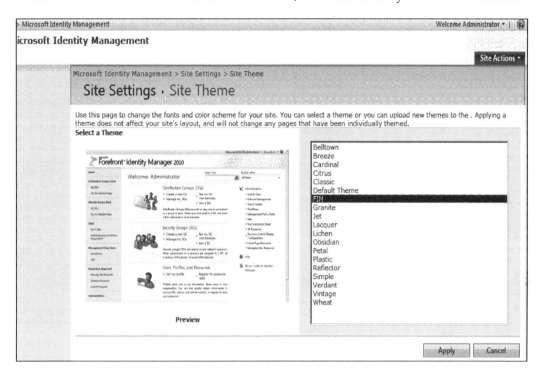

If you are thinking about trying to use another theme or trying to use this theme on other sites, forget it. I have made some tries in a few customer cases but have always realized the theme is quite specialized to use with the FIM Portal.

 If you are familiar with SharePoint, it would be easy to start making changes to **Site Settings** to modify the way the Portal looks. However, *do not!*

Changes should, as far as possible, be made using the FIM Portal interface, so that changes are stored in the FIM Service database and can be migrated and backed up.

But there are exceptions to this, of course. If you want to change the color scheme or other CSS-based items, you need to make modifications to the theme. How to do this and many other things is explained on `http://aka.ms/CustomizeFIMPortal`.

FIM Portal Customization

Then, we have the actual forms that we use to manage our objects like a user.

The forms are usually where projects spend most of the time during customization. It is quite common that customer demands force the project to build interfaces outside of the FIM Portal. If you need to build your own interface, you should visit http://fim2010client.codeplex.com, and you will find some useful components that you can use to communicate with the FIM Service.

In one of my bigger projects this last year, we built a wrapper WCF Service that exposed business usage of the FIM Service to internal applications, which needed to communicate with the FIM Service. In this way, the complexity of the underlying FIM Service was hidden, and also non-FIM Service functionality could be added.

Portal Configuration

All projects I have worked on have made some changes to the Portal Configuration. If we look at the Portal Configuration, we find some common settings to change.

Portal Configuration	
Common Attributes / **Extended Attributes**	
Branding Center Text The centered branding text that used by branding control	The Company
Branding Left Image * The left url image that is used by branding control	nages/MSILM2/logo.png
Branding Right Image * The right url image that used by branding control	~/_layouts/images/MSI
Global Cache Duration * This time how long the UI configuration element will be kept on the cache	86400
Is Configuration Type This is an indication that this resource is a configuration resource.	☐
ListView Cache Time Out * Specify the amount of time for the ListView cache to time out and expire.	120
ListView Items per Page * Specify the number of items to show per page in	30

The three branding settings are almost always changed, but sometimes settings such as **ListView Items per Page** are changed as well. At the bottom of the Portal Configuration form, you also have the **Time Zone** setting of the FIM Portal.

So what if we would like to change the logo in the upper-left corner that is **Branding Left Image**? We'll first take a look at the current value. It is `~/_layouts/images/MSILM2/logo.png`.

FIM Portal Customization

The ~ sign in the beginning is for showing that it is relative to the SharePoint site. The physical path of this file is `C:\Program Files\Common Files\Microsoft Shared\Web Server Extensions\14\TEMPLATE\IMAGES\MSILM2`.

So basically you have two options: you can either replace the `logo.png` file in the folder, or you can change the URL pointing to the image.

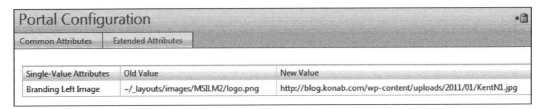

But after changing the setting, you will still see the old image in the UI. This is because many changes to the Portal UI require us to run **IISRESET** to make the changes visible.

Using an external URL as in my previous example will create a dependency to that external resource; but on the other hand, if you change the image in the folder, you need to make sure that the change is also made during disaster recovery or when scaling out the FIM Portal to multiple servers.

Best way? Well my very personal preference is to use an external URL, since I feel it is easier to maintain than the *local* files on the SharePoint server.

Navigation Bar Resource

Navigation bar resources are basically links we would like to expose in the Navigation section, on the left side of the Portal.

Display Name	Description	Parent Order	Order	Navigation Url
Administration		6	0	~/IdentityManagement/aspx/configuration/configuration
Approve Requests		5	2	~/IdentityManagement/aspx/requests/MyApprovals.aspx
Authentication Workflow Registration		3	3	~/IdentityManagement/aspx/authn/AuthNWFUserRegistr
Distribution Groups (DGs)		1	0	~/IdentityManagement/aspx/groups/DLs.aspx
Home		0	0	~/IdentityManagement/default.aspx
Manage My Requests		5	1	~/IdentityManagement/aspx/requests/MyRequests.aspx

Usually the URL points to a page within the FIM Portal, but you can also add external URLs if you like.

The **Order** and **Parent Order** attributes decide where they appear in the Navigation bar.

But if you look at one of them, for example the **Distribution Groups (DGs)** navigation bar resource, it has something called **Usage Keyword**.

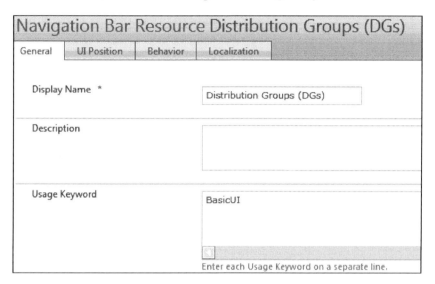

The value **BasicUI** in the **Usage Keyword** attribute means that the **Navigation Bar Resource** object will show up for all the users entering the Portal and not just for the administrators. This is why the Portal looks different when a user looks at it.

The **Usage Keyword** is a multivalued string attribute, with each entry delimited by a new line.

Portal administrators can use this attribute to customize which set of users can see which set of Navigation Bar resources, by following the given steps:

1. Create a set of Navigation Bar resources based on a particular **Usage Keyword** value.
2. Create a Management Policy rule, using this set to grant certain privileged users permissions to read these navigation bar resources.
3. To allow the same set of users to see a new **Navigation Bar Resource** object, you simply add that particular **Usage Keyword** to the new **Navigation Bar Resource** object. The new resource will automatically transit into the Navigation Bar set.

FIM Portal Customization

This is how the **BasicUI** usage keyword is also implemented.

If you look at **Sets**, in the FIM Portal there is one called **All Basic Navigation Bar Configurations**.

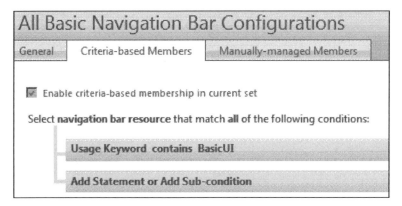

As you can see the criterion is **Usage Keyword contains BasicUI**.

This set is, in turn, part of a superset called **All Basic Configuration Objects**.

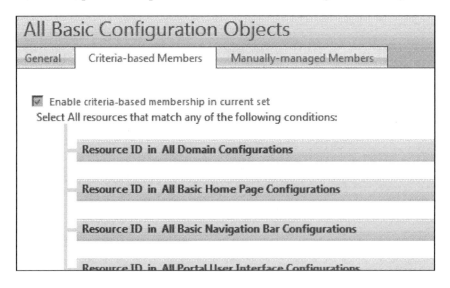

Chapter 10

Then there is an MPR, **General: Users can read non-administrative configuration resources**.

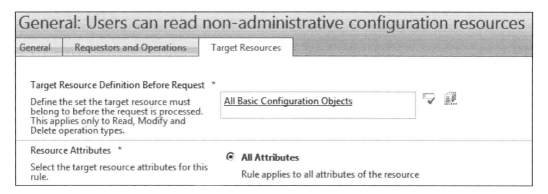

This allows the set **All Active People Read** on **All Basic Configuration Objects**.

If you recall from *Chapter 5, User Management*, this was one of the MPRs we needed to enable in order for a normal user to be able to view the FIM Portal.

The most common mistake when adding new navigation bar resources is that we forget to allow non-administrative users to see it.

Let's look at an example. Remember the report we wanted John (our manager) to have access to? Well we can just add that report as a Navigation Bar Resource for John to have access to, by following the given steps:

1. We need to decide where we want the new Navigation Bar item to appear. In my example, I would like it to appear below the **My Profile** item.

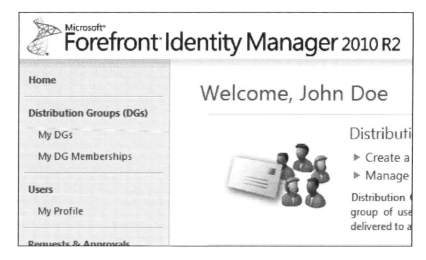

[305]

FIM Portal Customization

2. I therefore look at the **Parent Order** and **Order** attributes of that particular item. I can then see that my new item should have **Parent Order** 3 and **Order** 2, one below the **My Profile** navigation bar resource.

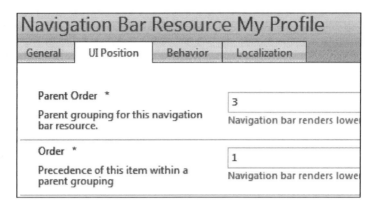

3. The **Display Name** attribute is the name we will see in the UI, so be careful not to give it so long a name that it will wrap in the UI. I then invent a *new* **Usage Keyword** attribute called ManagerUI. My intention is to use this to make sure only managers can see this **Navigation Bar Resource**.

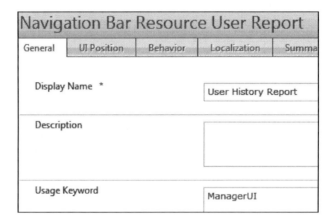

4. I place it at **Parent Order** 3 and **Order** 2. This will be below the **My Profile** navigation bar resource we checked earlier.

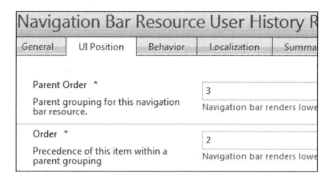

5. In the **Navigation Url** attribute we put the complete URL to the **User History Report** report.

6. We then need to create the set that will contain all our navigation bar resources with **Usage Keyword ManagerUI**. Create a set and give it a descriptive name such as **Company ManagerUI Resources**.

FIM Portal Customization

7. In the **Criteria** attribute for the set, we configure it to contain a Navigation Bar Resource where **Usage Keyword** contains **ManagerUI**. Make sure you click on **View Members** to verify that your newly created **Navigation Bar Resource** object appears.

8. One huge problem in this scenario is determining how the set allowing users to see this new **Navigation Bar Resource** should look. If we for example, would like to create a set called **Company Managers**, we could do it. But it is not possible to create a criterion that automatically takes all people, who are configured as managers of other people. One workaround would be to make this set manually-managed and create some workflow activity that updates this set automatically.

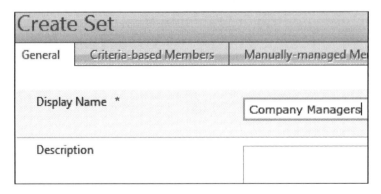

[308]

9. Finally, we need to create the MPR that allows the users in the **Managers** set to read the navigation bar resources in the **ManagerUI Resource** set. Give it a descriptive name. The **Type** option in this case is **Request**.

10. The requestor in this MPR is our **Manager** set. The **Operation** option is **Read resource** and we want to grant permission.

11. The target is our set of ManagerUI resources. For this type of MPR we usually give read access to **All Attributes**.

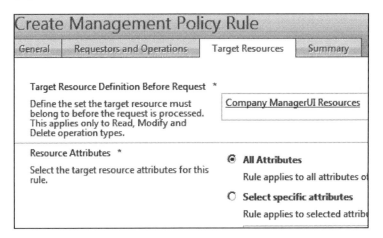

Once the MPR is created, John (our Manager) will have a new **Navigation Bar Resource** available when accessing the FIM Portal.

This was just one example to demonstrate how we can change navigation bar resources to customize the Navigation Bar.

As you can imagine there are always unique requirements in each project. And as the usage of FIM within a company evolves, the number of changes will increase.

Search scopes

In many of the interfaces of the FIM Portal there is an option to do searches.

If we go to **Users**, for example, we can search within **All Users**, and the result will be **All Users** and some of the properties of the users in columns.

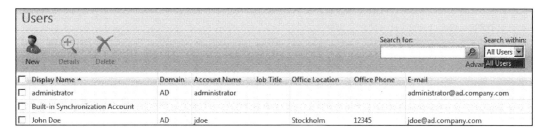

This is an example of a search scope. The name of the search scope is **All Users**. Let's take a look at this search scope.

Click on the **Search Scope** link in the **Administration** section of the FIM Portal, and search for **All Users** to find this particular search scope.

Usage Keyword

On the **General** tab we see the familiar **Usage Keyword** attribute again. Besides having the same purpose as the **Usage Keyword** attribute on the **Navigation Bar Resource** object, that is deciding who will be able to use the search scope, the **Usage Keyword** attribute on search scopes also decides where the search scope will appear.

The default list of keywords is described in the following table:

Keyword	Page where the Search Scope will appear
Global	Homepage
	When you use this Usage Keyword, either the GlobalSearchResult Usage Keyword or the Redirecting URL should be added. The default search result will direct the user to the Global Search Result page, which corresponds to GlobalSearchResult. If you do not add this Usage Keyword or Redirecting URL, the user will not see the results properly.
GlobalSearchResult	This is the search result page when a search is run from the homepage. (Also see keyword Global.)
AllDGs	All Distribution Groups
AllSecurityGroups	All Security Groups
MySecurityGroups	My Security Groups
MyDGs	My Distribution Groups
MySecurityGroupMemberships	My Security Group Memberships
MyDGMemberships	My Distribution Group Memberships
Security	Used in the Identity Picker to select members for a security group.
Distribution	Used in the Identity Picker to select members for a distribution group.
MailEnabledSecurity	Used in the Identity Picker to select members for an e-mail-enabled security group.
Customized	Used in any Identity Picker in the advanced detail view of a resource. By including this Usage Keyword, you include a generic list of search scopes, which will allow the user to search for all resources based on their resource types.
Forest	Used in the Identity Picker to select a forest configuration for a domain configuration.
Person	Users
AttributePicker	Used in the Identity Picker inside the Management Policy Rule Detailed View, to select an Allowed Attribute. It is also used in the Identity Picker to select Allowed Attributes for Filter Permission.
MyRequests	Manage My Requests
SearchRequests	Search Requests
MyApprovals	Approve Requests

Keyword	Page where the Search Scope will appear
Resource	All Resources
DeniedEmailTemplate	Used in the Workflow Definition detailed view in the Activity Definition UI when you create an owner approval activity. This is used in the Identity Picker for selecting Denied Email templates.
NotifictionEmailTemplate	Used in the Workflow Definition detailed view in the Activity Definition UI when you create an owner approval activity. This is used in the Identity Picker for selecting Notification Email templates.
TimeoutEmailTemplate	Used in the Workflow Definition detailed view in the Activity Definition UI when you create an owner approval activity. This is used in the Identity Picker for selecting Timeout Email templates.
SchemaObject	Used in all Schema pages, including All Resource Types, Attribute Types, and Bindings pages.

Search Definition

On the **Search Definition** tab, we will see how the search is made.

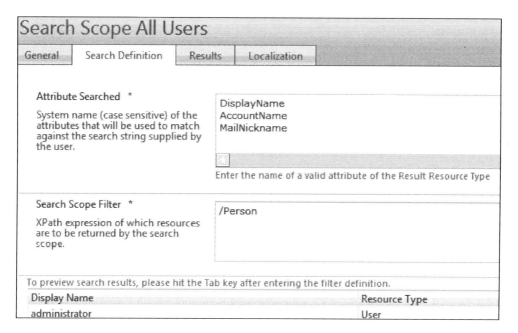

[313]

FIM Portal Customization

First we have the **Attribute Searched** field that defines the attributes that we can search for. If you would like to be able to search for other attributes, such as Employee ID, you need to add that attribute to the **Attribute Searched** attribute.

The **Search Scope Filter** is an **XPath** expression explaining which objects to return. In the All Users Search Scope it searches for all `Person` objects.

For a reference on how to write XPath queries, go to `http://aka.ms/FIMxPath`.

Results

The **Results** tab has three configuration options.

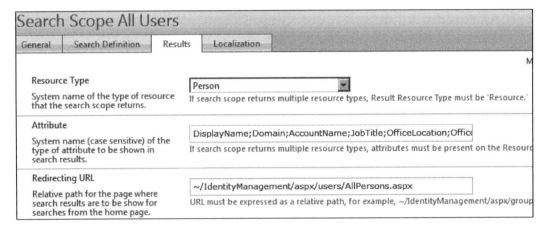

The configuration options are as follows:

- **Resource Type** will define the resource type returned. This is usually the same as the one used on the Search Scope Filter on the **Search Definition** tab, but in rare cases we would like to return multiple resource types. For example, when adding members to a group, it could be either a Person or a Group. In that case, we need to define the **Resource Type** on this tab to the base type `Resource`.
- **Attribute** is the list and order of the attributes returned. In the All Users Search Scope, I have always changed this in all my projects so far. Every customer has wanted some other columns to appear or to reorder them to fit their needs.
- The **Redirecting URL** is applicable if the search scope appears on the Home Page, and the search is made from the Home Page. We then need to define on which page the Result should be shown.

Creating your own search scope

In many projects we need to create our own search scopes. This could be because we changed the schema by adding attributes and/or resource types, or simply because we wanted to simplify some searches.

Let's look at a simple example. On the **Users** page, we would like to search for users within a Search Scope defined as **All Contractors**. That is, we would like to search only for people that are members of the set called **All Contractors**.

1. Navigate to the **Search Scopes** screen in the **Administration** section in FIM Portal.
2. Click on **New** to create a new search scope.
3. On the **General** tab, configure the **Display Name**; remember to keep it short. Regarding the appearance I only want the search scope to appear on the **Users** screen, and as I want it to appear for all users, I set the **Usage Keyword** attribute to BasicUI and Person. I give it the **Order** of 2 to appear right after All Users (which has the **Order** of 1).

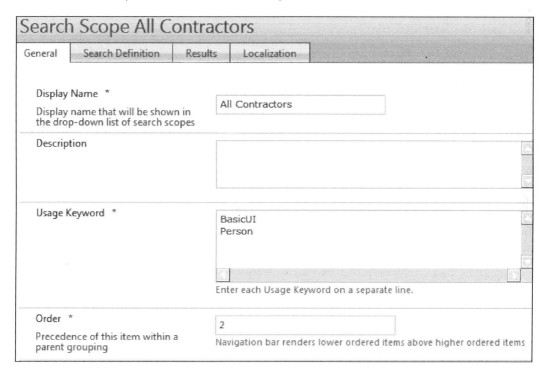

FIM Portal Customization

4. On the **Search Definitions** tab we define the search attributes and filter. For example, I make `AccountName` and `DisplayName` to be used for searching, but `FirstName` and `LastName` are also commonly used.

5. Then we have to define the **Search Scope Filter** attribute. We have two options in this example. We can define the filter the same way we defined the set **All Contractors**. If we look at the filter used in that set, it is defined as `/Person[EmployeeType=Contractor]`, but if we use that and later change the definition of members in the **All Contractors** set, we need to also remember to change the filter used in our Search Scope. I like the approach of using the set instead as a basis for my Search Scope Filter. The Search Scope Filter would then look like `/Person[ObjectID=/Set[ObjectID='479b9071-b9ad-48b6-b6fc-7c47237c7f51']/ComputedMember]`, where the GUID is the Resource ID of the set **All Contractors**. In this way, the search scope will show all the members in the set **All Contractors**, even if the set definition changes.

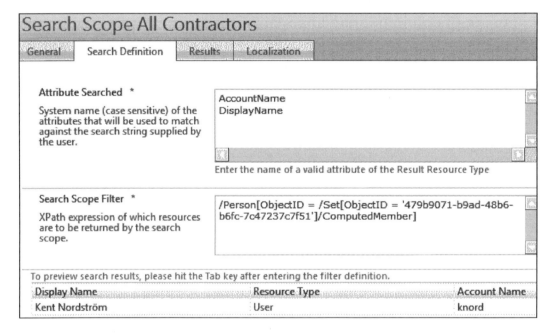

6. Finally, I define what the **Results** should look like. For simplicity, in this example, I give just three attributes in the result: `DisplayName`, `AccountName`, and `Manager`. Since I didn't configure it to show on the home page, I do not need to configure the **Redirecting URL** attribute.

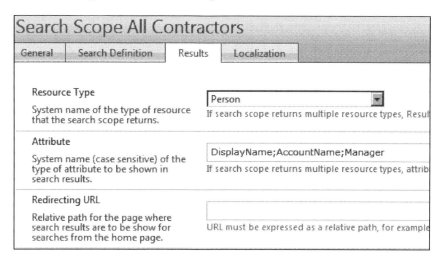

7. After a quick **IISRESET**, I make sure IIS picks up the new search scope at once, for me to test. Voilà! I can now search for **All Contractors**, and the result will show only members of the **All Contractors** set and my three defined attributes.

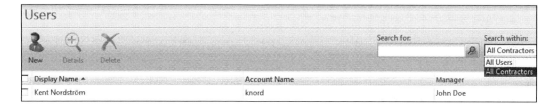

Filter Permissions

Filter Permissions are not so much about UI change, but they will affect how the UI behaves. Filter Permissions define which attributes we can use when defining filters for Sets and Groups.

Let's say you have added a new attribute to the schema called `Employee Status` and would like to create a set with all the users that have `Employee Status = Active`. Well this cannot be done, unless you add `Employee Status` to the correct **Filter Permission** object.

If we would like non-administrator users to be able to define this filter, we will need to add it to the **Non-Administrator Filter Permission** object. This is, however, not very common unless users can create dynamic groups.

Typically, the filters are changed by the administrators, after which we need to add the attribute to the **Allowed Attributes** list in **Administrator Filter Permission**.

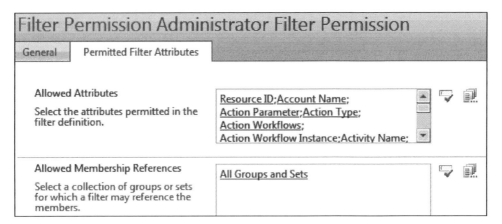

RCDC

RCDC is short for **Resource Control Display Configuration**. Don't ask me who came up with the name or why it got this name, but this is a form. Every form used in FIM to manage any kind of information is defined in what is called an RCDC.

All over the Internet, it is easy to find discussions on how to create and modify the RCDCs. I will give you some examples of typical changes I make to the RCDCs in my customer projects, but for a complete reference on the structure of the RCDCs, refer to `http://aka.ms/RCDCRef`.

Let's say we want to change how the form we get when looking at a user object looks. You then need to modify the RCDCs as per the following steps:

1. If you search for User RCDCs, you will find three. You will find three because we can define different forms depending on what kind of operation we are doing. So we have one for create, one for edit, and one for view. If we change the one for editing, it is most likely that we would also like to change the one for viewing, in a similar way.

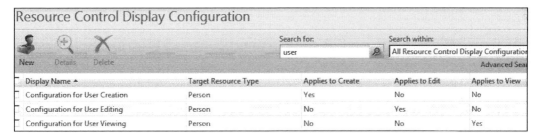

2. Open up the **Configuration for User Editing** RCDC. As you can see, it is not a graphical interface that will allow you to change the form.

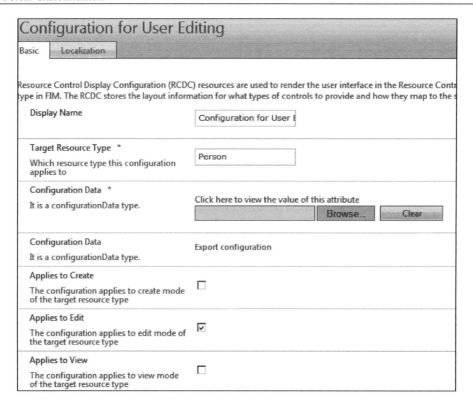

3. If you want to start editing the RCDCs, you need to make some preparations. I usually create a folder structure where I can export the configuration data, and make sure I keep backups in case I mess something up. It is very easy to make errors when working with RCDCs! So I say once again, keep backups!

4. You then click on the **Export configuration** link to export the RCDC to an XML file.

 If you are running this on a server, you might need to turn off the IE Enhanced Security Configuration in order to be able to download the XML.

5. When you download the file the default name is always configuration.xml for *all* RCDCs. So make sure you keep a track of what you are downloading, where you save it, and what you call it. Once you have downloaded it make sure to create a copy and make modifications to that one, to keep the originally working copy intact.

You can modify the RCDCs using Notepad, but I recommend that you use some XML-aware editor. I often use the Microsoft Visual Studio Tools for Applications myself, since I almost always have that one already on the Test/Dev FIM Server. It may then look like something similar to the following screenshot:

```xml
<?xml version="1.0" encoding="UTF-8" ?>
<my:ObjectControlConfiguration my:TypeName="UserProfileCodeBehind"
    xmlns:xsi="http://www.w3.org/2001/XMLSchema-instance"
    xmlns:my="http://schemas.microsoft.com/2006/11/ResourceManagement"
    xmlns:xd="http://schemas.microsoft.com/office/infopath/2003">
    <my:ObjectDataSource my:TypeName="PrimaryResourceObjectDataSource" my:Name="obje
    <my:ObjectDataSource my:TypeName="PrimaryResourceDeltaDataSource" my:Name="delta
    <my:ObjectDataSource my:TypeName="PrimaryResourceRightsDataSource" my:Name="right
    <my:ObjectDataSource my:TypeName="SchemaDataSource" my:Name="schema"/>
    <my:ObjectDataSource my:TypeName="DomainDataSource" my:Name="domain"/>
    <my:ObjectDataSource my:TypeName="TimeZoneDataSource" my:Name="timezone"/>
    <my:XmlDataSource my:Name="summaryTransformXsl" my:Parameters="Microsoft.Identit
    <my:XmlDataSource my:Name="regions">...</my:XmlDataSource>
    <my:Panel my:Name="page" my:Caption="%SYMBOL_EditUserPanelCaption_END%">
        <my:Grouping my:Name="caption" my:IsHeader="true" my:Caption="%SYMBOL_Caption
            <my:Control my:Name="caption" my:TypeName="UocCaptionControl" my:ExpandA
                <my:Properties>
                    <my:Property my:Name="MaxHeight" my:Value="32"/>
                    <my:Property my:Name="MaxWidth" my:Value="32"/>
                </my:Properties>
            </my:Control>
        </my:Grouping>
        <my:Grouping my:Name="BasicInfo" my:Caption="%SYMBOL_BasicInfoTabCaption_END%
            <my:Help my:HelpText="%SYMBOL_BasicInfoTabHelpText_END%" my:Link="01796f
            <my:Control my:Name="PhotoUpload" my:TypeName="UocFileUpload" my:Caption=
                <my:Properties>
                    <my:Property my:Name="MaxHeight" my:Value="100"/>
                    <my:Property my:Name="MaxWidth" my:Value="100"/>
                    <my:Property my:Name="Required" my:Value="{Binding Source=schema
```

Using Visual Studio allows you to add the RCDC schema to give you some intellisense and warnings when something is wrong. Henrik Nilsson has written a nice article about *Working with RCDCS in Visual Studio* at http://idmcrisis.com/post/2009/11/14/Working-with-RCDCe28099s-in-Visual-Studio.aspx.

The basic structure is not hard to understand if you know a little about XML. We have a `Panel` section that is our form. The panel has one or more `Grouping` sections corresponding to the tabs on the forms. And the `Grouping` section has controls, which contain the properties we would like to expose.

If you want to add a new attribute to be shown on a tab, I usually try to find some other attribute that has the same kind of control; `UocTextBox`, `UocDropDownList`, and so on. I then copy that control and modify it to point to the new attribute.

Once you have made the modifications you planned, save the XML file, and then go back to the RCDC UI and upload the new XML as configuration data.

In many of my projects there has been a need to modify the RCDCs in a way that we would like tabs to show only when a particular type of user is opened.

Let's take an example. Let us pretend that we would like a tab to show only if a user is a Consultant. What we need in order to make this happen is to have some Boolean attribute, `IsContractor` for example, on the user object, indicating that it's a consultant. We can then set the `my:Visible` property of the `Grouping` section to use that value. Instead of using `my:Visible="true"`, we would use something like `my:Visible= "{Binding Source=object, Path=IsContractor, Mode=TwoWay}"`.

This technique can also be used to hide specific controls if you like.

Just be prepared that, when starting to edit the RCDCs, you will have some trial and error before you get what you want, even if you have the RCDC reference guide beside you.

By now I also think you are wondering about all the values containing the `%SYMBOL_` prefix you see in the RCDC. These are pointers to the localized strings stored in the String Resources of the RCDC, as you can see on the **Localization** tab.

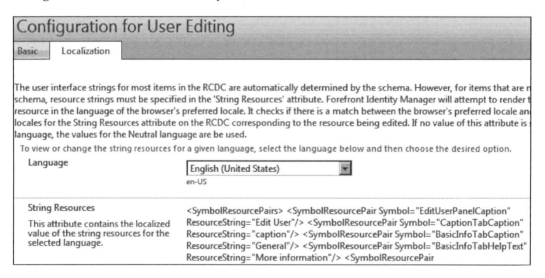

If you add your own attributes, and also need to support localization, you will also likely need to add some strings to the **String Resources** attribute in order for labels and other strings around your new attribute to appear in localized versions.

Summary

It is not easy to make changes to the FIM Portal, to make it better fitted for the tasks we will use it for. Just remember that UI changes are among the last things we do in an FIM project. First of all we need to make sure it works and then we can think about how we can change the UI to make the operation and usage of FIM easier.

The forms used in FIM have some limitations, but I usually try to convince my customers to use the FIM Portal first, before building a custom interface. In most cases, the cost for building the custom interface is too high compared to the gain in usability.

In this chapter I have showed some examples of typical changes made to the UI of the FIM Portal. We have seen how navigation bar resources and search scopes can dramatically change the look and operation of the FIM Portal depending on who the user is. I have also showed how difficult it is to modify the forms and RCDCs used in the FIM Portal.

As we have discussed in this chapter, it is quite common to customize the FIM Portal. In a typical FIM deployment, it is as common as customizing the data that FIM works with as well. In the next chapter we will take a look at how we can customize data transformations by using PowerShell, *classic* extensions, and SSIS.

11
Customizing Data Transformations

We have so far been able to solve our problems using built-in functionality in FIM. But in many cases the data you are managing is not structured or formatted in a way that FIM can manage.

I have so far showed you how to build a couple of synchronization rules, and we have used a few of the out of the box *functions* available in FIM. For a complete list of all FIM functions available in synchronization rules, please take a look at `http://aka.ms/FIMFunctions`.

What we will find is that the built-in functionality will not cover all our needs. In this chapter we will look at:

- Discussing the overall need and options for data transformation
- An example when managing Microsoft Lync
- Selective deprovisioning
- The case with strange roles

Our options

There are many different ways in which we can modify the data to fit our needs. I will show a few of the most common ones I use in my customer projects, but every project has unique requirements and also a unique set of competences which will govern the options we choose.

Customizing Data Transformations

When working with FIM, there are several places where data transformations can happen. They are as follows:

- At the Connected Data Source using, for example, an advanced SQL view
- During Import and Export using, for example, a custom Management Agent
- At inbound and outbound synchronization using both declarative and non-declarative synchronization rules
- In the FIM Service using workflows

Since we have the workflow engine in the FIM Service, you will find many examples of how to modify data using workflow activities. However, do keep in mind that using the synchronization engine will maintain data consistency in a way that is very hard to do using workflows.

PowerShell

If you look around the Internet, you will find many examples of PowerShell Workflow activities and PowerShell Management Agents.

If you do not have .NET development competence within the project, using PowerShell might be a good solution to manage data. Even if you have .NET competence, it may be that using PowerShell to solve the problem is the most cost-effective way.

Later in this chapter, I will show you an example of using PowerShell to manage Microsoft Lync users. We discussed this a little bit in *Chapter 8, Using FIM to Manage Office 365 and Other Cloud Identities*, when discussing managing cloud identities.

Classic rules extensions

I have focused in this book on how to use the new, declarative synchronization available in FIM rather than showing how to use non-declarative, *classic* synchronization used in MIIS and ILM.

But in some cases, using *classic* rules extensions, the way we have done for many years in MIIS and ILM, is the most effective way of solving a problem related to data transformations.

In this chapter, I will show you an example where we will use *classic* rules extensions to manage multivalued attributes in the Lync scenario. But there are numerous occasions when using classic rules extensions is the quickest way of solving odd data management problems.

SSIS

SQL Server Integration Services (SSIS) is a great tool to use when you need to modify the structure of data or read/write to odd data sources.

In many of my projects I prefer to use SSIS instead of having to build a custom Management Agent. The reason for this, is that in many cases I can solve the problem of using SSIS without having to write any code. You can then use the standard SQL MA in FIM to access the data.

But again it comes down to the competence you have within your company or within your project.

When starting a new **Integration Services Project**, we can examine the **Toolbox**, and we will find many out of the box, data transformation tools, which can be used without having to write code.

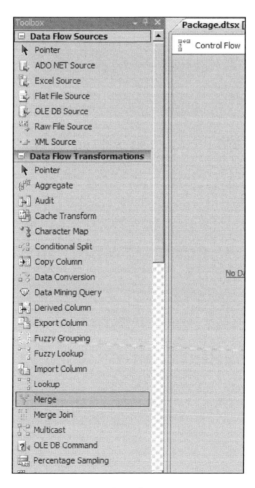

SSIS also allows you to add code activities. I have, for example, used this capability of SSIS in a project where photos needed to be scaled before importing them into FIM.

When doing exports in FIM, we have learned that we only do *delta* exports. Using SSIS, you can easily make a *full* export if the CDS requires it.

Another example of how to use SSIS, which I have in a customer solution, is to have SSIS create a CSV text file and send it using FTP to a remote data target.

Later in this chapter, there is an example where I have used SSIS to solve the problem with strange roles.

Workflow activities

In all the steps a request to the FIM Service is passing. We recall that there were three Workflow kickoffs; the authentication, authorization, and action workflows. For each workflow, we can create our own custom activities.

On the market today, there are several third-party workflow activities for FIM. In projects where I am subcontracted by MCS (Microsoft Consulting Services) I use a Workflow Activity Library with a bunch of nice functionalities, such as creating unique usernames and e-mail addresses, or generating complex passwords, among other things.

If you would like to start creating your own workflow activities, start off by looking at the simple example at `http://aka.ms/FIMWALExample`. From the example you will learn how to create your own Workflow Activity Library and how to add a logging activity.

Extensible Connectivity Management Agent

If you want FIM to talk to a data source for which no Management Agent exists, you can create your own Extensible Connectivity MA. The PowerShell MA I demonstrate in the *Managing Lync* recipe later in this chapter is an example of an Extensible Connectivity MA.

Lately, Microsoft has released the **Extensible Connectivity MA 2.0 (ECMA 2.0)** framework. If you are new to this and would like to get started on creating your own ECMA 2.0 MA, I suggest you take a look at `http://aka.ms/ECMA2`. There you will find some basic information about ECMA 2.0, as well as some code examples.

As with many other things, there are plenty of third-party MA suppliers. The FIM community tries to keep an up-to-date list on http://aka.ms/FIMPartnerMA. Here you can find many MAs; make sure you check it out before starting to develop your own.

Managing Lync

Microsoft Lync is one example where management cannot be made using built-in capabilities in FIM. As we saw in *Chapter 5, User Management*, the AD MA has some built-in functionalities to cover some Exchange management. And even though Lync also uses AD as its main source of information, the AD MA in FIM has no knowledge of Lync.

There are basically two problems we need to solve. They are as follows:

- Unlike with Exchange, as discussed in *Chapter 5, User Management*, FIM has no built-in, Lync *provisioning* capability. We need to add that capability. I will show you an example of how to use PowerShell to solve this problem.
- We need to manage the proxyAddresses attribute in AD. This is a multivalued attribute, and FIM does not have any built-in functions to do advanced management of multivalued attributes. I will show you how to use non-declarative, *classic* rules extension to manage the proxyAddresses attribute.

Provision Lync Users

Provisioning in a Lync perspective is to run a PowerShell command to enable a user for Lync. The command used is Enable-CsUser. In order for this command to be successful, the user object in Active Directory needs to be present.

The case that we use as an example here, used the mail address to also be the SIP address. In order for FIM to be able to enable and disable Lync users, we need to use a PowerShell MA. In this particular case, I added a Boolean attribute LyncEnabled to the FIM schema and used that to control the Lync users.

I used the PowerShell MA developed by Søren Granfeldt. We talked about this one in *Chapter 8, Using FIM to Manage Office 365 and Other Cloud Identities*, as well. More information on this MA can be found at http://aka.ms/PowerShellMA. However, any PowerShell MA should do.

Customizing Data Transformations

My strategy in this particular case was to use the Active Directory MA to flow the main part of the attributes and only manage a minimum number of attributes using the PowerShell MA.

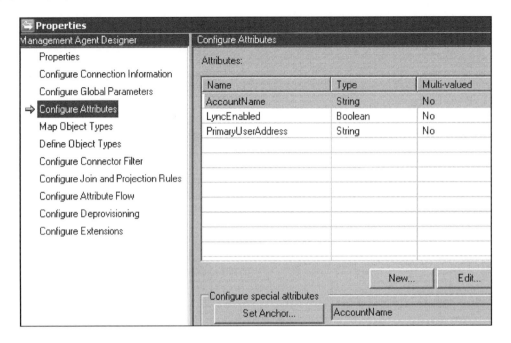

The idea was to use this MA to export the `LyncEnabled` value from FIM, to control the enabling and disabling of Lync, and to import the SIP address generated by Lync. So the outbound attribute flow had `LyncEnabled->LyncEnabled` and the inbound attribute flow had `PrimaryUserAddress->companySIP`. FIM was not configured to provision users to this MA, so instead I imported the users and joined them to the existing MV object based on **AccountName**, corresponding to the `sAMAccountName` attribute in AD.

I then created the PowerShell scripts required to import the data, and manage the enabling and disabling of the Lync user. The logic in the PowerShell scripts managing the export was quite simple. If `LyncEnabled` was `true` from FIM, call `Enable-CsUser` else call `Disable-CsUser`.

The key PowerShell commands look as follows (not a complete script, but just a snippet):

```
If ($LyncEnabled) {
Enable-CsUser -Identity $AccountName –RegistrarPool $LyncPool -
SipAddressType EmailAddress
}
Else {
Disable-CsUser -Identity $AccountName
}
```

Since I extended the schema with the `LyncEnabled` attribute, the problem was then reduced to deciding how to manage this attribute. At the time of my writing this, the customer used the FIM Portal to manage this attribute manually, since the Lync project was still running only for pilot users.

By adding attributes to the flow, it is quite easy to extend the attributes managed by the PowerShell MA. In larger Lync environments it is likely that you would also need to manage the `$LyncPool` attribute used in the previous PowerShell snippet. In this case they only had one pool, making it a constant in my PowerShell scripts. We might also have a need for more complex SIP address generation, if the e-mail address is not matching the SIP address.

Managing multivalued attributes

Managing multivalued attributes in FIM is sometimes challenging, and requires some coding or other special arrangements. The problem is that FIM does not contain functions to do advanced management of multivalued attributes.

One of the most common multivalued attributes FIM is managing is the `proxyAddresses` attribute in Active Directory. The `proxyAddresses` attribute is used by both Exchange and Lync to store the e-mail and SIP addresses a user has. In the case of Lync, the challenge is that we would like to add the SIP address to the `proxyAddresses` attribute in AD.

If you look at all the functions FIM has built-in (http://aka.ms/FIMFunctions), you will find none that operates by adding to or removing values from multivalued attributes. We need to add that functionality.

I will show you one way, but believe me when I say that there are numerous ways of solving this problem. But this is how I solved it for one of my customers.

The scenario with this particular customer is that FIM should *only* manage the SIP addresses in the `proxyAddresses` collection without messing up the other values.

Customizing Data Transformations

The solution in this case was to use non-declarative, *classic* rules extensions instead of declarative ones when managing this attribute. What this means is that I added some synchronization code to the synchronization engine instead of writing a custom workflow activity to use in the FIM Service.

In order for us to call custom code in the attribute flow of the synchronization engine, we need to add a rules extension `dll` to our solution and configure the Management Agent to use it. But if we look at the Management Agent of Active Directory on the **Configure Extensions** page, the option to select a **Rules extension name:** attribute is greyed out.

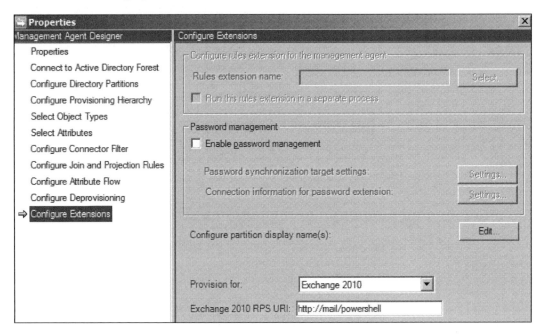

The reason is that we need to first define something that is in need of the extension. One such need could be that we use an **Advanced** attribute flow.

In this scenario when managing `proxyAddresses`, we need to add an attribute flow that uses an **Advanced** attribute flow requiring a Management Agent Rules Extension.

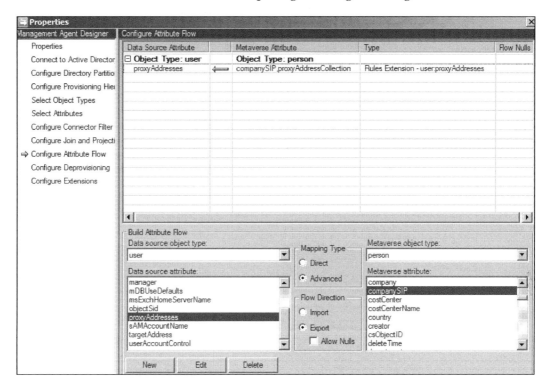

Since we have not talked about how to add these kind of classic attribute flow rules earlier in this book, it might need some explanation. To create the flow rule you see in the previous screenshot, I have added the attribute `companySIP` to the MV schema, after which you need to do the following:

1. Select **user** as **Data source object type**.
2. Select **person** as **Metaverse object type**.
3. In the **Data source attribute:** list select **proxyAddresses** (if it is not listed, you first need to add it to the list of attributes on the **Select Attributes** page in the MA).
4. In the **Mapping Type** setting, select **Advanced**.
5. In the **Flow Direction** setting, select **Export**.
6. In the **Metaverse attribute:** list select **companySIP**, and while pressing the *Ctrl* key on the keyboard, select **proxyAddressCollection** (the *Ctrl* key allows you to make multiple selections).

Customizing Data Transformations

7. When all the selections are done, click on the **New** button.

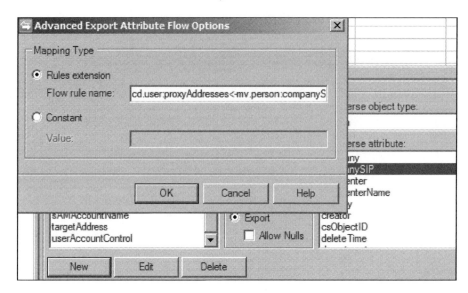

8. Change or note the **Flow rule name:** value. I usually change this to only the *target* name. In this case I have changed it to **user:proxyAddresses** by removing the rest of the name. When we later go into Visual Studio to build our `dll`, you will find why a less complex rule name is better.

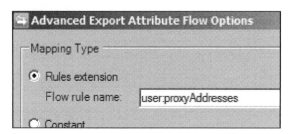

9. Click on the **OK** button, and you're done.

Once we have configured at least one attribute flow rule that uses the **Mapping Type** setting of **Rules extension**, the UI on the **Configure Extensions** page of the MA is changed.

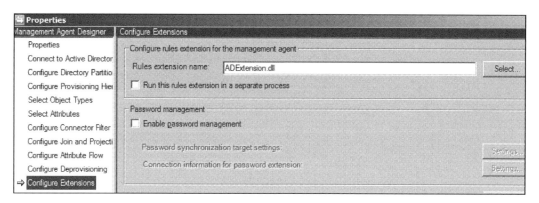

The UI suggests that the name of the extension `dll` should be **ADExtension.dll**; this is the default naming standard of using the MA name followed by `Extension.dll`. But we can choose whatever name we like, because as you might realize, this `dll` does not exist yet!

So our next goal is to produce this `dll` and put it into the extensions folder used by the Synchronization service. The default path of this folder is `C:\Program Files\Microsoft Forefront Identity Manager\2010\Synchronization Service\Extensions`.

There are a number of requirements on the `dll` in order for the Synchronization service to be able to use it, so the easiest way of creating the Visual Studio project required to build the `dll` is to have the Synchronization Service Manager create it for you.

Customizing Data Transformations

After creating the project, you then need Visual Studio to modify it. We have that on our FIM-Dev server where all the development is taking place. Follow the given steps to create the project:

1. In the **Actions** menu of the Synchronization Service Manager, we have the ability to **Create Extension Projects**.

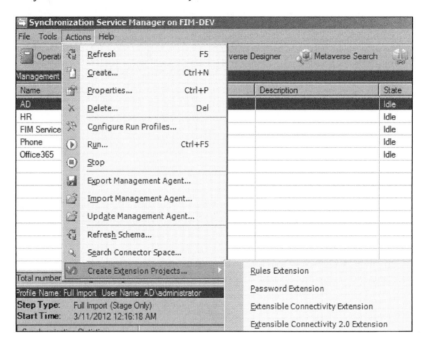

2. The Synchronization Service Manager will then create a project using the **Programming language** selection, VB or C#, and in the **Project location** you chose.

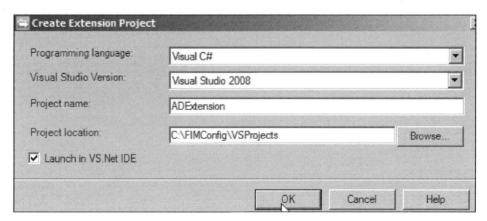

The project created will have settings which will make new builds that need to be made to the default Extensions folder; this makes testing of the code on the FIM-Dev environment easier.

If you need to debug your code, you will do this by attaching the debugger to the FIM Synchronization Service process (**miiserver.exe**). See `http://aka.ms/DebugExtension` for more information and details on how to debug your extension.

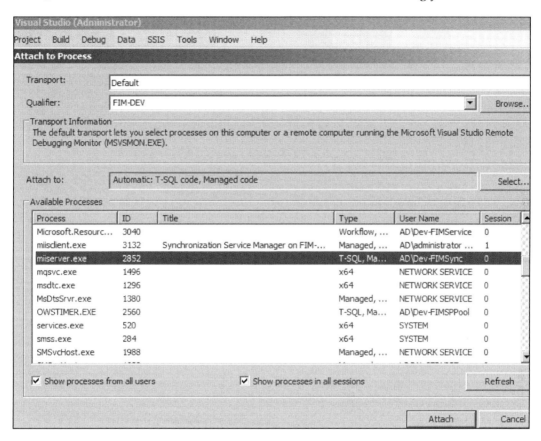

Once you have attached the debugger to the correct process, you can use the preview function in the Synchronization Service Manager to run your synchronization and put breakpoints into your code to find out why it is not working as expected.

If you need to debug the code you have to remember to launch Visual Studio with elevated privileges (**Run as administrator**).

Customizing Data Transformations

If you are looking on the Internet for help on how to work with Extensions, make sure you search for information regarding the older versions, ILM and MIIS, since using extensions was the main solution to add logic before FIM.

 When coding rules extensions, it is vital that we have good error management in the code since we might cause the synchronization job to stop if we make some mistakes in the code.

But let's take a look at some of the parts in the code (I use C# in my example) to help you on the way:

```
void IMASynchronization.MapAttributesForExport (string FlowRuleName,
MVEntry mventry, CSEntry csentry)
        {
            switch (FlowRuleName)
            {
                case "user:proxyAddresses":
```

Since we are doing *outbound* synchronization in our example, the code should go into the `IMASynchronization.MapAttributesForExport` method of our code.

The Synchronization engine will send the **Flow rule name** value to the code, to tell which synchronization rule we are handling. Now you realize why I usually shorten the **Flow rule name** value.

Usually we use a `switch` statement to separate the code blocks managing different rules. We then use the `FlowRuleName` parameter to make sure we run the correct code, depending on what attribute flow we are processing. You can now see why the shorter name `user:proxyAddresses` makes your code easier to write and read.

If we just need to add a value, we can use something like the following line to add a value to a multivalued collection:

```
csentry["proxyAddresses"].Values.Add(mventry["companySIP"].Value);
```

But usually we would need to add some logic that ends up with code, as follows:

```
Microsoft.MetadirectoryServices.Value existingSIP = null;

foreach (Microsoft.MetadirectoryServices.Value Items in
csentry["proxyAddresses"].Values)
{
 string strValue = Items.ToString().ToLower();
 if (strValue == mventry["companySIP"].Value.ToLower())
   {
     //Value already exists so let's skip the rest
```

```
    break;
  }
  else if (strValue.Contains("sip:"))
  {
    //There is an existing SIP address that we should remove.
    existingSIP = Items;
  }
}
//When finished walking through the collection we can add the new
value and remove any existing

if (existingSIP != null)
{
 //There is an old SIP address to remove
 csentry["proxyAddresses"].Values.Remove(existingSIP);
}

if (mventry["companySIP"].IsPresent)
{
 //We have a SIP address to add
 csentry["proxyAddresses"].Values.Add(mventry["companySIP "].Value);
}
break;
```

This is just to show you how it could look when starting to write your own rules extensions. Once again, please remember that there are other ways of solving problems like this, and each case is unique. This just happened to be the way I solved it in one of my projects.

Selective deprovisioning

The term **deprovisioning** is often used when talking about deleting objects in some CDS (Connected Data Source). But deprovisioning is much more than just that.

Carol Wapshere has written a great article explaining our options about deprovisioning. Go to http://aka.ms/FIMDeprovisioning and read it before you start using the option to deprovision.

A typical scenario related to what we have discussed in this book may be that we would like FIM to delete obsolete distribution groups in Active Directory based on some policy. But we do not want FIM to delete users or security groups in AD even if some FIM administrator makes a mistake in the FIM Service configuration.

We need to use code to make the decision.

Customizing Data Transformations

On the **Configure Deprovisioning** page of our AD MA, instead of having **Stage a delete on the object for the next export run**, we use the option **Determine with a rules extension**.

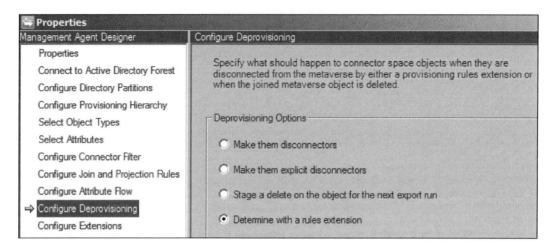

This means we need to make use of another method, `DeprovisionAction IMASynchronization.Deprovision (CSEntry csentry)`, in our `MA Extension.dll` DLL we talked about earlier in this chapter.

This method is called when a *CSEntry* is disconnected from its *MVEntry*. In this we can now have code logic checking the object type before setting the action that FIM should perform. For distribution groups, we can return the action `DeprovisionAction.Delete`, but for the other object types we can return `DeprovisionAction.Disconnect`.

This is, however, not the only place where deprovisioning actions can be triggered. Again, read `http://aka.ms/FIMDeprovisioning` before you decide how, when, and where deprovisioning should take place.

The case with the strange roles

This is an example where I used SSIS to solve a problem where the data structure in the data source did not meet the requirements of FIM. I then used SSIS to transform the data into a structure easily used by FIM.

The information in this case was defined in a database with two tables, of which one table contained information about the organizational units within the company.

OrgUnits	
OrgID	Name
101	Sales
102	Marketing

The other table contained information about the roles users had within each organizational unit. The screenshots are just showing an example and are not the actual roles and units that my customer was using.

Roles		
OrgID	RoleID	UserID
101	Manager	Mary
101	Secretary	John
102	Secretary	Lisa

The goal was to create groups in Active Directory with the users as members. But they didn't just want the organizational units as groups. They also wanted one group for each unique role within a specific organizational unit.

So the goal was to use SSIS to structure this data into the FIM-optimized structure you have seen in the HR database at The Company in this book.

From the small amount of previous example data, we would like to end up with two tables, one containing the objects and one containing the multivalued attribute members.

The `Objects` table would look like the following figure:

Objects	
ObjectID	ObjectType
101	group
102	group
Manager	group
Secretary	group
101_Manager	group
101_Secretary	group
102_Secretary	group
Mary	user
John	user
Lisa	user

Customizing Data Transformations

The MV table would look like the following figure:

MVData		
ObjectID	**Attribute**	**Member**
101	member	Mary
101	member	John
102	member	Lisa
Manager	member	Mary
Secretary	member	John
Secretary	member	Lisa
101_Manager	member	Mary
101_Secretary	member	John
102_Secretary	member	Lisa

As you can see, we have some data transformation to do in order for this to work.

One option would have been to create a custom Management Agent, but I decided to use SSIS instead, since the customer already had knowledge about SSIS among their database administrators.

Filling the Objects table is the easy part of this task. We just need to use the **Sort Transformation Editor** tool in SSIS, since it contains a function to remove duplicates, making sure we only add unique values from the Roles table. I also use some merging and adding of columns. When running the debug run on my SSIS project, I get the following output:

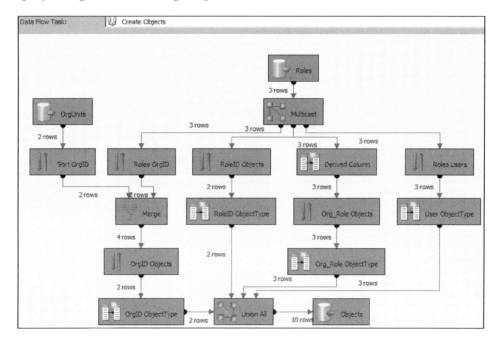

It is quite easy to follow the flow and notice any errors. This is one thing I like about SSIS! In order for me to get the Role objects read, I read the different sorts in different flows, before merging it all into one `Objects` table. If you are wondering about my double reading of organizational units, it was because the data quality of the sources sometimes made new organizational units appear in either of the two tables.

This is not the only way I could have solved it using SSIS. I know that many people out there who are experts on SSIS will argue that there are more efficient ways of solving my problem. But I am just happy I could solve it in a quick way. Building an SSIS package like the previous one takes about an hour's work. Building any kind of custom code and maintaining it, I would argue, would be much less cost effective.

After creating the `Objects` table, it is time to create the `MVData` table showing the memberships in each group object.

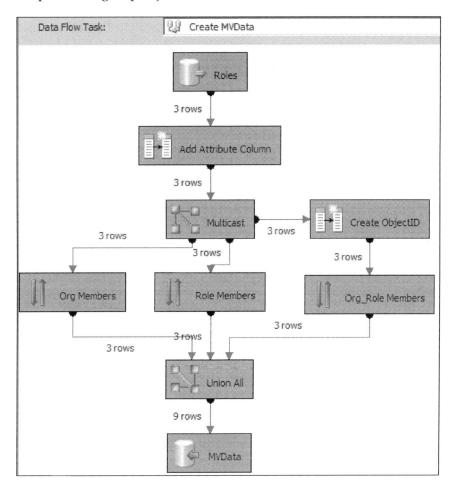

Customizing Data Transformations

The three different group types we should generate end up with three members each.

In the following **Sort Transformation Editor** tool ,you see how I transform the input columns to the output columns, which I need in the target table. The following screenshot is from the **Org Members | Sort Transformation Editor** tool:

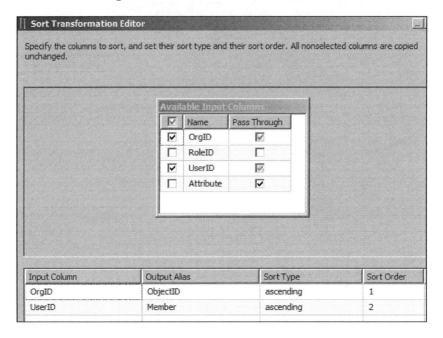

In the previous example, I only *fill* the **Objects** and **MVData** tables, but in order to do so, the full flow of the tasks also contains clearing the tables before refilling them.

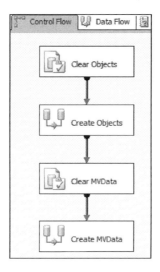

In many cases when using SSIS you cannot use the *clear-and-fill* flow approach I used in the previous example; you need to store the new data and update the existing data. In these cases, I use the **Lookup** tool to find out if it's a new record or if I need to update an existing record using the **OLE DB Command** tool.

Now that we have filled our `Objects` and `MVData` tables in SQL, it is a piece of cake to just create a standard SQL MA in FIM to import this group information in the same way that we discussed in *Chapter 6, Group Management*, maybe by joining existing users and groups in the MV if they already exist.

Summary

It is very rare to have a FIM project where the data in all CDSs (Connected Data Sources) are structured in a way that can be easily consumed and managed by FIM.

You will often need to use one or several of the transformation ways we have discussed in this chapter. I am personally a friend of limiting the code base in the FIM implementations, since I believe the cost of maintaining this code over time is often underestimated. This is why I have grown fond of using SSIS lately. SSIS is today a really powerful tool when it comes to data transformations.

In this chapter we have seen examples of how PowerShell, non-declarative, classic rules extensions, and SSIS can be used to transform data, making it manageable by FIM.

In the next chapter, we will take a look at the *outcast* member of the FIM products, FIM Certificate Management. It is time to show how FIM can be used to manage Smart Cards.

12
Issuing Smart Cards

We have earlier stated that FIM CM is the outcast of the FIM product family. In this chapter, we will take a look at how we can use FIM CM to issue Smart Cards. FIM CM is not a requirement for starting to use Smart Cards, but as you will see, FIM CM will add a lot of functionality and security to the process of managing the complete lifecycle of your Smart Cards.

In this chapter, we will look at:

- How to run the FIM CM configuration wizard
- Installing and configuring the FIM CM CA files
- An example of allowing a manager to enroll a certificate on behalf of a consultant

Our scenario

FIM CM can be used in many ways, but to show you a little bit about how we can use its basics, *The Company* will use it to allow managers (like John) to issue Smart Cards to consultants (like Kent).

For reference purposes I give you, once again, the FIM CM overview image I showed you in *Chapter 2, Overview of FIM 2010 R2*:

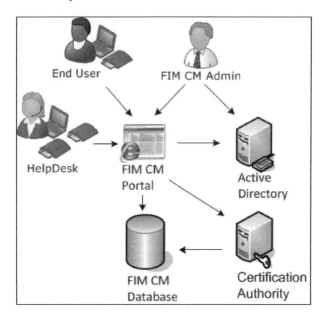

We have also, in *Chapter 3, Installation*, discussed how to install the FIM CM website. But with that we have only just begun our FIM CM deployment. So, let's move on and take a good look at FIM CM.

Assurance level

When discussing **PKI (Public Key Infrastructure)** and Smart Cards, you usually need to have some discussion about what level of assurance you would like for the identities secured by your PKI.

For some basic insight on PKI and assurance, please have a look at http://aka.ms/CorePKI.

In typical scenarios, many PKI designers will argue that you should use **HSMs (Hardware Security Modules)** to secure your PKI, in order to get the assurance level to use Smart Cards. My personal opinion in this discussion is that HSMs are great if you need high assurance on your PKI, but Smart Cards will increase your security even if your PKI has medium or low assurance.

Using FIM CM with HSM will not be covered in this book, but if you take a look at http://aka.ms/FIMCMandLunaSA, for example, you will find some guidelines on how to use FIM CM and the HSM Luna SA.

The Company actually has a low-assurance PKI, with only one enterprise root CA issuing the certificates as well. *The Company* does not use any HSM with their PKI or their FIM CM. If you are running a medium- or high- assurance PKI within your company, policies on how to issue Smart Cards may differ from my example.

Extending the schema

Before we can do anything, we need to extend the Active Directory schema to support FIM CM.

 All schema changes in Active Directory should be planned carefully.

If we don't, **Configuration Wizard** will stop and tell us to extend the Active Directory schema if we try to run it.

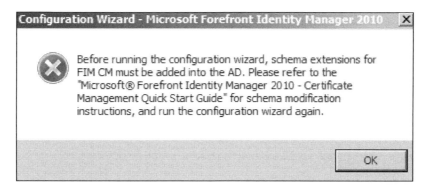

 Remember that all modifications to the Schema require Schema Admins permissions.

If you look at the FIM 2010 R2 media in the `\Certificate Management\x64` folder, you will find a `Schema` folder where you can run the script `ModifySchema.vbs`.

```
D:\>cd "Certificate Management\x64\Schema"
D:\Certificate Management\x64\Schema>ModifySchema.vbs
```

If you just run that script, you will get a **Success** message:

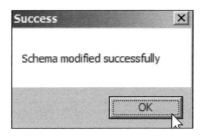

However, this hasn't made any changes; it's a false **Success** message.

In order to actually change your schema, you need to modify the script and the files it used to match your environment before running the script.

1. Copy the Schema folder from the FIM R2 2010 media to a local folder, C:\Temp\FIM CM Schema for example.
2. If you look at the content of the folder, you will see four files.

```
Directory of C:\Temp\FIM CM Schema
05/17/2012  03:22 AM    <DIR>          .
05/17/2012  03:22 AM    <DIR>          ..
11/04/2011  03:26 PM             8,439 clm.ldif
11/18/2011  11:46 PM            12,635 ModifySchema.vbs
11/18/2011  11:46 PM            12,688 ModifySchemaOnlineUpdate.vbs
11/04/2011  03:26 PM             1,112 onlineupdate.ldif
               4 File(s)         34,874 bytes
```

3. What we need to do is make changes to the ModifySchema.vbs and the clm.ldif files.
4. Open up the ModifySchema.vbs file and change the line in the **RunLDIF** function that points to the forest. The default value is DC=company,DC=com. In my scenario, I change it to **DC=ad,DC=company,DC=com**.

```
Function RunLDIF(DmnPath)
        Dim path
        path = "ldifde -i -v -f """ & GetCurrentDir & "clm.ldif""" -k -c ""DC=ad,DC=company,DC=com"" "
```

In your environment, you would of course change it to your AD forest name.

5. Open up the **clm.ldif** file and replace all occurrences of **DC=company,DC=com** with your AD forest name. In my case it is **DC=ad,DC=company,DC=com**.

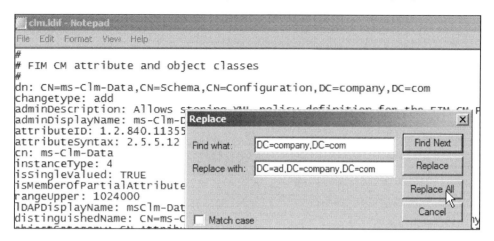

6. Now run the `ModifySchema.vbs` file from your modified, local folder. The **Success** message you will get this time will be true.

The Schema in AD is now upgraded to support FIM CM.

The configuration wizard

If we knew what was coming in the configuration wizard, we might have prepared a bit more before starting it. But one way of configuring FIM CM is to solve the problems as they arise in the configuration wizard. It is quite common to cancel out from the wizard to fix something, and then start it again.

Since I know what is coming, I will make some preparations before I start it.

Create service accounts

We have so far, in our FIM deployment, created quite a few service accounts. FIM CM, however, requires that we create a few more. During the configuration wizard, we get the option of having the wizard create them for us, but I always create them manually in my FIM CM deployments.

One reason is that a few of them need to be assigned some certificates. If we use an HSM, we have to create them manually, in order to make sure the certificates are indeed using the HSM.

The wizard will ask for six different service accounts, but we actually need seven.

In my example, I have created the following seven accounts to be used by FIM CM:

1. `svcFIMCMAgent`
2. `svcFIMCMAuthZAgent`
3. `svcFIMCMCAMngr`
4. `svcFIMCMEnrollAgent`
5. `svcFIMCMKRAgent`
6. `svcFIMCMPool`
7. `svcFIMCMService`

The last one, `svcFIMCMService`, will not be used during the configuration wizard, but will be used to run the FIM CM Update Service.

Create certificate templates for FIM CM service accounts

Three of the service accounts will require a certificate, and during the configuration wizard we will be asked which template to use when requesting the certificate. This can be ignored during the wizard, but then we need to make sure that the three accounts are configured manually with each certificate. In the case of using an HSM, this is how you need to do it.

We will, however, let the wizard request the certificates we need, but we need to create the templates.

The service accounts using a certificate are:

- `svcFIMCMAgent`: This account needs a *User* certificate
- `svcFIMCMEnrollAgent`: This account needs an *Enrollment Agent* certificate
- `svcFIMCMKRAgent`: This account needs a *Key Recovery Agent* certificate

There are templates already present in AD, but we need to create our own versions to work with FIM CM.

All three of these accounts will be given much power within your organizations and should be handled carefully. If you are not using an HSM, the certificates need to be backed up in a secure way.

So for each of the three, we need to create a new certificate template.

> FIM CM does not support **Cryptography Next Generation (CNG)**, which is turned on when Windows Server 2008 Enterprise certificate templates are used. You must therefore select Windows 2003 Server Enterprise for the templates, which you are creating in this procedure, to work properly with FIM CM.

One common parameter among all three is the validity period. In my opinion, the validity period on the FIM CM certificates should always exceed the maximum validity period of the certificates managed by it. Renewing these certificates might also be challenging. In my example in this book, I use a five-year validity period on these certificates. The idea is that the Smart Cards will have a maximum two-year validity period.

When you look in my guides, as follows, please remember that I only show you the minimum requirements to work with FIM CM. Your PKI might have quite a different set of requirements for the templates.

Please make sure your PKI supports the usage of the custom templates needed for FIM CM. Peter Geelen has made a note about this at `http://identityunderground.wordpress.com/2010/05/17/clm-vs-key-recovery-agent-certificate-template`. You need to have the correct version on the operating system used on your Enterprise CA.

FIM CM User Agent certificate template

The FIM CM User Agent needs a User certificate, so let's just use the existing User template as a basis for our template. This certificate is used to secure (encrypt) a lot of data used in FIM CM.

> Once you have used the certificate in FIM CM, make sure you never lose track of the certificate and the private keys. If you do, you may create a situation where all data in FIM CM is useless, since it is unable to decrypt it.

1. Right-click on the **User** template and select **Duplicate Template**.
2. Select **Windows Server 2003 Enterprise** as **Version**.
3. Give it a descriptive name. In my example I called it **The Company FIM CM User Agent**.

4. Change **Validity period** to something appropriate; in my example I use **5 years**. Also, extend **Renewal period** to something like **6 months**.

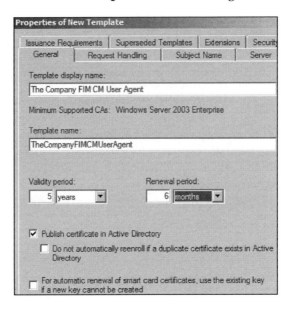

5. In the **Request Handling** tab, modify the CSPs and select **Microsoft Enhanced RSA and AES Cryptographic Provider**.

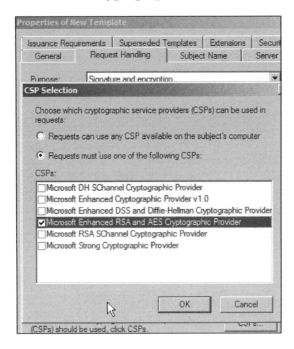

6. In the **Subject Name** tab, clear the **Include e-mail name in subject name** and **E-mail name** checkboxes.

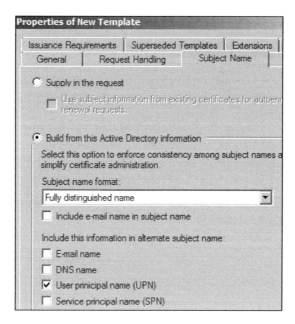

7. In the **Security** tab, remove the **Domain** users.

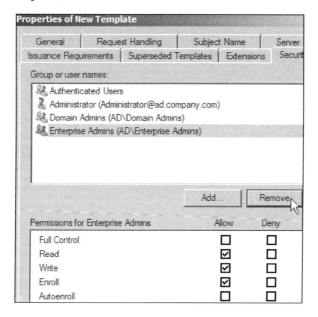

8. Click on **OK** to save the new template.

FIM CM Enrollment Agent certificate template

The Enrollment Agent certificate is used to sign off all certificate requests made by FIM CM. An Enrollment Agent basically has the ability to request a certificate to impersonate all users, including the administrator. This is one reason why many people like to use HSMs, since it will protect the private keys from being stolen.

1. Right-click on the **Enrollment Agent** template and select **Duplicate Template**.
2. Select **Windows Server 2003 Enterprise** as **Version**.
3. Give it a descriptive name. In my example I called it **The Company FIM CM Enrollment Agent**.
4. Change the **Validity period** to something appropriate; in my example I use **5 years**. Also, extend the **Renewal period** to something like **6 months**.
5. On the **Request Handling** tab, select **Allow private key to be exported** if you are not using HSMs.

FIM CM Key Recovery Agent certificate template

The Key Recovery Agent is used if FIM CM needs to restore private keys.

1. Right-click on the **Enrollment Agent** template and select **Duplicate Template**.
2. Select **Windows Server 2003 Enterprise** as **Version**.
3. Give it a descriptive name. In my example I called it **The Company FIM CM Enrollment Agent**.
4. Change the **Validity period** to something appropriate; in my example I use **5 years**. Also, extend the **Renewal period** to something like **6 months**.

Enable the templates

Once the templates are created, you need to remember to enable them on your CA.

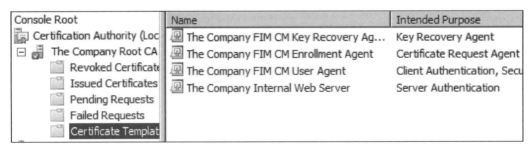

Require SSL on the CM portal

It is highly recommended to configure your FIM CM portal to require SSL. If not, you will get a message during the configuration wizard as follows:

In IIS manager, you need to configure the virtual directory **CertificateManagement** to require SSL. **CertificateManagement** is the default name, but if you configured the installation to create a site with a different name, you need to change it.

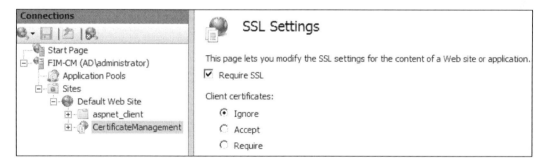

Kerberos again!

Well now that we have created the accounts used by FIM CM we might as well verify that all Kerberos Constrained Delegation and SPNs are in place.

Issuing Smart Cards

Most of the job is done by the `svcFIMCMPool` account, the one that will be running the FIM CM portal.

1. First we need to make sure the correct SPNs are configured for this account. Since this is the web-portal application pool account, there will be some HTTP services that need to be registered. We have talked a little about them in *Chapter 3, Installation*, but let's verify the services to be registered. As implemented in *Chapter 3, Installation*, I will use the alias **cm** for the FIM CM portal.

```
C:\>setspn -L svcFIMCMPool
Registered ServicePrincipalNames for CN=svcFIMCMPool,OU=FIM
Service Accounts,DC=ad,DC=company,DC=com:
        http/fim-cm
        http/fim-cm.ad.company.com
        http/cm
        http/cm.ad.company.com
```

2. **svcFIMCMPool** then needs to be trusted for delegation against the `rpcss` service on the CA server.

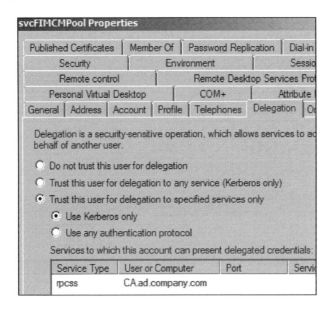

Install SQL Client Tools Connectivity

If you, like me, are using SQL aliases, you will need to install SQL Client Tools Connectivity. I usually do this from the SQL Server media, but there are other sources for this software. In my experience, though there are some differences between the versions that you will find, I tend to use the SQL media all the time.

I also usually install SQL Management Tools to make it possible to configure and troubleshoot the FIM CM database directly from the FIM CM server.

None of this is required, however, unless you use SQL aliases. If you use SQL aliases and do not have the SQL Client Tools, you will get an error similar to the following screenshot when running the configuration wizard:

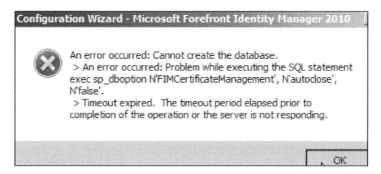

Run the wizard

After some preparations, it is time to run the wizard. It is not uncommon to rerun the wizard a few times, but be careful. It does not remember your current settings, so running it a second time may well break your working FIM CM environment.

1. To run the wizard, you need to be a domain admin and also use an account with permission to create the database in SQL.

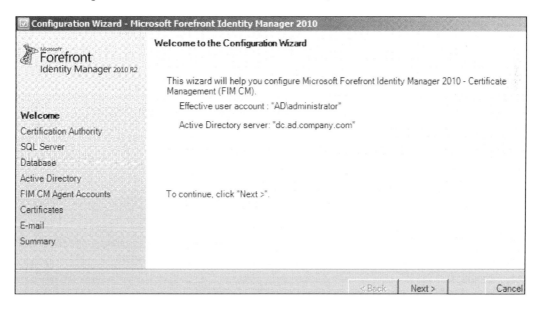

Issuing Smart Cards

2. If you have multiple Enterprise CAs, select the one that FIM CM should use. We can later configure FIM CM to use multiple CAs if we like.

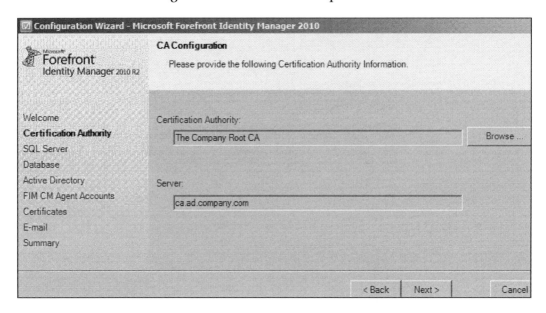

3. Since we use the SQL alias, we set **dbFIMCM** as the SQL Server name. If you are not logged on with an account that has permission to create the database, you need to provide credentials for such an account.

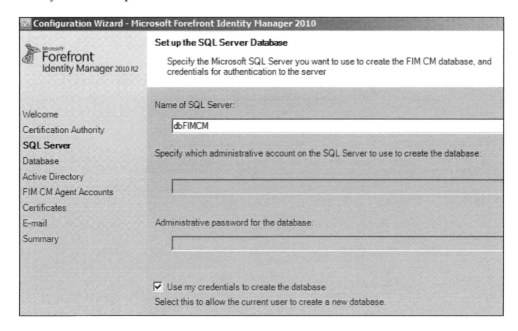

4. Leave the default settings on the **Database Settings** page.

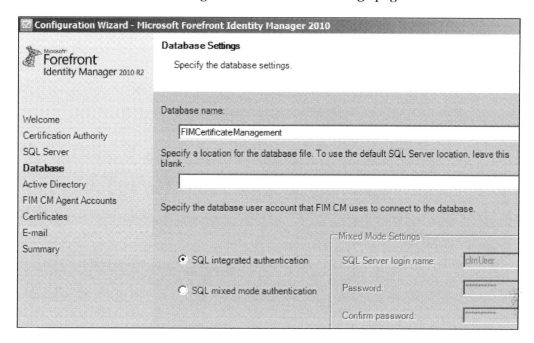

5. On the **Active Directory** page, note the AD path for the so-called Service Connection Point. We will need to configure some permission on this object later on. I have never dared to change the location, even if it points to an old location referencing the older version of FIM CM, Certificate Lifecycle Manager.

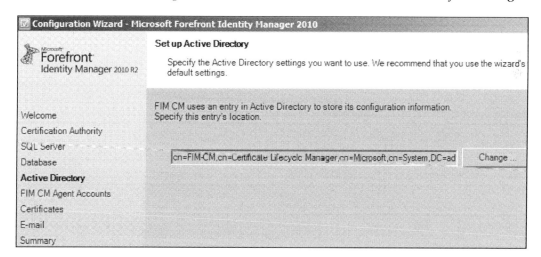

Issuing Smart Cards

6. So far I guess it has been an easy wizard to follow, but now it is time to really pay attention, especially if it is the first time you are running the wizard.

7. On the **FIM CM Agent Accounts** page, you need to configure every one of the agents with the correct information. Clear the **Use the FIM CM default settings** checkbox and click the **Custom Accounts...** button.

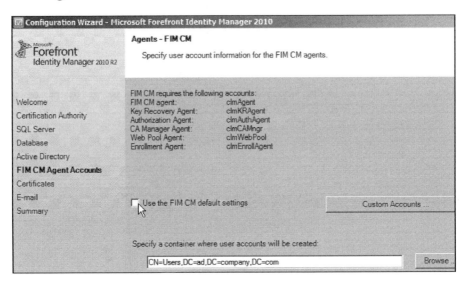

8. On all the six agent accounts, select the **Use an existing user** checkbox and fill in the **User name** and **Password** textboxes for the account. Now you see why I named my accounts the way I did. It makes it easy to understand which account to use for which agent.

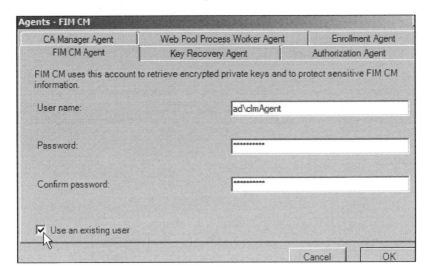

9. On the **Certificates** page, we select the corresponding template we would like each account to use. Some people argue that we should always use the option **Create and configure certificates manually**. When using HSMs, I always do that. It is, however, nice to allow the wizard to configure the certificates and put all the information about the certificates into the configuration files.

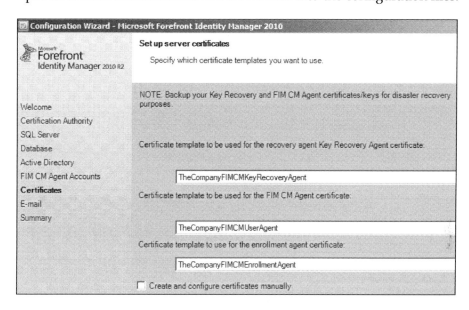

10. On the **E-mail** page, we just point FIM CM to an SMTP server it can use to send e-mails. Also note the default path for print documents. In this short coverage of FIM CM, I will not show you how to use printing and e-mail in workflows.

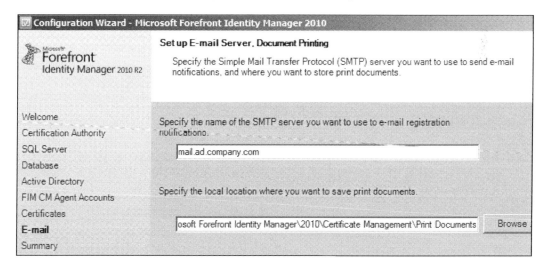

11. Before you click the **Configure** button, verify all the settings. If something is wrong, just use the **<Back** button and change whatever value is wrong.

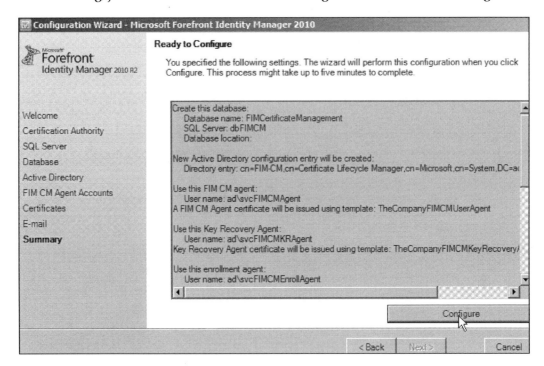

12. The wizard will take a few minutes to complete the execution. It is not uncommon for it to fail, as there may be many parameters that might not have been correctly set.

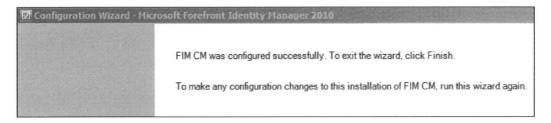

Backup certificates

As soon as your configuration wizard is finished, you need to log in to the FIM CM server as the three users, svcFIMCMAgent, svcFIMCMEnrollAgent, and svcFIMCMKRAgent, and make sure you get a backup of the certificates. Do not forget the private keys they received.

Do not ever lose track of the agent certificates!

Rerunning the wizard

If something goes wrong or you need to change something, you might need to rerun the wizard. This is fine as long as you keep a close eye on what you are changing.

There are two critical parts where you might end up destroying your FIM CM deployment.

The accounts

If you have successfully generated and requested certificates for the three FIM CM accounts, make sure to configure the wizard with the same accounts, but also to check the **Create and configure certificates manually** checkbox. Otherwise you might end up creating new certificates without this actually being your intention.

If you generate new certificates, make sure to also create backups, including the private keys. And remember that once a FIM agent certificate has been used by FIM CM, you have to keep track of it until you are certain that no data is encrypted using its keys. If FIM CM is unable to use the private key to decrypt data, the data is lost. I have seen cases where every Smart Card had to be thrown away and new ones bought due to the loss of the private keys.

The database

If there is already a FIM CM database, we will receive an option to either use the existing one or create a new one. Make sure you select the correct option. Answering **No** will delete all the data that FIM CM has so far stored in the database and a new database will be created.

Issuing Smart Cards

Configuring the FIM CM Update Service

By default, the Forefront Identity Manager CM Update Service runs under the local system account. It is considered the best practice to change it and use a service account instead.

We have already created the `svcFIMCMService` user that we intend to use for this purpose. Before we can configure it for the service, we need to assign a few user rights to it.

The account needs the following User Rights Assignment:

- To act as part of the operating system
- To generate security audits
- To replace a process-level token
- To log in as a service

It then needs to be added to the following local groups on the FIM CM server:

- Administrators
- IIS_IUSRS

After that, we reconfigure the service to use the account and start automatically.

Database permissions

Once the database is created by the configuration wizard, we need to assign permissions to it. If you are not comfortable managing your SQL database, your DBA can help you with this.

On the **FIMCertificateManagement** database, we need to allow the CA server and the FIM CM Update Service with the **clmApp** role.

Usually, this also means that we need to create the logins since these accounts never had any.

Chapter 12

So what we need is to create logins for AD\CA$ and AD\svcFIMCMService, and then assign them the **clmApp** role in the FIM CM database.

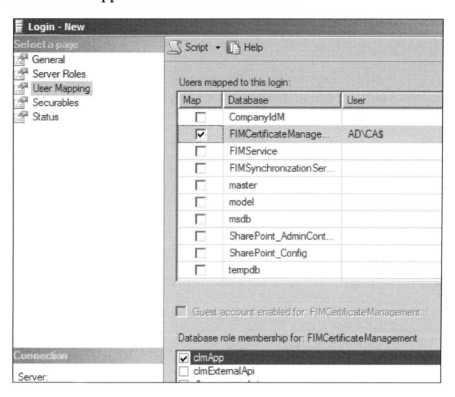

Configuring the CA

The CA used by FIM CM needs to be configured before we can use it.

First, we need to install the FIM CM CA files, and then we need to configure the modules we just installed.

Installing FIM CM CA files

You install the CA files by running the same setup as when installing the FIM CM server.

Issuing Smart Cards

The only trick is to remember to deselect the **FIM CM Portal** and **FIM CM Update Service** options in the feature selection during setup. We only want to install **FIM CM CA Files**.

Configuring Policy Module

Once we have installed the modules, we need to configure them with some information regarding the FIM CM.

In the properties of **Exit Module**, we need to tell the CA how to connect to the FIM CM database by supplying it with a connection string.

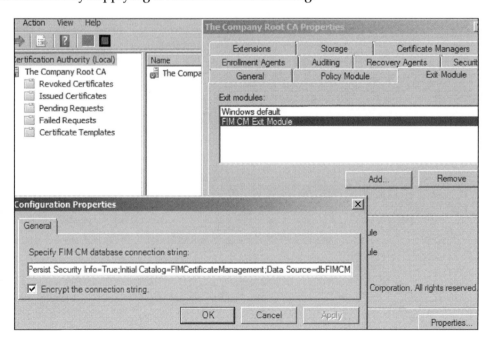

Chapter 12

A typical connection string might look as follows:

```
connect Timeout=15;Integrated Security=SSPI;Persist Security
Info=True;Initial Catalog=FIMCertificateManagement;Data Source=dbFIMCM
```

In this example, I am using a SQL alias on the CA server as well.

Check for errors in the event log when restarting the CA service to verify that the connection to the FIM CM database is successful.

The FIM CM **Policy Module** requires a bit more attention. In this we can make some adjustments depending on how we would like FIM CM to be in charge of all the certificate issuances. For now you can leave the **General**, **Default Policy Module**, and **Custom Modules** tabs. The only part we must configure is the **Signing Certificates** tab.

On this tab, we need to add the hex-encoded hash value of the certificate the FIM CM Agent will use to sign requests.

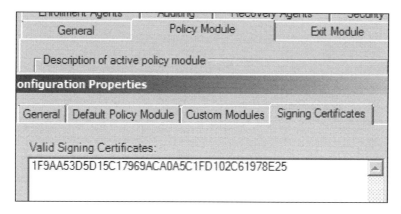

You can get this value by either checking out the certificate or by looking into the configuration file of FIM CM. I almost always get this from the configuration file, since reading the information from the certificate requires me to re-format them.

Issuing Smart Cards

The configuration file I am talking about is the `Web.config` file used by the FIM CM portal. If you open up IIS Manager, and right-click on the **CertificateManagement** site and choose **Explore**, you will end up in the right spot.

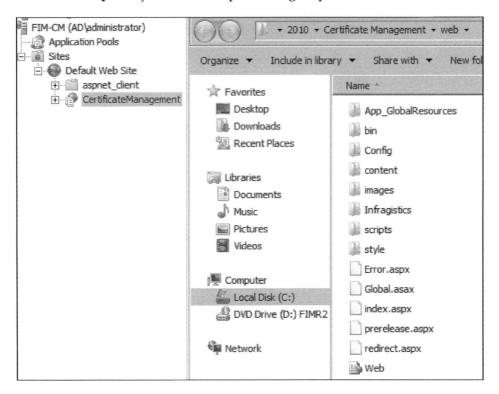

The default path is `C:\Program Files\Microsoft Forefront Identity Manager\2010\Certificate Management\web`.

As a FIM CM administrator, you will find yourself looking at this `Web.config` file quite often.

Within this configuration file you will find the hash of the currently used certificate as well as hashes of previous certificates, if any. Locate the following section in the `Web.config` file:

```
<!-- hex-encoded certificate hash. -->
<add key="Clm.SigningCertificate.Hash" value="1F9AA53D5D15C17969ACA0A5C1FD102C61978E25" />
```

In my example environment, the hash was on line 126.

Now you can copy the hash value and place it into the **Policy Module Signing Certificates** setting.

If you have renewed your User Agent certificate, you might also have additional valid signing certificates that you need to add. These should be listed a few lines below, in your configuration file.

```
<!-- comma-separated list of hex-encoded certificate hashes. -->
<add key="Clm.ValidSigningCertificates.Hashes" value="1F9AA53D5D15C179
69ACA0A5C1FD102C61978E25" />
```

Since in my case this is a new installation, I only have one certificate and the same value for `SigningCertificate` and `ValidSigningCertificate`.

The Policy Module will only accept an input in uppercase without spaces when entering the value. Be sure to stop and restart the certificate service on the CA, after configuring the Policy Module.

Installing the FIM CM client

On the client computers where users will manage Smart Cards (in some cases all workstations), you will need to install some client components.

> You should install the x86 client software, even if the operating system is 64-bit. You have to match your FIM CM client with the type of IE that the users are using. (Even on 64-bit Windows we almost always use the 32-bit version of IE.)

The installation can be automated and settings controlled using GPOs, but showing the few manual steps gives you an idea of what might need to be changed.

1. Usually we select all the components of the client software since we would like to support all the features. If you are using a separate tool for the PIN reset, for example, you might exclude this component.

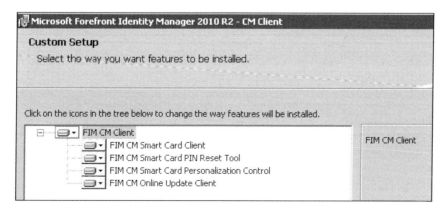

Issuing Smart Cards

2. We then need to tell the component the name of the sites it should trust to run the ActiveX controls. In my example, I use the alias **cm.ad.company.com** for access to the FIM CM portal.

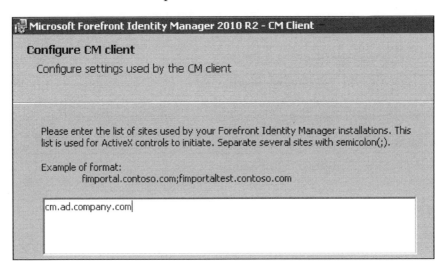

If you are not using the self-service option while using the FIM CM portal, I still suggest you install the client components in case you decide to start using some workflows within CM, which require the users to interact with FIM CM.

FIM CM permissions

Permissions for FIM CM are set in five different places, sometimes making it hard to troubleshoot permission errors. On the other hand, the granular permission model makes it possible for a granular policy to be defined.

If, for example, you have a policy that managers in the USA should only be able to issue Smart Cards for consultants in the USA but not in Europe, you can do so.

Service Connection Point

The **Service Connection Point**, **SCP**, permissions determine whether a user is assigned a management role in the FIM CM deployment.

When you run the configuration wizard, the SCP is decided but the default is the one shown in the following figure:

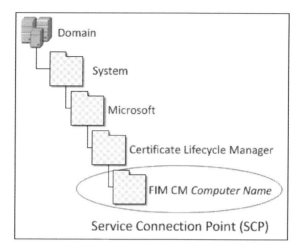

If a user is assigned any of the FIM CM permissions available on the SCP, the administrative view of the FIM CM portal will be shown.

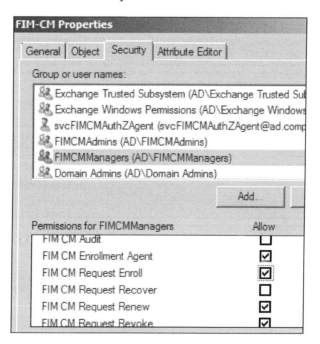

The FIM CM permissions are defined on Microsoft Technet, http://aka.ms/FIMCMPermissions. For your convenience, I have copied parts of the following information:

- **FIM CM Audit**: Generates and displays FIM CM policy templates, defines management policies within a profile template, and generates FIM CM reports.
- **FIM CM Enrollment Agent**: Performs certificate requests for the user or group on behalf of another user. The issued certificate's subject contains the target user's name, not the requester's name.
- **FIM CM Request Enroll**: Initiates, executes, or completes an enrollment request.
- **FIM CM Request Recover**: Initiates encryption key recovery from the **Certification Authority (CA)** database.
- **FIM CM Request Renew**: Initiates, executes, or completes an enrollment request. The renewal request replaces a user's certificate that is near its expiration date, with a new certificate that has a new validity period.
- **FIM CM Request Revoke**: Revokes a certificate before the expiration of the certificate's validity period. This can be necessary, for example, if a user's computer or Smart Card is stolen.
- **FIM CM Request Unblock Smart Card**: Resets a Smart Card's user **Personal Identification Number (PIN)** so that he/she can access the key material on a Smart Card.

For example, if a user must initiate requests on behalf of other users, the user is assigned the **FIM CM Request Enroll** permission at the service connection point.

Users and groups

On user and group objects we can define who has what permission on other users. A user or group that is assigned a management role in the FIM CM environment must have permissions assigned on the users or groups that they will manage in the environment.

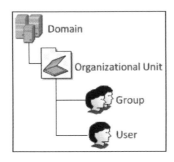

If, for example, you have defined that the group **FIMCMManagers** has the **FIM CM Request Enroll** permission on the SCP, you can use users and groups to define which users will be allowed to request an enroll. You may do this by allowing them the appropriate permission on the target group, like in the following example, **FIMCMConsultantSubscribers**:

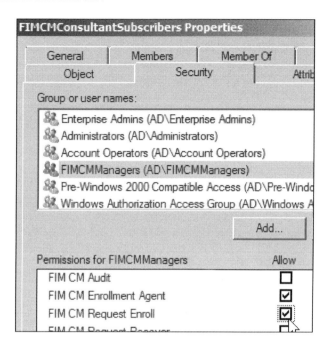

Certificate Template

To manage **Certificate Templates**, we use the **MMC Snap-In** option available on the CA and on computer with **RSAT**, **Remote Server Administration Tool**, for Active Directory Certificate Services.

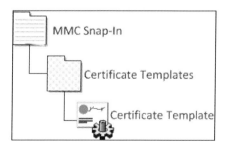

Issuing Smart Cards

As with all certificates, the certificate templates we would like to use need to be defined. FIM CM will act impersonated against the CA. This means that the user and, if applicable, the enrollment agent need the **Enroll** permission on the actual certificate template.

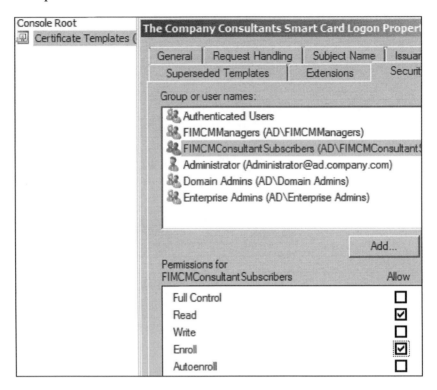

Certificate Templates also need to be added to the list of templates that are issued by the CA that FIM CM is configured to enroll the certificates from.

I do not have room for a complete guide on how you should design your certificate templates, since this is not a PKI book. But if you are trying this out and lack experience, I suggest you create a copy of the **Smartcard Logon** template and build your certificate template from that one.

Chapter 12

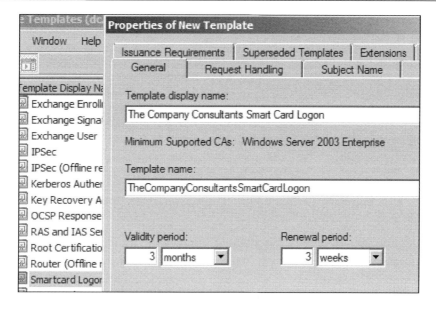

In the examples in this chapter, I am using two templates, one for consultants and one for employees. The key difference is that the consultant template has only a three-month validity period.

Profile Template object

Profile Templates are the objects we create as administrators within the FIM CM portal. These objects are then stored in Active Directory. This is, in my opinion, the easiest one to forget.

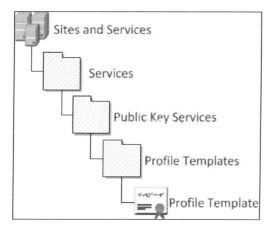

On these objects in AD, we need to assign the **FIM CM Enroll** permissions in order for someone to use it.

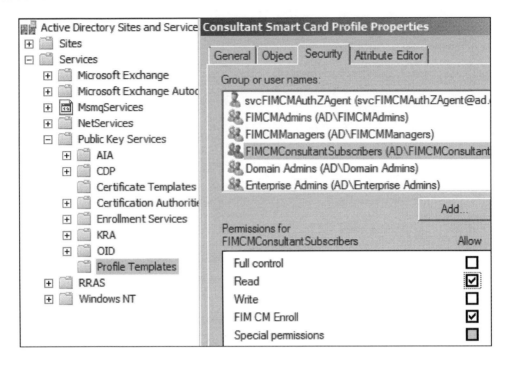

Why is this causing errors then? Well in the FIM CM portal, we define these Profile Templates, and within the template we also define permissions. And since the Profile Template object does not exist until we have defined it in the FIM CM portal, it is easy to forget that we also need to give permission to the groups involved in the Profile Template on the AD object.

Profile Template settings

Even though I take this last, we usually start off by creating the Profile Template, and during the design of this Profile Template we will find out the groups and users we would like to assign different roles to and define the other permissions as described previously.

Chapter 12

In Profile Template, we define a number of workflows that can be triggered. And within each, we define who has the permission to initiate the action.

Workflow: Initiate Enroll Requests
The following users and groups can initiate an enroll request for this profile template:

Selected	Principal (click to edit)	Enroll Initiate
☐	AD\FIMCMManagers	Grant

Allowing managers to issue certificates for consultants

To allow our managers to issue the consultant Smart Cards using the FIM CM portal, we need to define the Profile Template and then configure the correct permissions.

The following guide shows what you need to consider. Prepare yourself for some trial and error before you are satisfied with the behavior and settings in all aspects of the process.

Creating a Profile Template for consultant Smart Cards

When you create a Profile Template, you always start by copying an existing one. If you are planning this for Smart Cards, you start off by copying the **FIM CM Sample Smart Card Logon** template. You can then change it to fit your needs.

1. Start of by creating a copy of the **FIM CM Sample Smart Card Logon** template.

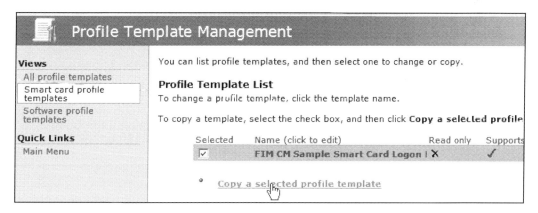

Issuing Smart Cards

2. You can give it a descriptive name.

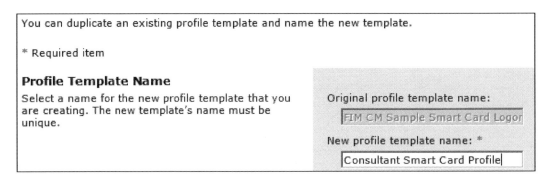

3. We need to configure the Certificate Template we would like to use, and in this case also remove the old one that we do not want to use.

4. Within the **Smart Card Configuration** option, we will configure how **PIN** and other items should be handled. I recommend that if this is a test/PoC environment, do not use the **Diversify Admin Key** setting. If you set this, the Admin Key of your Smart Card will be randomized and encrypted by FIM. Basically this means that FIM CM will be the only one able to manage the Smart Card. I also usually start off by using the **User provided** setting for the PIN, which in our example means that the manager will manually provide a PIN during enrollment.

Smart Card Configuration

This section displays smart card settings, including information about the card provider and certifi

Provider name:	Microsoft Smart Card Base CSP
Provider id:	MSBaseCSP
Initialize new card prior to use:	✓
Reuse retired card:	✓
Use secure key injection:	✗
Install CA Certificate(s):	✓
Certificate label text:	{Template!cn}
Maximum number of certificates:	Unlimited
Diversify Admin Key:	✗
Card Initialization Provider Type:	Default
Card Initialization Provider Data:	
Admin Key initial value:	
Admin PIN rollover:	✗
Admin PIN length:	Not Applicable
Admin PIN character set:	Not Applicable
Admin PIN initial value:	Not Applicable
User PIN policy:	User provided
User PIN character set:	Numeric
Print card:	✗

○ Change settings

5. For each workflow step in the Profile Template, you will then need to configure the settings and determine who will be able to initiate it. In the **Enroll Policy** option, you need to define the **Enrollment agent required** setting in this scenario.

Select a view
- Profile Details
- Duplicate Policy
- Enroll Policy
- Online Update Policy
- Replace Policy
- Recover On Behalf Policy
- Renew Policy
- Suspend and Reinstate Policy
- Disable Policy
- Retire Policy
- Temporary Cards Policy
- Unblock Policy
- Offline Unblock Policy

You can set properties related to enrollment for this profile template, including items rel; distribution.

Workflow: General

This section displays workflow information related to enrollment of this profile template.

Policy enabled:	✓
Self service enabled:	✓
Enrollment agent required:	✓
Allow collection of comments:	✓
Allow collection of request priority:	✗
Default request priority:	0
Number of approvals:	0
Number of active or suspended profiles/smart cards allowed:	Unlimited

Configuring permissions for consultant Smart Cards

Assuming that the managers (like John) are a member of the FIMCMManagers group and the consultant (like Kent) is a member of the FIMCMConsultantSubscribers group, we need to assign the following permissions for the managers to be able to use the FIM portal to request a Smart Card for the consultants:

1. At the Service Connect Point, you must assign FIMCMManagers with two permissions—**FIM CM Request Enroll** and **FIM CM Enrollment Agent**.
2. On the FIMCMConsultantSubscribers group, you must assign FIMMManagers with two permissions—**FIM CM Request Enroll** and **FIM CM Enrollment Agent**.
3. On the Profile Template object in AD, you must assign both the FIMCMManagers and FIMCMConsultantSubscribers groups with **Read** and **FIM CM Enroll** permissions.
4. On the Certificate Templates included in the Profile Template, you must assign the FIMCMManagers group with **Read** and **Enroll** permissions.
5. In the Enroll policy of the Profile Template, you must enable the **Require enrollment agent** checkbox, and grant FIMCMManagers with the **Enroll Initiate** and **Act as Enrollment Agent** permissions for **Enroll**.

John enrolls a Smart Card

The actual enrollment of the Smart Card can now take place:

1. John goes to the FIM CM portal and starts the wizard **Enroll a user for a new set of certificates or a smart card**.

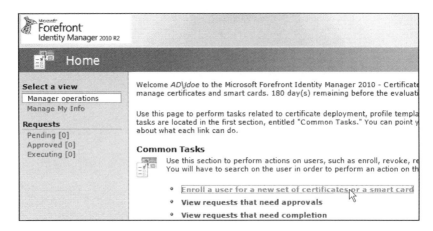

2. He searches for the user Kent and starts the process of enrolling a Smart Card for Kent, **AD\knord**. A few clicks later he can review the request and hit the **Execute** button to start the actual enrolment process.

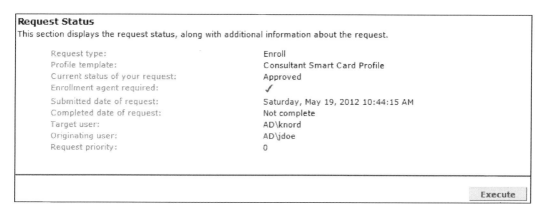

3. John will then **Assign** a physical Smart Card to the user. If John himself is using a Smart Card to log in, he might have trouble selecting the correct reader where the card is inserted.

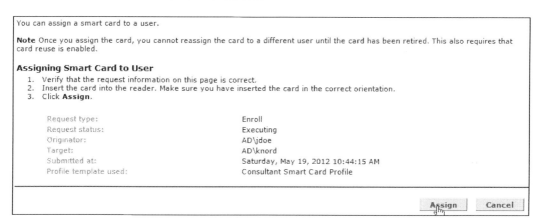

Issuing Smart Cards

4. Since I am using the **User provided PIN** setting, John will be asked to set a PIN for the Smart Card.

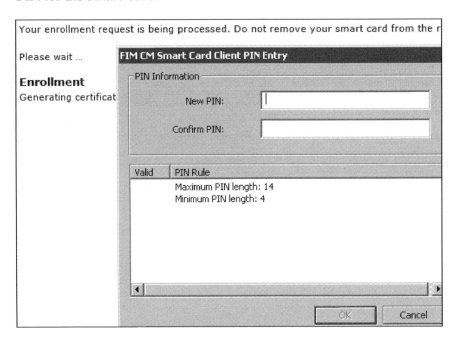

5. John will then see on the screen, the request being made and certificates being generated, as defined in the Profile Template.

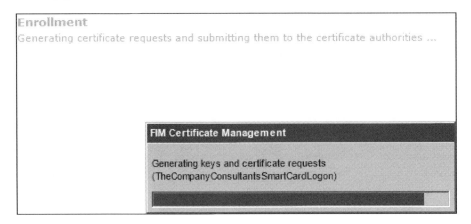

6. If everything is working as expected, John will then succeed and the request will be complete. He can now hand over the Smart Card to the consultant, who can use it to log in.

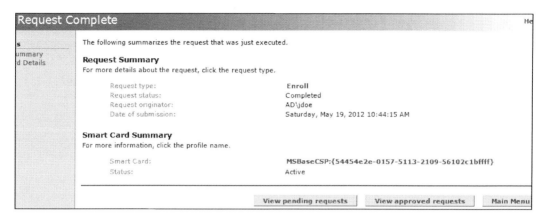

7. He can also look at the details of the card and take actions allowed by the Profile Template.

RDP using Smart Cards

If, like me, you are using **RDP (Remote Desktop)** during testing and would like to try this from a computer that is not part of the domain where the Smart Cards are to be tested, you are likely to hit some problems:

1. The RDP server needs to have **Allow connections from computers running any version of Remote Desktop (less secure)**.
2. If you get the error **This computer can't connect to the remote computer because the smartcard credentials are not available...**, you might need to import the certificate (not the private key, just the certificate) from the Smart Card, into your certificate storage.

CM Management Agent

So what about connecting FIM CM to FIM Synchronization and FIM Service?

If you look at your FIM Synchronization Service, you will find that you can create a Management Agent for Certificate Management. This MA is used to connect to FIM CM.

This MA is not used very often, since it is basically not that good. In FIM CM, the ID used for users is AD GUID. So in order for us to join our users with the objects in FIM CM, we need the **objectGUID** attribute from AD in our MV. And for some unknown reason the MA is preconfigured to *Join* using guid.

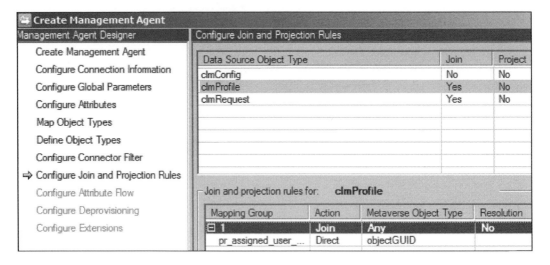

The usage of this MA, as I have said, is limited. If you initiate a request using this MA, the request would end up as pending in the FIM CM portal and the user would still be required to go to the FIM CM portal to finalize the request.

I have also used this MA to import the status from FIM CM into FIM, in order to gather the current status of FIM CM requests into FIM, and then use the FIM Service to act in case the request or profile show something odd. We could, for example, have a Set in FIM called *Smart Card Users* and use the information imported from FIM CM to dynamically assign users to this Set. This information could then be tracked as part of the normal FIM reports, showing other FIM data.

On CodePlex, http://fimcmextensions.codeplex.com, Craig Martin has started a project to try and build something better when it comes to integrating FIM CM with the rest of FIM. If you are running FIM CM and would like to integrate it with the rest of FIM, I suggest you keep an eye on that project.

Summary

FIM CM is indeed the outcast of the FIM product family. Nevertheless, it is a very powerful component in an overall identity management perspective.

Enrolling certificates using FIM CM adds a layer of permission and workflow capabilities, which are not available using built-in functionality, in Active Directory Certificate Services.

In this chapter, we have seen how to configure FIM CM and also looked at one example of allowing a manager to issue a Smart Card to consultants.

In the next and final chapter, we will take a look at troubleshooting FIM. Troubleshooting might sometimes force us to do some recovery, so we will look at backup and recovery as well.

13
Troubleshooting

We have finally reached the last chapter of this book. In general, this is also the one part you would hope never to have to read—troubleshooting!

In this chapter I will:

- Give you hints on how I usually go about troubleshooting
- Explain how to perform a backup and restore

Reminder

First, let me give you a short reminder. Microsoft Forefront Identity Manager 2010 R2 (FIM 2010 R2) is not *one* product but a family of products working together to solve problems surrounding identity management.

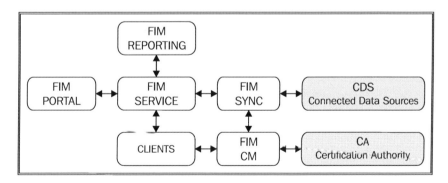

Troubleshooting, backup, and restore will differ, depending on the part that is failing.

Troubleshooting

Depending on the part where we see the failure and the type of failure, the first problem is to isolate where the problem is.

Let's look at an example. If a user reports that he is unable to reset his password using his Windows client, there are a number of errors that might have occurred, such as:

- The client is missing the add-ins and extensions
- The add-ins and extensions are not configured correctly
- The user is not part of the required set
- The MPR is misconfigured
- The workflow activity is not working
- FIM Service is missing some permissions in FIM Sync
- The AD MA is not configured correctly
- FIM Sync is unable to reset the password on the DC
- The DCs are not replicating as expected

A long list, and I have probably still missed some. What I am trying to show is that we need quite a bit of information about the error, in order to narrow down where the problem lies.

I will not be able to give you a complete guide to all scenarios, I won't even try. Instead I will give you some common errors and point you to resources where you will find the tools and guidelines to troubleshoot FIM.

The starting point for you when troubleshooting FIM will be `http://aka.ms/FIMTroubleshooting`.

Kerberos

Almost every guideline on troubleshooting any part of FIM mentions Kerberos. If you have read this book, I imagine you have already realized that Kerberos plays a vital part in many scenarios. And because of that, it will also be a major cause of errors.

In all cases where communication is made between clients and servers, and from server to server, we need to make sure that all the accounts, SPNs, and delegations are in place.

A common mistake when troubleshooting FIM is to actually create an error during troubleshooting. Let me show you what I mean.

Let's say you're an admin and you have trouble accessing FIM Portal. You get some **Access denied** or **Unable to show page** error message.

What many admins tend to do is to try and remove DNS from the error list by accessing the portal using not the alias but the server name or its IP address. But using another name or the IP address will break Kerberos. So, by trying to use an alternative way of accessing FIM Portal, the administrator has introduced an error into his troubleshooting.

 Keep in mind that Kerberos does not work when using IP addresses.

In *Chapter 3, Installation*, I talked a little about the Kerberos configuration required to get FIM to work. But we have added several SPNs, aliases, and so on, in other chapters as well.

When your FIM deployment is finished, you need to make a chart (Excel spreadsheet, maybe) showing all the DNS names, aliases, SPNs, and delegations you have used in your FIM deployment. A chart like that will make it much easier to eliminate Kerberos as the source of error.

If you search the Internet on how to troubleshoot Kerberos, you will get hundreds of thousands of hits, making it hard to find an exact match to your case.

When I work with FIM and get errors that I suspect are Kerberos-related, I use the following guideline, or variations of it, to check whether Kerberos is the cause:

- What is the URL we are trying to access?

    Example: `https://fimportal/identitymanagement`.

- Who owns the SPN of that service for that hostname?

    Example: `SETSPN -Q HTTP/fimportal` shows the owner to be the `svcFIMSPPool` account.

- Is the IIS or Service configured to use this account?

    Example: Is the application pool using this account and is the site configured to use the application pool identity?

- Is the site trying to impersonate a second service?

    Example: `FIMService/FIM-Service`.

- Who owns the SPN of that service for that hostname?

    Example: `SETSPN -Q FIMService/FIM-Service` shows the owner to be the `svcFIMService` account.

Troubleshooting

- Is the Service actually running using the account that owns the Service?

    Example: Is FIM Service running as `svcFIMService`?

- Is the first owner trusted to delegate to the service owned by the second owner?

    Example: Is `svcFIMSPPool` trusted for delegation to `FIMService/FIM-Service`?

What I am trying to say is that you need to follow the request flow and verify Kerberos settings in each step. Do not ever just *think* you have the correct configuration—verify it!

The first step, "What is the URL?", might in some cases be a problem. If, for example, we are using the client add-ins, you might need to verify what URLs the client is configured to use. In this case, the easiest way is to look in the registry of the client. In the `HKEY_LOCAL_MACHINE\SOFTWARE\Microsoft\Forefront Identity Manager\2010` part, you will find the setting for the Outlook add-in and the extensions.

Also remember that Kerberos requires time synchronization. You should make sure all servers and machines are time synchronized.

To summarize, FIM is heavily dependent on Kerberos configuration being correct. Make sure you have full control over your aliases, SPNs, and delegations.

Connected Data Sources

In many projects I have worked with, FIM has been accused of doing the wrong thing or of being misconfigured. While, in fact, the problem was flawed data from a CDS.

FIM is in many cases just reacting to the input data. If the HR system tells it that the user's employment has ended, it will disable the AD account if we have told it to do so.

We might be left trying to configure FIM to correct mistakes or bad data from a CDS. What we then end up with is a complex configuration that might be very hard to troubleshoot.

Let's say you have an HR system that is supposed to give you the home phone number of the user. But the people in the HR system sometimes use this field to store other notes. Suddenly, the requirement of you as FIM admin is to implement some logic to verify that the data in the field is indeed a phone number before importing it. The complexity of this inbound synchronization will increase dramatically. It might even cause you to have to write an extension to FIM. Troubleshooting this will then be even harder.

In my opinion, we should not try to solve the problem with flawed data in FIM, but instead solve it by making sure the data quality in the CDS is sufficient. In the previous example, I would make sure that the HR people stop using the field for non-phone number data. If they don't, I would stop using that as the source for this attribute and look for some other source with better data quality.

FIM Sync

Unless you have implemented some classic rules extensions, the FIM Sync service is quite simple to troubleshoot. If we are troubleshooting some scenario where data in a CDS is not looking the way we expect it, we always start the troubleshooting in FIM Synchronization Service Manager.

In this case, I remind you that FIM Service, and therefore FIM Portal, is also a CDS from the FIM Sync perspective.

Troubleshooting in FIM Sync usually starts off by finding the object in the FIM Synchronization Service Metaverse.

We can use the **Metaverse Search** tool to find the object of interest but also to find out if we have objects that are in a state that they shouldn't be in.

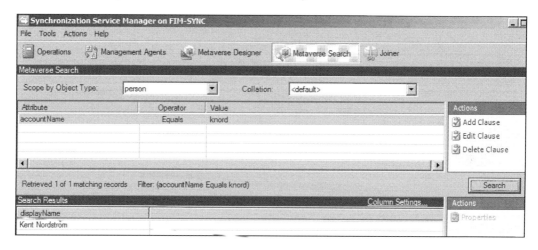

We can, for example, quickly find out if there are any users without **accountName** and then try to find out why. Or we can, as in the previous example, add some clause to find a particular user or set of users.

Troubleshooting

I have found it very useful to modify **Column Settings...** to display more than just the **displayName** attribute, to make it easier to get a quick overview of the objects.

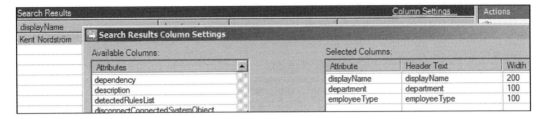

The search result will then make it easier to do quick error checking but also to make sure that I indeed have found the correct object.

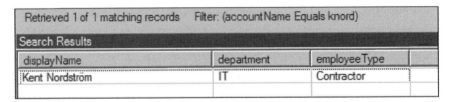

When we open up **Metaverse Object**, we can start to do some more advanced troubleshooting. This view of the object will show all **Attributes** and **Contributing MA**, where the contributing MA is the MA where the value came from.

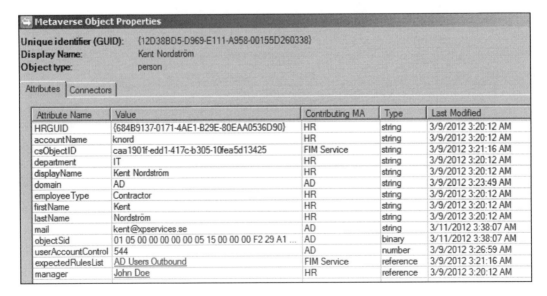

Chapter 13

If something is wrong, we then open up the **Connectors** tab to look at the object from a specific CS perspective; we might also detect a missing connector.

If I look at the object in one of the connector spaces, I will then be able to see what the object looks like in that particular CS. But usually, the main reason I navigate here is to use the **Preview...** button to see what would happen if I synchronized the object in this CS.

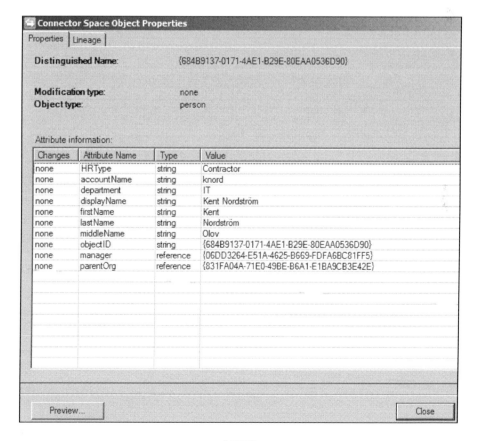

Troubleshooting

In the preview pane, we can see what would have happened had we synchronized this object. We also have the opportunity to commit the synchronization to basically synchronize a single object as part of our troubleshooting. After doing any kind of reconfiguration, I always use this method to test the effect on individual objects before enabling the synchronization schedule. We start off by clicking on the **Generate Preview** button to generate a preview to examine.

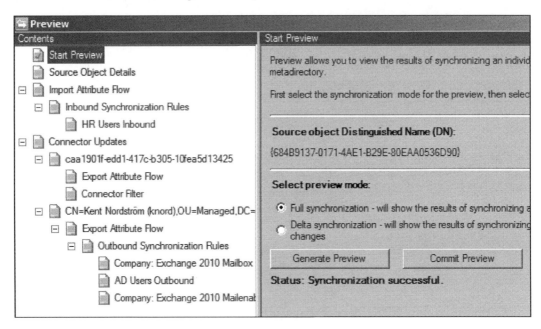

A typical problem when troubleshooting FIM Sync is that attributes do not flow as we expect them to. In the **Preview** window we can detect why. The most common problem is the Attribute Flow Precedence problem. In the **Preview** window, we will detect these problems as **Skipped: Not Precedent**, when looking at the attribute flows.

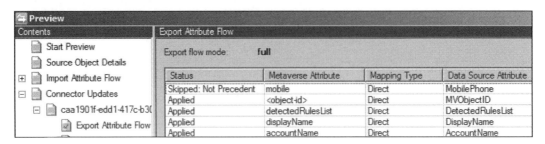

[396]

When this happens, we know we have a precedence problem and can use the **Metaverse Designer** tool to look at the **Attribute Flow Precedence** settings and figure out if we would like to change them or if this is actually the way we want it to be.

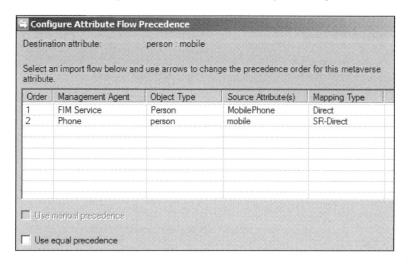

In the previous example, the **mobile** attribute from the **Phone** MA will not export to the **FIM Service** MA, since the FIM Service MA has higher precedence. Therefore, the mobile phone attribute you enter in the phone system will not show up in the FIM Portal.

In my experience, the precedence problem is the most common problem, when it comes to the FIM Synchronization Service.

To learn how to troubleshoot the FIM Sync Service is to learn how to follow the object within Synchronization Service Manager and use the Preview function to determine the cause of the error.

But what if the object is not present in the Metaverse? Well, then you need to search for the user in the CS, where you know it should be present. The **Connector** column should then have the value of **False**, indicating that the object in the CS does not have a connector to any object in the Metaverse.

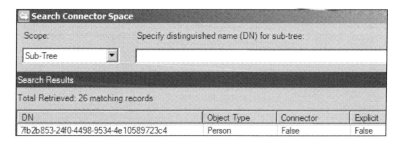

Troubleshooting

We can then look at the object and use the preview to determine why the object is not joined or projected as we expected.

In some cases, you might find that the object indeed has a connector, but to the wrong Metaverse object. You can then disconnect it from the wrong object and use the preview function to verify that it will connect to the correct MV object, and if it is not you can find out why it is connecting to the wrong one.

When we troubleshoot FIM Synchronization Service, we will also detect any errors or misconfigurations we might have caused in FIM Service when configuring, say, the Synchronization Rules or MPRs.

FIM Service

Problems within FIM Service are usually detected when trying to use FIM Portal or another client but can also be detected when looking at objects in the FIM Synchronization Service.

Request errors

If a user or administrator tries to make a change using FIM Portal and that somehow fails, FIM will present a dialog with a summary of the failure.

Forefront Identity Manager -- Webpage Dialog

Summary
The following summarizes the operation or operations that you are requesting.

User Creation

Status

Description	Date	Status
User Creation	5/30/2012 4:28:47 AM	Access denied. View Details

If we need some more information, we can click on the **View Details** link to get some interesting information.

In the detailed error message, we are able to copy the message to the clipboard or e-mail it, as shown in the preceding screenshot. The interesting part in the message, if we need to dig deeper, is the **Correlation Identifier**. This is an identifier FIM used to track this error.

If we then move over to the FIM Service server, we can find the event or events generated by this error based on **Correlation Identifier**.

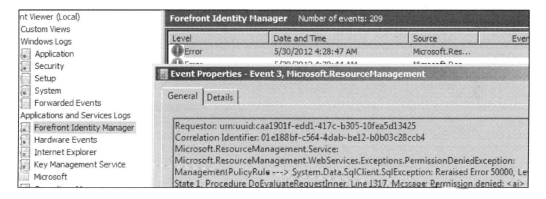

In this example, it was just a simple "access denied" message, but in more complex error situations, the ability to have this correlation identifier is vital to our tracking down the source of the error.

Troubleshooting

Whenever a request is made to FIM Service, we can find the request by using **Search Requests** and can take a look at the request to find out what might have gone wrong.

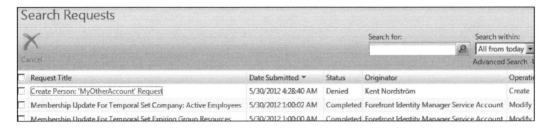

When we have found the request, we can look at **Detailed Content** for the request and at **Applied Policy** (MPRs) to determine what might be wrong.

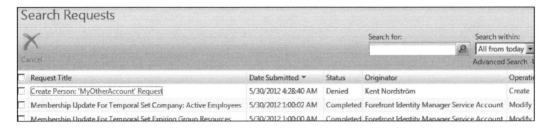

If this does not give you enough information to track down the cause of the problem or the error, you might consider running some tracing while repeating the error situation.

If you open up the FIM Service configuration file, the default path is `c:\\Program Files\Microsoft Forefront Identity Manager\2010\Service\Microsoft.ResourceManagement.Service.exe.config`, and you will find instructions on how to collect the ETW traces for FIM and change the diagnostics configuration.

```
<!-- Instructions for collecting ETW Traces

     To collect ETW traces for Microsoft.ResourceManagemen
     an elevated command prompt.

     1. To start a new etw trace session    : logman st
     2. To stop a running etw trace session : logman st

     To format the collected traces run any of the foll
     on the required output format.

     1. tracerpt FIMETWtrace.etl -o logdmp.xml  -of XML
     2. tracerpt FIMETWtrace.etl -o logdmp.evtx -of EV
     3. tracerpt FIMETWtrace.etl -o logdmp.csv  -of CSV
-->
<!--
     Full Diagnostics configuration.

     Uncomment the following section and replace the default
     enable all trace sources and obtain all available trace
```

Sync errors

If you have detected an error in the FIM Synchronization service and have decided that the cause is some misconfiguration within FIM Service, we need to first of all decide what we would have wanted and then look at why it didn't react in the way we had hoped.

Let's say you have a user that has not been *provisioned* to AD as you had hoped.

Using FIM Synchronization Service Manager, you have:

- Checked that **Enable Synchronization Rule Provisioning** is turned on
- Found that the ERE (Expected Rule Entry) is not within the ERL (Expected Rule List)

You then turn to FIM Service to try to figure out why the ERE is not in the ERL of the user.

What we need to do is to backtrack this.

Troubleshooting

Look at the Synchronization rule that is supposed to trigger the provisioning—**Create resource in external system**. On the **General** tab of the rule, make sure **Apply Rule** is configured in the correct way.

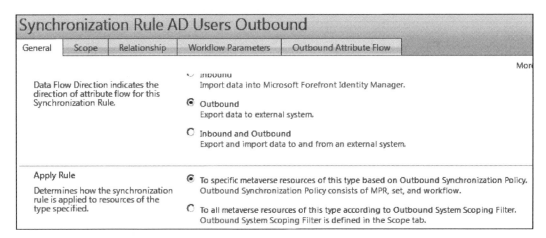

If the rule is configured to use **Outbound System Scoping Filter**, there shouldn't be any ERE, and the problem is likely in the filter used for outbound scoping.

Make sure **Create resource in external system** is correctly set on the **Relationship** tab.

Once we are sure that the Synchronization rule is configured correctly, we open up the MPR that is supposed to make sure the rule is applied to the user. First of all, just make sure you haven't disabled the MPR.

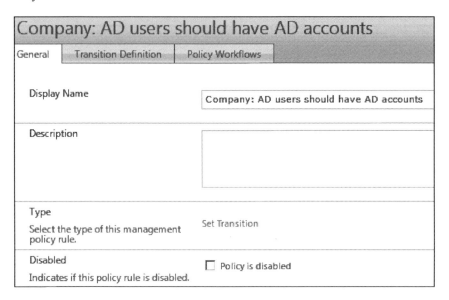

On the **Transition Definition** tab, verify that the correct set is used. If you click on the set, you will be able to verify that the user is indeed part of the set.

If the user is not part of the set, we have to review the criterion and verify that the attributes required to fulfill the criterion are correctly configured. In the previous example, we need to verify that the user's **Employee Type** attribute is either **Employee** or **Contractor**. If not, we usually need to return to the FIM Synchronization service to find out why not.

Troubleshooting

Finally, we check that the MPR is indeed configured to add the correct **Synchronization Rule** to the user.

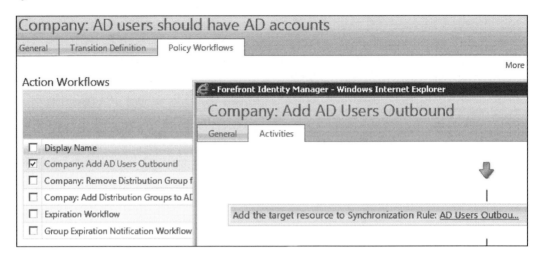

When we troubleshoot MPRs that trigger a workflow, we need to check that the workflow has the correct **Run on Policy Update** setting. The user might have been a member of the set before you started using it in your MPR. In that case, the *transition in* event might never happen on that particular user. A workaround in those cases might be to change the user in a way that he *transitions out* of the set and then change him back so that he transitions back in to trigger the MPR you are troubleshooting. Just make sure that the *transition out* event doesn't trigger any dramatic MPRs, if you use this workaround.

Reporting

Troubleshooting any Reporting related problems in many cases means you hand over the problem to the guys running the SCSM environment.

If the reports do not show the data from FIM that you hoped for, what you can do is verify that the Reporting job is working. If you open up the latest Reporting job you can verify that its status is **Completed**, indicating that FIM has successfully transferred the data to SCSM Data Warehouse.

What I have found is that the most common problem with Reporting is that the users looking at the reports are not filtering them correctly, making the reports show other data than what the viewer expected.

FIM CM

Troubleshooting FIM CM has, as with setup and configuration, very little to do with the rest of FIM.

To get a good guideline on troubleshooting FIM CM, please visit http://aka.ms/FIMCMTroubleshooting. At the time of my writing, it shows you how to troubleshoot CLM 2007. But don't worry. Almost everything is the same in FIM CM as in the older version.

The most common problem with FIM CM is that the permissions are not set correctly. So, make sure that you check out *Chapter 12*, *Issuing Smart Cards*, and review the permissions required to get FIM CM to work.

If you need more information to troubleshoot your FIM CM instance, you can enhance the tracing levels. You do this by modifying the Web.config file used by FIM CM. The default path is C:\\Program Files\Microsoft Forefront Identity Manager\2010\Certificate Management\web\Web.config. In this file, there is a section on **SERVER TRACING**. Here, you configure the file you would like FIM CM to write the tracing information to and also the level of tracing.

```
Web.config
    <!-- SERVER TRACING ***************************************************-->
    <!--
    The trace file specified will contain trace messages as configured in the
    switches section of the system.diagnostics section below. The Everyone
    group must have write access to the directory specified in order for the
    file to be created and have all configured events written.
    -->
    <add key="Clm.TraceFile" value="c:\temp\clm.txt" />

    </ClmConfiguration>


    <system.diagnostics>

    <trace autoflush="true" indentsize="2">
        <listeners>
        </listeners>
    </trace>


    <!-- TRACE SWITCHES ***************************************************-->
    <!--
    Logging levels are 0 - None, 1 - Error, 2 - Warning, 3 - Info, 4 - Verbose
    -->

    <switches>
        <add name="Microsoft.Clm.Security.Principal" value="0" />
        <add name="Microsoft.Clm.Security.Principal.Logon" value="0" />
```

Troubleshooting

Due to the complexity of many operations within FIM CM, I have found myself enabling **Verbose** logging for different parts and then trying to decipher the information in the trace file a number of times over the years.

If you enable **Verbose** logging, you will for the most part be drowned in information. So, try to be careful when setting the logging levels.

In some cases, the error is already displayed in the Event viewer of the FIM CM server. FIM CM writes most of its events to the FIM Certificate Management log, but you also need to look into the Application log to find IIS related errors, for example.

Agent certificates

It does not happen often, but when it does all hell breaks loose if you are not aware of it. I am talking about the expiration of the certificates used by the FIM CM agents. Remember from the setup in *Chapter 12, Issuing Smart Cards*, when we generated three certificates to be used by the FIM CM agents?

At some point, these are going to expire and you should never allow them to expire without having already renewed them and configured FIM CM to use the new certificate. The problem here is that from the original setup it will take years for this event to occur. What I have seen is that it is quite common for it to come as a surprise to the FIM CM admins.

What we need to do is to renew the certificates. This can be done by using the configuration wizard or manually. If you are using an HSM, it will be a manual task in most cases. Whatever method you use, you need to verify that the configuration file is updated with information about the new certificates.

Do not throw away the old certificates! FIM CM needs the keys from the old certificates to decrypt information it encrypted using the old ones.

It is actually one of the most common errors I have seen in FIM CM: losing certificates, causing FIM CM to be unable to decrypt old data in the database.

The worst case scenario could be that all Smart Cards you have deployed need to be replaced, since FIM CM has no way of reading the admin key from its database. This would make many operations, such as retiring the Smart Card, impossible.

CA

If a certificate request from FIM CM fails, you will likely need to examine the configuration of the FIM CM module on the CA.

The most common error here is the SQL connection string in the exit module. But once you get that one right, it shouldn't fail again unless you move the database.

A recurring error is the failure of the CA server to access the FIM CM database.

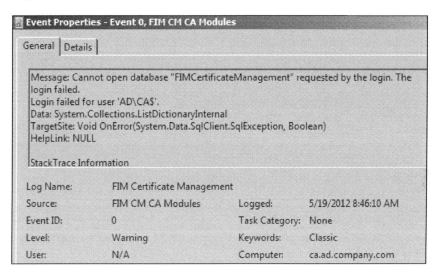

This might happen when we have made a restore and did not get the user login mapping correctly restored on the SQL server. I have also had a case where a DBA just removed the login because he thought it looked stupid to have a login with a dollar sign in it.

If you have renewed the FIM User Agent certificate, you also need to remember to update the Signing Certificates configuration in the FIM CM Policy Module.

FIM clients

Errors on the client side are usually a question of configuration settings.

You need to validate the settings and verify that URLs are reachable and Kerberos is configured correctly.

A common mistake on the client side is that the websites used by FIM have been assigned to the **Trusted Sites** security setting in Internet Explorer. In this security zone, IE is by default not configured to use Integrated Authentication. This will cause login prompts for the user. Making sure that the sites are in the Local Intranet security zone is usually the best way to make sure that Kerberos will work as expected and that security settings in IE will be correct.

For FIM CM to work, you also have to verify that the settings of the security zone you are using allow the ActiveX controls to operate in order to manage the user certificates and Smart Card.

Backup and restore

As with troubleshooting, the backup and restore procedures depend on what part of FIM we are talking about. As always, the FIM CM part is basically treated as a standalone product in this case.

Initially, I planned to have many pages in this book dedicated to this topic but realized it would end up being more or less a copy of the online guidelines Microsoft provides. So instead, I will point you to those guidelines and give you a short summary of the main problems I have seen when it comes to backup and restore.

So first of all the guidelines can be found at:

- `http://aka.ms/FIMBackup`
- `http://aka.ms/FIMCMBackup`

Now, on to my personal thoughts and experiences, when it comes to the backing up and restoring of FIM.

FIM Sync

The question around FIM Sync is whether to back up the Metaverse or not.

If you back up the database, your entire configuration including the schema and MAs will be in it. But I have found that having a manual export of the configuration together with a backup of any Extension DLLs is quite handy as well. Even exports of individual MAs might sometimes be good to have. Having manual exports of MAs, the configuration, and schema allows you to import them into a freshly installed FIM Synchronization server for troubleshooting.

The most common error when it is time to restore the FIM Synchronization Service database is that the encryption key is missing. If you need to restore the database without providing the encryption key, you will lose all MA connection settings and will have to reconfigure them. So, in most cases, this is not a big deal. However, you will also lose any initial passwords of users in the process of being provisioned.

If you look at the pending exports in your MAs, you can track if any users are in the process of being provisioned and if the initial password is used. If so, you can disconnect the user and re-provision them or export them and then manually set the passwords for these users.

FIM Service and Portal

Apart from backing up the databases, I always try to keep a configuration export as backup as well. If you look in *Chapter 4, Basic Configuration*, you will find the PowerShell scripts needed to export the schema configuration and policy configuration for FIM Service.

In many of my FIM cases, we have also made some modifications to the FIM Portal, involving modifications of the underlying SharePoint installation. If you have done that, you also need to look at guidelines to back up your SharePoint configuration and database. A guide on how to back up SharePoint Foundation can be found at `http://aka.ms/SPFoundationBackup`.

In comparison to the FIM Synchronization Database, I personally feel that backing up the FIM Service database is much more important. Why? Well, the Metaverse can be repopulated relatively easily by resynchronizing.

The FIM Service database however will contain object relations and request history. If we reimport all the users, we will lose all history and manually set information referring to an object might also be lost.

So, whatever you do, make sure you have a working backup of your FIM Service database.

FIM CM

Ok, I know I am starting to get a little repetitive, but don't forget to make sure you have a procedure in place to be able to restore the FIM CM Agent certificates.

With FIM CM, you have the same story as with the FIM Service database. Please make sure you have a working backup of it.

Troubleshooting

But with FIM CM, it is also vital that you back up the *config* files, even if you haven't made any changes to them manually. The backup guide tells you that, within the `C:\Program Files\Microsoft Forefront Identity Manager\2010\Certificate Management` folder, there are four configuration files you need to back up. They are as follows:

- `\web\Web.config`
- `\Bin\Microsoft.CLM.service.exe.config`
- `\Bin\Microsoft.Clm.Config.exe.config`
- `\Bin\ClmUtil.exe.config`

What I usually do is back up the entire `\web` folder, so that I also catch any customizations that might have been made to the FIM CM Portal.

As part of your FIM CM backup strategy, you also need to look at how you back up the CA and the CA database of the CA used by FIM CM. If you lose the CA database, you will not, for example, be able to renew a certificate. So make sure you also take a look at the guidelines available at `http://aka.ms/CABackup` on how to perform backups for your CA.

Source code

We have mentioned a few times in this book that you might also have to write extensions or custom workflow activities. In *Chapter 11, Customizing Data Transformations*, we also mentioned the use of SSIS. In all these cases, you will have some source code related to your FIM deployment.

Make sure you have some kind of backup and source control to manage the code you are using. Not too long ago, I was in a project where the source code of an old ILM Metaverse Rules Extension was missing. This made it impossible to figure out the exact logic used in the provisioning of users to Active Directory. So, instead of doing a quick look in the source code to see how the logic was implemented, we had to guess.

If you have a source code management solution, such as *Microsoft Visual Studio Team Foundation*, I suggest you also use that to check your manually exported configuration files or *config* files. This way, you will get version handling of your configuration, preventing you from accidentally overwriting a working configuration backup with a non-working version.

Summary

Since Microsoft Forefront Identity Manager 2010 R2 is not just one product but a family of products, troubleshooting and disaster recovery will vary a lot, depending on which part you're dealing with. The backup strategy will, in most cases, involve both automated backups as well as manual ones, as part of the configuration process.

In this chapter, I have given you some hints on how to troubleshoot common errors in FIM and how to perform backup and restore of the critical parts of FIM.

This was the last chapter in this book. To continue your journey, or if you have any unanswered questions, I hope that you will visit my blog at `http://blog.konab.com/fim-2010-r2-book`, where I will answer questions and post downloads and corrections, if any.

Afterword

The end of the book is just the next step forward!

But at least now you've got a good baseline and reference to continue exploring the FIM universe.

You'll certainly enjoy the online references that Kent has pointed out in the book.

The online experience is a perfect complement to the book. Even better is sharing knowledge and discussing questions and issues, the perfect means to build your knowledge.

Join the FIM Forum at Microsoft TechNet (`http://aka.ms/FIMForumTN`).

Check out the TechNet Wiki for FIM 2010 (`http://aka.ms/FIM2010Resources`), or surf `http://aka.ms/FIM2010Wiki`.

If you feel that information on the TNWiki is missing or needs an update, be the first to add or update it.

There is so much more out there!

Don't be afraid to ask for help; the community is there for you!

Looking forward to seeing you online, fellow FIMster!

Peter Geelen

`http://blog.identityunderground.be`

`https://twitter.com/geelenp`

Index

A

ACCOUNTDISABLE flag 171
Action workflow 22, 159
Active Directory (AD)
    about 18, 90, 160
    directory replication 93
    inbound synchronization 183-185
    least privileged approach 91, 92
    password management, enabling in 240, 241
    schema, extending 349-351
    Self-service Password Reset feature 93
    users, managing in 170
    users, provisioning to 173
Active Directory Federation Services (AD FS)
    about 10, 274-276
    URL, for overview 10
Active Directory Lightweight Directory Services (AD LDS) 279
Active Directory Management Agents. *See* AD MA
Active Directory schema
    extending 349-351
AD MA
    about 93
    creating 94-104
    pre-import filtering feature 101
Alacris 16
AllDGs keyword 312
AllSecurityGroups keyword 312
Alternate Access Mapping 42
anonymous request 239
AttributePicker keyword 312
Authenticate workflow 22

Authentication workflow (AuthN) 22, 239
Authorization workflow (AuthZ) 22
Authorize workflow 22

B

backup certificates 364
BeginExportScriptname 278
BitAnd function 172
BitOr function 172

C

Capacity Planning
    about 30
    URL, for guide 30
CAS (Client Access Server) 195
case study, SSIS 340-345
Certificate Lifecycle Management (CLM) 25
Certificate Lifecycle Manager (CLM) 16
Certificate Management portal (CM) 10, 26
certificate templates
    creating, for FIM CM service accounts 352, 353
    managing 375-377
Certification Authority (CA) 70, 374
challenges, Identity Management
    Highly Privileged Accounts (HPA) 8
    lifecycle procedures, identifying 8
    password management 9
    provisioning, of users 8
    traceability 9
classic rules extensions 326
Client Access Licenses (CALs) 27
cloud computing 7
CodePlex 387

Collation settings 35
configuration
  moving, from dev to production 131, 132
configuration options, Results tab
  Attribute 314
  Redirecting URL 314
  Resource Type 314
configuration triple 159
configuration wizard, FIM CM
  about 351
  backup certificates 364
  certificate templates, creating for FIM CM service accounts 352, 353
  Kerberos 357, 358
  rerunning 365
  running 359-364
  service accounts, creating 351
configuring
  FIM CM CA 367
  FIM CM Policy Module 368-371
  FIM CM Update Service 366
  FIM Portal 301, 302
  FIM Service 246
  One Time Password (OTP) gate 251-254
  Question and Answer (QA) gate 249-251
Connected Data Source (CDS) 17, 150, 240
Connectors 18
Connector Space (CS) 18
consultant Smart Cards
  permissions, configuring for 382
  Profile Template, creating for 379-381
Cryptography Next Generation (CNG) 353
custom code
  importing 137
customizations
  in DirSync 271-273
Customized keyword 312

D

database permissions, FIM CM 366
databases
  about 31, 34
  collation and languages 35
  FIM-Dev 38
  SCSM 39, 40
  SQL 38
  SQL aliases 36, 37
data synchronization
  from FIM to SCSM 283-285
data transformation
  options 325, 326
data transformation, options
  about 325, 326
  classic rules extensions 326
  Extensible Connectivity MA 2.0 (ECMA 2.0) 328
  PowerShell 326
  SQL Server Integration Services (SSIS) 327, 328
  workflow activities 328
Data Warehouse
  FIM Post Install Scripts 87
  SCSM Manager, registering in 82-86
DateTimeFormat function 185
db_datareader permissions 106
declarative synchronization
  verus non-declarative synchronization 20
default reports
  about 285
  Group History 286
  Group Membership Change 285
  Management Policy Rule History 286
  Request History 286
  Set History 286
  Set Membership Change 286
  User History 286
delegation 52
delta 93
DeniedEmailTemplate keyword 313
deprovisioning
  about 103, 126, 339
  URL, for info 104
Detected Rule Entry (DRE) 160, 161
development environment
  versus production environment 29, 30
Dev-FIMMA account 45, 91
Dev-FIMService account 46, 52
Dev-FIMSPPool account 46, 52
Dev-FIMSync account 46
dev to production
  configuration, moving from 131, 132

difference files, generating 136
policy difference, generating 136
schema difference, generating 136
directory replication 93
directory synchronization product 16
DirSync
  about 267
  configuration, tips 268-271
  customizations 271-273
  downloading 267
disabling
  maintenance mode 133
Discovery import 128, 183
Distinguished Name (DN) 91, 176
Distribution keyword 312
DONT_EXPIRE_PASSWORD flag 171
DONT_REQ_PREAUTH flag 171

E

Enable-CsUser command 329
ENCRYPTED_TEXT_PWD_ALLOWED flag 171
EndExportScriptname 278
Enrollment Agent certificate template, FIM CM 356
ERL (Expected Rules List) 182
Exchange
  managing 194
Exchange 2007
  about 194
  managing 194
Exchange 2010
  about 195
  managing 195
Exchange Recipient Management group 194
Exchange, synchronization rules
  about 195
  mailbox users rules 196, 197
  mail-enabled users rules 197, 198
Expected Rule Entries (EREs) 159
ExportScriptname 278
Extensible Connectivity MA 2.0 (ECMA 2.0) 20, 328
Extract, Transform and Load (ETL) process 286

F

features, Self-service Password Reset (SSPR) 249
federation
  about 273-276
  implementing 10
Filter Accounts, in FIM Service MA 128, 129
filter permissions 318
FIM
  features 31
  used, for obtaining OTP for Office 365 279
FIM 2010 R2 Synchronization Service 16
FIM Certificate Management
  about 44, 70
  installing 70, 71
FIM Certificate Management (FIM CM)
  about 25, 26, 347
  Active Directory schema, extending 349, 350, 351
  assurance level 348, 349
  CA, configuring 367
  CA files, installing 367
  client, installing 371, 372
  configuration wizard 351
  database permissions 366
  Enrollment Agent certificate template 356
  Key Recovery Agent certificate template 356
  Management Agent 386, 387
  permissions 372
  Policy Module, configuring 368-371
  scenario 347, 348
  Update Service, configuring 366
  User Agent certificate template 353-355
FIM CM accounts 365
FIM CM Audit 374
FIM CM CA
  configuring 367
FIM CM CA files
  installing 367
FIM CM client
  installing 371, 372
FIM CM components
  installation order 32, 33
  installation prerequisites 34

FIM CM configuration wizard
  about 351
  Kerberos 357, 358
  rerunning 365
  running 359-364
  service accounts, creating 351
  SSL requisites, on CM portal 357
FIM CM configuration wizard, rerunning
  accounts 365
  database 365
FIM CM databases 365
FIM CM Enrollment Agent 374
FIM CM Enrollment Agent certificate template
  about 356
  enabling 356
FIM CM Key Recovery Agent certificate template
  about 356
  enabling 356
FIM CM, permissions
  about 372
  Certificate Template, managing 375-377
  FIM CM Audit 374
  FIM CM Enrollment Agent 374
  FIM CM Request Enroll 374
  FIM CM Request Recover 374
  FIM CM Request Renew 374
  FIM CM Request Revoke 374
  FIM CM Request Unblock Smart Card 374
  groups 374, 375
  profile template object 377, 378
  profile template settings 378
  Service Connection Point (SCP) 372, 373
  users 374, 375
FIM CM Request Enroll 374
FIM CM Request Recover 374
FIM CM Request Renew 374
FIM CM Request Revoke 374
FIM CM Request Unblock Smart Card 374
FIM CM service accounts
  certificate templates, creating for 352, 353
FIM CM Update Service
  configuring 366
FIM CM User Agent certificate template
  about 353, 355
  enabling 356

FIM-Dev server 34, 38
FIM family 15
FIM Licensing
  URL 28
FIM Password Reset 42-44
FIM Password Reset portal
  installing 67-70
FIM Password sites
  edit binding, in IIS 82
  FIM Post Install Scripts, for Data Warehouse 87
FIM Portal
  about 24, 41, 42, 297
  configuring 301, 302
  installing 58-67
  logging in 186
  Self Service Password Reset (SSPR) 24
  UI, modifying 298-300
FIM portal, self service
  about 186, 187
  attributes, managing 190-194
  direct reports, sending 188-190
FIM Portal UI
  filter permissions 318
  modifying 298-300
  navigation bar resources 302-310
  RCDC 319-322
  search scopes, creating 315-317
  search scopes, customizing 311
FIM Portal URL
  redirecting, to IdentityManagement 81
FIM Post Install Scripts
  for Data Warehouse 87
FIM Reporting 25
FIM reports
  viewing 289-291
FIM Service
  about 21
  access, granting to FIM Sync 80
  configuring 246
  installing 58-67
  management agent 23
  Management Policy Rules (MPRs) 23
  multivalued attributes, managing 331-339
  Password Reset Users Set 247, 248
  permissions, for setting password 242-246
  placing, into maintenance mode 133

request pipeline 22
schema, exporting 135
security context 247
settings, exporting 134, 135
FIM Service Database 22, 122
FIM Service MA
  about 120
  accounts, filtering 128, 129
  creating 120-126
  run profiles, creating 127
FIM Service mailbox
  securing 80
FIM Service Management Agent 21, 23
FIM Service policy
  exporting 135, 136
  importing 140
FIM Service schema
  exporting 135
  modifying 118-120
  URL 118
  versus FIM Sync 116
FIM Service settings
  exporting 134, 135
FIMSyncAdmins group 80, 94
FIM Synchronization Service (FIM Sync)
  about 15, 17, 53
  FIM Service access, granting to 80
  FIM Service Management Agent 21
  installing 53-58
  Management Agents (MA) 19
  non-declarative vs. declarative synchronization 20
  password synchronization 21
  placing, into maintenance mode 132
  settings, exporting 134
  versus FIM Service schema 116
FIM Synchronization Service settings
  exporting 134
FIM, to SCSM
  data, synchronizing from 283-285
First import profile 128
FlowRuleName parameter 338
Forefront Identity Manager 30
Forefront Identity Manager 2010 (FIM 2010) 16
Forest keyword 312
Full Import profile 128

G

Global keyword 312
GlobalSearchResult keyword 312
Group History report 286
Group Membership Change report 285
groups 148

H

Hardware Security Module (HSM) 9
Highly Privileged Accounts (HPA) 8
holograms 18
HOMEDIR_REQUIRED flag 171
HR (SQL Server)
  about 105-107
  SQL MA, creating 107-115
HSMs (Hardware Security Modules) 348
Human Resource (HR) system
  about 18
  scenario 18, 19

I

IBM Lotus Notes 194
Identity Lifecycle Manager 2007 (ILM 2007) 16
Identity Management
  about 7, 15
  challenges 8
  FIM Portal URL, redirecting to 81
  lifecycle procedures 8
IdNexus 16
IISRESET 302, 317
ImportScriptname 279
inbound synchronization
  from Active Directory 183-185
inbound synchronization rules 150-158
indexing
  disabling, in SharePoint 80
initial load
  versus scheduled runs 130, 131
installation order, FIM CM components 32, 33
installation prerequisites, FIM CM components
  about 34
  databases 34

Kerberos configuration 48-50
service accounts 45-48
web servers 41
installing
FIM Certificate Management 70, 71
FIM CM CA files 367
FIM CM client 371, 372
FIM Password Reset portal 67-70
FIM Portal 58-67
FIM Service 58-67
FIM Synchronization Service 53-58
SCSM console 53
SQL Client Tools Connectivity 358
INTERDOMAIN_TRUST_ACCOUNT flag 171

J

Join and Projection rules 102
Joining 18

K

Kerberos
enforcing 81
Kerberos configuration
about 48-50
delegation 52
SETSPN utility 50, 51
Kerberos Constrained Delegation (KCD) 48, 357, 358
Key Recovery Agent certificate template, FIM CM 356

L

least privileged approach 91, 92
lifecycle procedures
identifying 8
LOCKOUT flag 171
Lockout Gate activity 249
Lync
about 329
managing 329
LyncEnabled attribute 331
Lync Users
provisioning 329-331

M

MailEnabledSecurity keyword 312
maintenance mode
disabling 133
FIM Service, placing into 133
FIM Synchronization Service, placing into 132
for production 132, 133
Management Agent, FIM CM 386, 387
Management Agents (MAs)
about 18, 19, 36, 90, 277
Active Directory 90
creating 90
HR (SQL Server) 105-107
run profiles, creating for 116
Management Policy Rule History report 286
Management Policy Rules. *See* **MPRs**
MCS (Microsoft Consulting Services) 328
Metaverse (MV) 17, 18
Microsoft Consulting Services solution 16
Microsoft Forefront Identity Manager 2010 R2 (FIM 2010 R2)
about 7, 15, 29
capacity planning 30
development versus production 29, 30
hardware 32
high-level overview 15
history 16
implementing 9
licensing 27
reporting feature 281
reports, modifying 294-296
Microsoft Identity Integration Server (MIIS) 16
Microsoft Lync 277
Microsoft Metadirectory Services (MMS) 16
Microsoft System Center Service Manager (SCSM) 25
MNS_LOGON_ACCOUNT flag 171
MPRs
about 23, 30, 143, 159
creating 181-183
enabling 255
modifying, for user management 144-148
multi-step option, Run Profiles 116

multivalued attributes
  managing, in FIM 331-339
MV schema
  object, deleting 117, 118
MyApprovals keyword 312
MyDGMemberships keyword 312
MyDGs keyword 312
MyRequests keyword 312
MySecurityGroupMemberships keyword 312
MySecurityGroups keyword 312

N

navigation bar resources 302-310
New-MsolFederatedDomain cmdlet 265
non-declarative provisioning 162, 163
non-declarative synchronization
  verus declarative synchronization 20
NORMAL_ACCOUNT flag 171
NOT_DELEGATED flag 171
NotifictionEmailTemplate keyword 313

O

object deletion
  in MV 117, 118
Object Deletion Rules 117
Office 365
  about 263
  FIM used, for obtaining OTP 279
  overview 264-267
  services 264
  UAG used, for obtaining OTP 279
  URL, for info 10
One Time Password (OTP) gate
  about 24, 240
  configuring 251-254
  versus Question and Answer (QA) gate 240
OTP
  FIM, used for obtaining 279
  UAG, used for obtaining 279
Outbound Attribute Flow option 198
outbound synchronization policy 159
outbound synchronization rule
  about 158, 159
  creating 174-176

outbound system scoping filter 159, 160

P

PARTIAL_SECRETS_ACCOUNT flag 171
PASSWD_CANT_CHANGE flag 171
PASSWD_NOTREQD flag 171
password
  setting, FIM Service used 242-246
Password Authentication Challenge activity 249
Password Change Notification Service (PCNS) 21
PASSWORD_EXPIRED flag 171
password management
  about 9
  enabling, in Active Directory 240, 241
Password Reset AuthN workflow
  about 248
  One Time Password (OTP) gate, configuring 251-254
  Question and Answer (QA) gate, configuring 249-251
Password Reset Users Set 247, 248
password synchronization 21
permissions
  configuring, for consultant Smart Cards 382
Personal Identification Number (PIN) 374
Person keyword 312
phone system
  about 163
  users, managing in 163-169
post-installation configuration
  edit binding, in IIS for FIM Password sites 82
  FIM Portal URL, redirecting to IdentityManagement 81
  FIM Service access, granting to FIM Sync 80
  FIM Service mailbox, securing 80
  indexing, disabling in SharePoint 80
  Kerberos, enforcing 81
PowerShell 131, 265, 277, 326
PowerShell scripts 141
pre-import filtering feature, AD MA
  about 101

[421]

URL, for info 101
production environment
  changes, importing to 137
  custom code, importing 137
  versus development environment 29, 30
Profile Template
  creating, for consultant Smart Cards 379-381
profile template object 377, 378
profile template settings 378
Projection 18
property flags
  ACCOUNTDISABLE 171
  DONT_EXPIRE_PASSWORD 171
  DONT_REQ_PREAUTH 171
  ENCRYPTED_TEXT_PWD_ALLOWED 171
  HOMEDIR_REQUIRED 171
  INTERDOMAIN_TRUST_ACCOUNT 171
  LOCKOUT 171
  MNS_LOGON_ACCOUNT 171
  NORMAL_ACCOUNT 171
  NOT_DELEGATED 171
  PARTIAL_SECRETS_ACCOUNT 171
  PASSWD_CANT_CHANGE 171
  PASSWD_NOTREQD 171
  PASSWORD_EXPIRED 171
  SCRIPT 171
  SERVER_TRUST_ACCOUNT 171
  SMARTCARD_REQUIRED 171
  TEMP_DUPLICATE_ACCOUNT 171
  TRUSTED_FOR_DELEGATION 171
  TRUSTED_TO_AUTH_FOR_DELEGATION 171
  USE_DES_KEY_ONLY 171
  WORKSTATION_TRUST_ACCOUNT 171
provisioning
  about 19, 161, 162
  non-declarative provisioning 162, 163
proxyAddresses attribute 329, 331
Public Key Infrastructure (PKI) 9, 348

Q

Question and Answer (QA) gate
  about 240
  configuring 249-251
  versus One Time Password (OTP) gate 240

R

RCDC 319-322
RDP
  about 386
  using Smart Card 386
Remote Desktop. *See* **RDP**
Remote Server Administration Tool. *See* **RSAT**
Replicating Directory Changes permission 93
Report Definition Language (RDL) file 295
report reading
  access, providing to users 291-294
reports
  modifying 294-296
  viewing 289-291
Request History report 286
Request MPR 23
request pipeline, FIM service 22
Request Processor workflow 22
re-registration, Self-service Password Reset (SSPR) 254
Resource Control Display Configuration. *See* **RCDC**
Resource keyword 313
Results tab
  about 314
  configuration options 314
roles
  separating 31
roles, separating
  about 31
  databases 31
  FIM features 31
RSAT 375
Run Profiles
  creating, for FIM Service MA 127
  creating, for Management Agents 116
  first import 128
  multi-step profiles option 116
  single-step option 116
RUS (Recipient Update Service) 194

S

scheduled runs
 vesus initial loads 130, 131
schema management
 about 116
 FIM Service schema, modifying 118-120
 FIM Sync versus FIM Service schema 116
 object deletion, in MV 117, 118
SchemaObject keyword 313
SCRIPT flag 171
SCSM
 about 39, 40
 requisites 39
 setup, verifying 281-283
SCSM console
 installing 53
SCSM Data Warehouse
 about 76
 setting up 76
 79
SCSM-DW 34
SCSM ETL process 286
SCSM management
 about 71
 setting up 72-75
SCSM Manager
 registering, in Data Warehouse 82-86
SCSM-MGMT 34
SCSM setup
 verifying 281-283
Search Definition tab 313, 314
SearchRequests keyword 312
search scopes
 about 311
 creating 315-317
 keywords 312, 313
 Results tab 314
 Search Definition tab 313, 314
 usage keyword 311
security context, FIM Service 247
Security keyword 312
selective deprovisioning 339, 340
Self-service Password Reset (SSPR)
 about 24, 93, 239
 features 249
 MPRs, enabling 255

 re-registration 254
 user experience 255-262
SERVER_TRUST_ACCOUNT flag 171
service accounts
 about 45
 creating 351
 Dev-FIMMA 45
 Dev-FIMService 46
 Dev-FIMSPPool 46
 Dev-FIMSync 46
 svcFIMCMPool 47
 svcFIMMA 46
 svcFIMPWService 47
 svcFIMService 47
 svcFIMSPPool 47
 svcFIMSync 47
 svcSCSMAdmin 47
 svcSCSMReport 48
 svcSCSMService 48
 svcSCSMWF 48
Service Connection Point (SCP) 372, 373
Service Level Agreement (SLA) 41
Service Manager 291
Service Principal Name (SPN) 42, 48
Service schema difference
 importing 137
Set History report 286
Set Membership Change report 286
sets
 about 148, 159
 configuring, for user management 148-150
 creating 177, 178
SETSPN -L 50
SETSPN -Q 50
SETSPN -S 50
SETSPN utility
 about 50, 51
 switches 50
SETSPN utility, switches
 SETSPN -L 50
 SETSPN -Q 50
 SETSPN -S 50
Set Transition MPR 23
SharePoint
 indexing, disabling in 80
Single Sign On (SSO) 20, 273
single-step option, Run Profiles 116

Smart Card enrollment 382-385
SMARTCARD_REQUIRED flag 171
smart cards
  about 16, 347, 348
  using 10
SQL 34, 38
SQL aliases 36, 37
SQL Client Tools Connectivity
  installing 358
SQL feature requirements
  for SCSM-DW 40
  for SCSM-MGMT 40
  for service database 39
SQL MA
  creating 107-115
SQL Server Integration Services (SSIS)
  about 34, 105, 327, 328
  case study 340-345
SSL requisites
  on CM portal 357
Subject Alternative Name (SAN) 42
svcFIMCMAgent account 352
svcFIMCMAuthZAgent account 352
svcFIMCMCAMngr account 352
svcFIMCMEnrollAgent account 352
svcFIMCMKRAgent account 352
svcFIMCMPool account 47, 52, 352, 358
svcFIMCMService account 352
svcFIMMA account 46, 91
svcFIMPWService account 47, 52
svcFIMService account 47, 52
svcFIMSPPool account 47, 52
svcFIMSync account 47
svcSCSMAdmin account 47
svcSCSMReport account 48
svcSCSMService account 48
svcSCSMWF account 48
switch statement 338
synchronization rule
  about 174
  creating 150-176
Synchronization Rule object 153
synchronization rules, for Exchange
  about 195
  mailbox users rules 196, 197
  mail-enabled users 197, 198

Synchronization Service settings
  importing 137-140
systems
  CA 11
  DC 11
  FIM-CM 12
  FIM-Dev 12
  FIM-PW 12
  FIM-Service 12
  FIM-Sync 12
  MAIL 11
  RD 11
  SCSM-DW 12
  SCSM-MGMT 12
  SQL 11
  TMG 11
  UAG 12

T

TEMP_DUPLICATE_ACCOUNT flag 171
temporal set 185
TimeoutEmailTemplate keyword 313
TRUSTED_FOR_DELEGATION flag 171
TRUSTED_TO_AUTH_FOR_
    DELEGATION flag 171

U

UAG
  used, for obtaining OTP for Office 365 279
Unified Access Gateway. See UAG
usage keyword 303, 304, 311
USE_DES_KEY_ONLY flag 171
userAccountControl attribute 170-173, 184
User Agent certificate template, FIM CM
    353, 355
user experience, Self-service Password Reset
    (SSPR) 255-262
User History report 286
user management
  about 143
  MPRs, modifying for 144-148
  sets, configuring for 148-150
User Rights Assignment 366
users
  access providing, for report reading 291-294

managing, in Active Directory 170
managing, in phone system 163-169
provisioning 8
provisioning, to Active Directory 173
users, provisioning to Active Directory
  about 173
  MPRs 181-183
  sets 177, 178
  synchronization rule 174-176
  workflow 178-180

V

VIA 16

W

web servers
  about 41
FIM Certificate Management 44
FIM Password Reset 42-44
FIM Portal 41, 42
Windows Management Instrumentation (WMI) 53, 242
workflow
  for synchronization rule 178-180
workflow activities 328
WORKSTATION_TRUST_ACCOUNT flag 171

X

XPath expression 314

Z

Zoomit 16

Thank you for buying Microsoft Forefront Identity Manager 2010 R2 Handbook

About Packt Publishing

Packt, pronounced 'packed', published its first book "Mastering phpMyAdmin for Effective MySQL Management" in April 2004 and subsequently continued to specialize in publishing highly focused books on specific technologies and solutions.

Our books and publications share the experiences of your fellow IT professionals in adapting and customizing today's systems, applications, and frameworks. Our solution based books give you the knowledge and power to customize the software and technologies you're using to get the job done. Packt books are more specific and less general than the IT books you have seen in the past. Our unique business model allows us to bring you more focused information, giving you more of what you need to know, and less of what you don't.

Packt is a modern, yet unique publishing company, which focuses on producing quality, cutting-edge books for communities of developers, administrators, and newbies alike. For more information, please visit our website: www.packtpub.com.

About Packt Enterprise

In 2010, Packt launched two new brands, Packt Enterprise and Packt Open Source, in order to continue its focus on specialization. This book is part of the Packt Enterprise brand, home to books published on enterprise software – software created by major vendors, including (but not limited to) IBM, Microsoft and Oracle, often for use in other corporations. Its titles will offer information relevant to a range of users of this software, including administrators, developers, architects, and end users.

Writing for Packt

We welcome all inquiries from people who are interested in authoring. Book proposals should be sent to author@packtpub.com. If your book idea is still at an early stage and you would like to discuss it first before writing a formal book proposal, contact us; one of our commissioning editors will get in touch with you.

We're not just looking for published authors; if you have strong technical skills but no writing experience, our experienced editors can help you develop a writing career, or simply get some additional reward for your expertise.

Mastering Microsoft Forefront UAG 2010 Customization

ISBN: 978-1-849685-38-2 Paperback: 186 pages

Discover the secrets to extending and customizing Microsoft Forefront Unified Access Gateway

1. Perform UAG extension magic with high level tips and tricks only few have had knowledge of – until now!
2. Get to grips with UAG customization for endpoint detection, client components, look and feel, and much more in this book and e-book
3. An advanced, hands on guide with customization tips and code samples for extending UAG

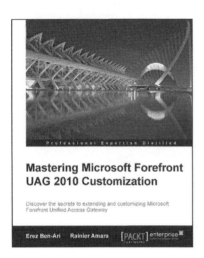

Microsoft Forefront UAG 2010 Administrator's Handbook

ISBN: 978-1-849681-62-9 Paperback: 484 pages

Take full command of Microsoft Forefront Unified Access Gateway to secure your business applications and provide dynamic remote access with DirectAccess

1. Maximize your business results by fully understanding how to plan your UAG integration
2. Consistently be ahead of the game by taking control of your server with backup and advanced monitoring
3. An essential tutorial for new users and a great resource for veterans

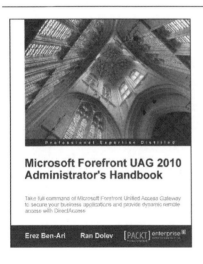

Please check **www.PacktPub.com** for information on our titles

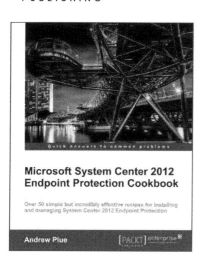

Microsoft System Center 2012 Endpoint Protection Cookbook

ISBN: 978-1-849683-90-6 Paperback: 350 pages

Over 50 simple but incredibly effective recipes for installing and managing System Center 2012 Endpoint Protection

1. Master the most crucial tasks you'll need to implement System Center 2012 Endpoint Protection

2. Provision SCEP administrators with just the right level of privileges, build the best possible SCEP policies for your workstations and servers, discover the hidden potential of command line utilities and much more in this practical book and eBook

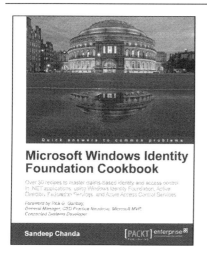

Microsoft Windows Identity Foundation Cookbook

ISBN: 978-1-849686-20-4 Paperback: 294 pages

Over 30 recipes to master claims-based identity and access control in .NET applications, using Windows Identity Foundation, Active Directory Federation Services, and Azure Access Control Services

1. Gain a firm understanding of Microsoft's Identity and Access Control paradigm with real world scenarios and hands-on solutions.

2. Apply your existing .NET skills to build claims-enabled applications.

3. Includes step-by-step recipes on easy-to-implement examples and practical advice on real world scenarios.

Please check **www.PacktPub.com** for information on our titles

Made in the USA
Lexington, KY
25 September 2012